Saying I No More

Saying I No More

Subjectivity
and Consciousness
in the Prose
of Samuel Beckett

DANIEL KATZ

Northwestern

University Press

Evanston

Illinois

Northwestern University Press
Evanston, Illinois 60208-4210

Copyright © 1999 by Northwestern University Press.
Published 1999.
All rights reserved.
Printed in the United States of America
ISBN 0-8101-1682-0 (cloth)
ISBN 0-8101-1683-9 (paper)

Library of Congress Cataloging-in-Publication Data

Katz, Daniel.
Saying I no more : subjectivity and consciousness in the prose of
Samuel Beckett / Daniel Katz.
p.   cm. — (Avant-garde and modernism studies)
Includes bibliographical references and index.
ISBN 0-8101-1682-0 (alk. paper)
ISBN 0-8101-1683-9 (pbk. : alk. paper)
1. Beckett, Samuel, 1906–   —Prose.   2. English prose literature—
Irish authors—History and criticism.   3. Modernism (Literature)—
Ireland.   4. Consciousness in literature.   5. Subjectivity in
literature.   6. Self in literature.   I. Title.   II. Series.
PR6003.E282 Z7539   1999
828'.91208—dc21

                                                    99-34853
                                                    CIP

The paper used in this publication meets the minimum requirements
of the American National Standard for Information Sciences—
Permanence of Paper for Printed Library Materials, ANSI Z39.48-1984.

Contents

Acknowledgments

This book began as a doctoral dissertation written under the direction of Marjorie Perloff, and her contributions both to the elaboration of the initial project and to its transformation into book form have been inestimable. Other friends and colleagues have also read portions of the manuscript at various stages, and I would especially like to thank H. Porter Abbott and Jean-Michel Rabaté for decisive interventions at various points.

My friends Dina Alkassim, John Culbert, David Fussner, and Richard Sieburth have helped me in a number of ways, not least through their brilliant conversation and critical perspicacity, though certainly not only. Thinking things through in their company has been one of the greatest pleasures of the writing of this book.

I would also like to thank my family for considerable support, financial and otherwise, and especially my daughter, Lisa.

I am grateful to my editors, Susan Harris and Susan Betz, for so skillfully managing the at-times considerable tribulations of a transatlantic book project. The friendship and hospitality of David and Hannah Fussner made my research trips to London far more pleasurable than I had any right to suspect, and, finally, the companionship of Dorothée Bonnigal has produced a similar effect on my life as a whole.

Some of this book has already appeared in print. Chapter 1 was published in slightly different form in *Beckett avant Beckett: Essais sur les premières oeuvres*, Jean-Michel Rabaté, ed. Paris: Presses de l'Ecole normale supérieure, 1984. A section of chapter 5 appeared in significantly different form in *Samuel Beckett Today/Aujourd'hui 5: Beckett & Psychoanalysis*, Editions Rodopi, 1996, and part of chapter 2 was published in French in *Samuel Beckett: L'écriture et la scène*, Evelyne Grossman and Régis Salado, eds. Paris: Editions SEDES. I thank the respective publishers for permission to reprint here.

En principe, l'attitude de l'homme est le refus. L'homme s'est cabré pour
ne plus suivre le mouvement qui l'emportait, mais il ne put, de cette façon,
que le précipiter, qu'en rendre la rapidité vertigineuse.

[As a rule, man's attitude is one of refusal. Man reared up against the
movement that was carrying him away but in so doing only hurried it along,
made its speed dizzying.]
    —Georges Bataille [1]

Dont you know you are happiest while I withold and not confer—dont you
know that "No" is the wildest word we consign to Language?
    —Emily Dickinson [2]

Introduction
Expression and Refusal

Impossible Texts and Possible Approaches

In recent criticism, Samuel Beckett's prose has been increasingly described as a labor of refusal—a refusal not only of what traditionally has
made possible narrative and the novel, but also of the major conventional
suppositions concerning the primacy of consciousness, subjectivity, and
expression for the artistic act.[3] With regard to these issues the startling
proposal of 1949 concerning the task of the "maker" remains crucial, as
Beckett invokes, "The expression that there is nothing to express, nothing
with which to express, nothing from which to express, no power to express, no desire to express, together with the obligation to express."[4] In its
literal disavowal of consciousness and expression, much of Beckett's prose
takes place in the hypothetical mode, against its own stated impossibility.
These lines from the *Texts for Nothing* pose the problem starkly: "Where
would I go, if I could go, who would I be, if I could be, what would I say,
if I had a voice, who says this, saying it's me?" (91). As there is no voice, no
being, no movement, the discussion can only proceed in the conditional,
marked by the auxiliary *would*. However, the discussion does in fact go
on: "who says this, saying it's me?" Beckett never betrays his belief in
"the impossibility to express," first posited in the "Three Dialogues," and
as we shall see in this study, the conventional romantic and metaphysical
notions of "expression" are resolutely rejected in Beckett's postwar prose.

But if the "I" and its "voice" are both eliminated, language and speech are allowed to continue. The expression of voicelessness is not silence in Beckett, on the contrary, and "nothingness" does not follow from the I's failure to be. This study will build itself around the Beckettian refusal, around the "no" that Beckett can only paradoxically address to his readers, as even this refusal must in spite of itself permit address. But parallel to this, perhaps even in consequence of it, the negativity and negation so evident in Beckett's work are not simply affirmed. Beckett fully realized that the valorization of abnegation, of emptiness, impotence, or the "no," can too easily become itself an inverted imposition of force, the mirror of every act of affirmation or assertion of power. Refusal too must come to be refused, or as the eighth *Text for Nothing* ruefully puts it, "ah if no were content to cut yes's throat and never cut its own" (113–14). "No" is only cutthroat if it denies to denial the same authority it denies to affirmation. Thus, although there is nothing from which or with which to express, Beckett constantly stages this nevertheless obligatory, agentless, content-less "expression." Moreover, Beckett's texts consistently ironize the common critical recuperations of impotence, loss, and lack. Speaking, perhaps pointedly, about his "stick," Malone discusses its loss in these terms:

> It is a disaster. I suppose the wisest thing now is to live it over again, meditate upon it and be edified. It is thus that man distinguishes himself from the ape and rises, from discovery to discovery, ever higher, towards the light. Now that I have lost my stick I realize what it is I have lost and all it meant to me. And thence ascend, painfully, to an understanding of the Stick, shorn of all its accidents, such as I had never dreamt of. What a broadening of the mind. So that I half discern, in the veritable catastrophe that has befallen me, a blessing in disguise. How comforting that is. (*Three Novels*, 254)

This "impossible" or conditional status that Beckett confers on much of his work remains at the heart of the critical disagreements around his texts. Humanist and existentialist critics will stress the "affirmation" deriving from continuing within the space of the impossible; Blanchot's thoughts on the "neutral," on the other hand, inspire a focus on the elimination of subjectivity and the refusal to say "I." Others cast the issue in Kantian terms and discuss Beckett within the problematics of the sublime and the expression of the inexpressible, while the last few years have seen an increased emphasis on the prose and an explosion of "poststructuralist" readings. Indeed, the history of Beckett criticism, although not long, for obvious reasons, is amazingly voluminous and varied. It is doubtful that any other postwar literary figure has generated as much critical work as Beckett with as great a variety of approaches, and one of the oddities of Beckett's reception is the scope of the critical differences of the attempts to explain him. In the introduction to their recent collection of articles, Lance Butler and Robin Davis list some of the startlingly different "Becketts" we have been given: "Beckett as the quintessential *nouveau romancier,* Beckett the Cartesian, Beckett the Existentialist, these have rubbed shoulders with Beckett the nihilist, Beckett the mystic and, of course, Beckett the dramatist of the Absurd and Beckett the explorer of the limitations of language" (x). This list shows a recuperation of Beckett by almost every major school of critical thought since his arrival on the scene, and Butler and Davis could easily have gone on to add Beckett the "postmodernist" or Beckett the avant-gardist. That Beckett has been read through both mysticism and Cartesian skepticism, both Wittgensteinian and Heideggerian lenses, both existentialist affirmation and new novelistic formalism, can certainly be seen as evidence of the "inexhaustible quality of the challenge he offers" (x), as Butler and Davis assert, but to others this variety seems on the contrary indicative of a certain critical bewilderment.

Thus, in the preface to his recent book, Leslie Hill also comments on the breadth of Beckettian criticism, remarking "over several decades, in countless books and articles, the search for stable and satisfactory meanings in Beckett's writings has carried on unabated" (ix). But for Hill, this avalanche is more a symptom of failure than a mark of richness: "Set beside the emotional fervour and intellectual disarray voiced in Beckett's own writing, the critical response to the task of interpreting Beckett's work has been, to a large degree, bland and unconvincing" (x). Although Butler and Davis work from a premise of overflowing plenitude and Hill from that of a series of failures, these two major publications of 1990 reach similar conclusions regarding the "new" direction for Beckettian studies. Butler and Davis write that Beckett seems to be, in addition to everything else, "the poet of the post-structuralist age" and "deconstructionist *avant la lettre*" (x). There is now, they assert, "a new Beckett, thinkable only in the most recent critical terms" (x). Although Hill avoids terms like "deconstruction" and "poststructuralist," his emphasis on language as constitutive of subjectivity, his references to the "signature" and "textual perplexity," his rejection of "transcendence" or "an all-embracing authorial vision" in Beckett, and his statement "The concern here is not with presumed authorial concepts, but with textual affects" (x) are resonant of the interests and vocabulary of thinkers like Derrida, de Man, Kristeva, and Lacan, whose work Hill draws upon in his readings.

Without entering into a discussion of the ultimate utility and precision of the term "poststructuralist," [5] it is undeniable that the theories, speculations, and approaches usually grouped together (for better or worse) under this aegis, and particularly the critical approaches usually associated with Jacques Derrida, have been an extremely powerful force in works on Beckett over the last several years.[6] Certainly, the wave of poststructuralist work on Beckett is to some extent simply part of the larger poststructuralist wave of the late eighties and early nineties generally. If that wave seems largely to have subsided, Beckett nevertheless represents a special case. For beyond any wider interest in poststructuralism, there is also widespread sentiment that Beckett is in certain ways particularly close to the writers and questions associated with this movement.[7] The feeling is especially acute with regard to Derrida, and Stephen Barker speaks for many when he states: "One's first reaction to reading Beckett is that he is not only the most obvious choice of an author to whose works one can apply poststructuralist strategies but that he is almost too good, programmed, it seems, for a Derridean treatment" (Butler and Davis, 200). Meanwhile, Richard Begam, carefully cataloguing the manifold occurrences of the term "unnamable" in Derrida (149–55) and artfully comparing the Derridean "tympanum" to the famous tympanum passage of *The Unnamable* (175–79), almost seems to hint that Derrida is willfully alluding to Beckett in these places.

I too share the sense of an almost privileged relationship between Beckett's texts and those usually associated with poststructuralism, and this study will make frequent reference to "poststructuralist" issues and practices. In this introduction, through detailed examination of certain questions that Beckett's texts raise, I will attempt to show the utility of various poststructuralist and structural linguistic approaches. But for the moment let us note that should one evoke only the most general and cliché issues of "deconstruction," for example, the relationships between linguistic structure and subjectivity, language and intention, "iterability" and context, and the deconstruction of subjective presence as a source of linguistic meaning, it is difficult not to be reminded of Beckett. It is, then, hardly surprising that I am not alone in my methodological approach, but this sort of company, as readers of Beckett well know, is both comforting and haunting. If it is reassuring to have one's critical suppositions seconded by others, this companionship also strips one of the sense of originality, singularity, and, in the end, purpose, which a more solitary endeavor might grant. It is often hard to avoid the impression with regard to Beckett that all has either been said or else is unsayable, and I cannot deny that a certain sense of futility has at times accompanied me during the writing of this study. Yet in this very futility I once again find company, it being itself a rather frequent theme of Beckettian criticism, particularly in recent years,[8] and interestingly, one sounded by Jacques Derrida precisely in relation to the question of the proximity of his work to Beckett's. Asked by Derek Attridge in a recent interview why he has never written on Beckett, although he has given seminars on his work, Derrida responds, "This is an author to whom I feel very close, or to whom I would like to feel myself very close; but also too close. . . . I have perhaps avoided him a bit because of this identification." Derrida then goes on to echo Stephen Barker's perception of the almost overappropriateness of Beckett as a subject for "deconstructive" criticism, responding guardedly in the affirmative when Attridge asks, "Is there a sense in which Beckett's writing is already so 'deconstructive,' or 'self-deconstructive,' that there is not much left to do?"[9]

If I have perhaps too much company in the feeling that there is not much left to do, or even nothing to be done, what needs to be remembered is that my most notable companion in this respect would be Beckett himself, and not primarily because of his tendency to discount critical approaches to his work. Rather, the obligation to say, or express, along with the impossibility of ever saying what needs to be said, of saying the thing that would allow a silence, is one of the central Beckettian textual scenes. Beckett's own prose is filled with the assertions of futility, unoriginality, repetitiousness, and inadequacy that often come to haunt its exegetes. The common critical perception that the thing that needs to be said about Beckett has yet to be said, or that we have yet to receive the ideally adequate account of Beckett, sufficient to obviate the current torrent of criticism,[10] is very likely due less to the criticism than to its object. It is worth quoting at length Derrida's own perplexity regarding the problem of responding to or writing on Beckett. In the Attridge interview, speaking of the question of Beckett's "nihilism" or lack thereof, Derrida says:

Above all, this question should not be treated as a philosophical problem outside or above the texts. When I found myself, with students, reading some Beckett texts, I would take three lines, I would spend two hours on them, then I would give up because it would not have been possible, or honest, or even interesting, to extract a few "significant" lines from a Beckett text. The composition, the rhetoric, the construction and the rhythm of his works, even the ones that seem the most "decomposed," that's what "remains" finally the most "interesting," that's the work, that's the signature, this remainder which remains when the thematics is exhausted (and also exhausted, by others, for a long time now, in other modes). (Derrida, *Acts of Literature*, 61)

For a Beckett scholar, immediately notable is Derrida's automatic assumption that Beckett's texts need to be approached through minute analyses of short passages. A novel like *Molloy* instantly invites narratological analyses, whereas *Malone Dies* is obviously friendly to a focus on metafictionality. Consequently, in addition to thematic and philosophical interpretation, there is a long tradition of structuralist and formalist analysis of Beckett's prose. It is only relatively recently that critics have begun to rely more heavily on close readings and tropological analyses of Beckett's sentences, paragraphs, and rhetoric, with emphasis on the sorts of effects of repetition, syntax, rhythm, and figure more usually found in criticism of poetry.[11]

Derrida's emphasis on close reading goes hand in hand with the central difficulty he raises in terms of reading Beckett—the need not to remain "above" or "outside" the texts along with the inability to find an "inside" to crawl into. This is, in a nutshell, the dilemma every conscientious reader of Beckett's prose has had to face, in one way or another.[12] Indeed, Beckett's refusal and thwarting of this sort of interiority, whether subjective or textual, are perhaps his most significant achievement. I agree with Derrida that the "thematics," in the narrow sense, is not what is most "interesting" about Beckett; however, Derrida's subsequent reliance on the vaguest, most aestheticized terms of stylistic analysis to account for Beckett—terms which his own work has brought into question as much as anyone's—seems noteworthy. One of my tasks here will be to attempt to establish a critical vocabulary for responding to these texts which present the obstacles for "thematic" analyses that Derrida rightly sees. Assuming that Derrida and Attridge are right that Beckett's texts are largely "self-deconstructive" (and for the most part I will argue that they are), I would like to investigate in this study just what is left for a "deconstructionist" or "poststructuralist" critic to do with them. The implications of the responses to this question go beyond Beckett and would be of crucial importance for the study not only of other writers who might have paralleled Derrida, but for the increasing number who have been directly influenced by him. For if Derrida is no longer the preeminent figure of current literary critical methodology, his enduring place in the intellectual history of the latter part of the twentieth century seems increasingly assured. So, in addition to "reading" Beckett, in this study I will also investigate implicitly the question of what is to be done with a "self-deconstructive" text. Therefore, I certainly do not propose this project as a "deconstruction" of Beckett, nor even primarily as an investigation of "deconstructive motifs" in Beckett's prose. Rather, I hope to begin to find a way of discussing "what remains" in Beckett, the singularity of Beckett's prose, in terms of its inscription and composition, in addition to examining what "remains" for poststructuralist criticism to do with an author who in many ways anticipates and obviates classic poststructuralist critical moves. Derrida's own bafflement concerning where to locate the singularity of Beckett's achievement, his difficulty in determining what there is in Beckett to discuss and where it might be, are typical. But of course it is Derrida more than anyone who has made contemporary critics rethink their own conceptions of textual borders, boundaries, and interiors. It is around the questions of subjective and textual boundaries that Derrida and Beckett probably are closest.

This study will examine these questions primarily through a focus on Beckett's prose. The first chapter will look at *Murphy* and the early poem "Whoroscope" to investigate Beckett's initial attempts to inscribe the Cartesian model of consciousness and subjectivity into a larger reflection on filiation, debt, authorship and authority, narcissism, and obsessional ritual. Beckett's focus on auto-inscription, which he finds to be both the mode of the cogito and the key to the interest both Descartes and Murphy show in horoscopes, leads him to certain distinctive stances regarding the status of proper names, reading and interpretation, and language and desire that remain central throughout his oeuvre. An understanding of Beckett's early onomastic play is crucial for an understanding of the rejection of the proper name that the title *The Unnamable* seems paradoxically to imply. Chapter 2 will examine *Watt* as Beckett's most extended investigation of the relationship between individual subjectivity and the plural group structures like language and culture which must inevitably precede it. *Watt* is Beckett's most explicit reflection on the issues of cultural and linguistic appurtenance—issues which underlie all of this bilingual author's subsequent writing—and is also the site where Beckett most rigorously considers the concept of the "we" in relation to his severely problematic "I." On a narrative level, this "anthropological" concern shifts Beckett away from the intense focus on the first-person pronoun which characterizes most of his later prose, and our reading of *Watt* will also necessitate a detour from some of the central critical practices and questions which will occupy us subsequently. Chapters 3 and 4 will look at Beckett's extension of the problem of the proper name into a consideration of pronouns and reference and will focus on the issues of expression, self-consciousness, and textual inscriptions of subjectivity in the trilogy, with specific emphasis in chapter 4 on *The Unnamable*. The accent here will be on close reading, in the attempt to show Beckett's ability to break down traditional assumptions and practices concerning these issues on the most fundamental levels of linguistic construction. Chapter 5 will continue to examine these questions as they are explored in the *Texts for Nothing* but will also focus on the Beckettian problematics of belatedness and response. To this effect, consideration will be given to the manner in which the trilogy might be seen as post-Joycean, as a response to Joyce. Meanwhile the *Texts*, which Beckett himself described as an attempt to move out of the impasse of *The Unnamable*, will be examined as the first "post-Beckettian" work, trying to discover what can come "after" the trilogy. A look at a highlighted auto-citation in the *Texts* will show another variation on the Beckettian mechanics of responding to "oneself," of the "self" as a network of echoes. Chapter 6 will return to the question of impasse and impossibility, specifically that of "going on" when one "can't go on," or its converse, that of allowing oneself not to "go on" when one must. To do this, we will look at how Beckett discusses progress, continuation, or any sort of "onward" movement generally in the late prose, specifically *Company, Worstward Ho,* and "Stirrings Still."

In terms of the totality of Beckett's oeuvre, even the brief sketch above shows a very obvious gap: the near total absence of the drama. The source of this omission is a difference between the "prose" and the "drama" which I would rather call "technical" than "generic." To investigate the questions of expression, subjectivity, and consciousness in Beckett, I have found it necessary to focus above all on Beckett's manifold dismantlings of the concept of the narrational or subjective *source*. This dismantling of the source effect in Beckett is conducted largely through extremely complex interrogations of pronouns and proper names. One of the major burdens of this study will be to show how Beckett disrupts the traditional function of the first-person pronoun as mark of the source of utterance, either through constructions of the sort found throughout *The Unnamable* and the *Texts for Nothing*, which amount to an "I" saying "I am not speaking," or through what seems to be a replacement of an "I" with a "you" in

Company, or through various other structural devices which highlight the role of the "speaker" or narrational source as citing and repeating rather than "expressing." Certainly, much of the theater addresses similar questions. One might think of the auto-citational structure of "Krapp's Last Tape," in which the aged Krapp obsessively listens to himself listening to himself, or even more of the interminable denial of subjective appropriation which makes up "Not I." But drama, of course, is also obviously different from prose and poetry in that it consists of a *staging* of events in addition to a linguistic account of them and offers an entirely different surface of inscription and signification. This introduces crucial differences in terms of the interpretive position of the audience and, equally important, tends to eliminate one of the key structural elements Beckett's prose often troubles—the necessary temporal difference between the "moment" of the recounting of events and the events that are recounted. Beckett's prose continually harps on the problem of the spacing and temporality of a fictive narrativized voice on which textual production depends. The staging of the theater, on the other hand, automatically dispenses with this problem of "sourcing." Admittedly, the distinctions between the drama and the prose start to be blurred when one considers the radio and television plays—the reduction of the stage to the sound of voices in radio would perhaps offer an opening to the kinds of work I will do on the prose here, though already the tactile markers provided by the differences in voice of the different actors along with the sound effects provide an element of differentiation and ontological grounding of the sort the prose enthusiastically refuses. To a considerable extent, the postwar prose and the theater seem to respect a division, the concerns with language as space of auto-affect and auto-inscription belonging to the prose while the theater focuses on the exposure of the spectacle of subjective debacle to the gaze of the other. In certain respects, the epitome of Beckett's theatrical representation of subjectivity is "Film," focused on "perceivedness" and paranoia, the eye of the other, rather than voices, hearing, and repetition, as in so much of the prose. That Beckett's notes to "Film" inform us that the "pursuing perceiver is not extraneous, but self" (*Collected Shorter Plays,* 163) shows how the specularity of the theater rejoins the problematics of self-recognition in the prose, but the extremely complex tactics of Beckett's specular play in the drama would require a study in itself.

As we have already seen, Beckett's work poses formidable problems for exegesis, and in this book I have, I hope, devised a set of approaches which will allow us to see exactly what the stakes are in Beckett's manipulations of written prose forms and conventions and, more important, exactly how these manipulations do their work. An attempt to extend the arguments I will be making here to the major drama would be an interesting and necessary project, but it would also be a different one, entailing an elaboration of a critical vocabulary capable of responding to the formal structures and signifying economies of drama and theater, in addition to a look at Beckett's relationship to and subversions of theatrical traditions, expectations, and predecessors. In terms of the latter point, I would think a focus on Yeats might have to replace the recurrent emphasis on Joyce to be found in this study.[13] To put it another way, if the subject is largely seen as constitutionally "textual" in Beckett, as I will go on to argue, an investigation of the drama would necessitate a methodology capable of responding to the textual space, in the wide sense of the term, of the theater, including the textuality and temporality of performance—a worthy task, but one I have not been able to undertake here. My entire project is based on the assumption that what is crucial and difficult in Beckett is not mostly the intellectual positions or philosophical problematics which can be abstracted from his work—Derrida's "thematics"—but how in "technical" terms his texts pursue, enact, and implicate the reader within them (as if the language and signifying economy of a work were "only" technical). For this reason it is only after having examined closely the workings of the prose that we will be in a position to clearly gauge the relationship the drama might maintain with it. Therefore, I will await the conclusion to return to the crucial question of the theater.

Regarding the questions of subjectivity and consciousness, it is in the prose and particularly in the trilogy that we find the central questioning of the Cartesian grounding of self-consciousness and self-knowledge which is Beckett's focal point in his investigation of these issues. Throughout the trilogy, Beckett obsessively returns to the cogito and its triple suppositions concerning the ability to produce thought, represent thought linguistically, and recognize oneself as the producer of the linguistic thought thus produced. Beckett's attack on the cogito in the trilogy and later works comes from within the first-person structure necessary to the cogito's success, but takes the form of voiding—systematically—all of the cogito's assumptions and deductions. In this introduction we will give an overview of some of the central recurrent tropes and strategies Beckett uses to accomplish this, along with their implications for analysis, theory, and simply reading. Thus, in terms of the function and implications of the first-person pronoun, we will need to examine Blanchot's thoughts on the "neutral," and look at linguistic analyses of deixis and reference with regard to the pronominal system. To begin, however, we should return to the assertions of impossibility, incomprehensibility, and illegibility mentioned above, which are among other things attacks on the limpid transparency of intention to linguistic signification which the cogito assumes. Beckett's prose consistently affirms the absence of all that the cogito is meant to guarantee, presenting subjective constructions of language as everything but the proof of self-consciousness and self-recognition. Central, then, both to the cogito and to the structure of the trilogy is Beckett's treatment of linguistic expression and vocal expressing, whether "internalized" or no, and it is around these issues that we shall begin.

Expression and Voice: Catachresis and Prosopopoeia

Perhaps the central Beckettian paradox or "impossibility" in the prose is the one evoked above in the passage from the *Texts for Nothing*—that of the absence of subjectivity, expressed content, expressing consciousness, and expressive signification, along with the presence of linguistic expression. However, the disavowal of the (non)speaking subjects in Beckett of the speech they (don't) utter partakes, in paradoxical form, of an extremely old literary tradition—that of the "orphic" moment in poetry, when speech is somehow given to the mute, expression to the inexpressive. What is often at stake in Beckett, then, is one of the most traditional poetic conceits: that of giving voice to the voiceless. How Beckett turns this trope, however, is hardly traditional and reveals problems that have always been implicit in the orphic stand. To get a clearer view of this, it is instructive to look at the investigations into these problems of an earlier Irish writer—William Butler Yeats.

Around the end of the last century, the symbolist Yeats struggled toward defining the distinction between symbol and allegory, finally settling on the following terms. Allegory, Yeats suggested, "said things which could be said as well, or better, in another way," while symbolism, on the other hand, "gave dumb things voices, and bodiless things bodies."[14] The symmetry that might seem to obtain between these two terms is illusory: allegory, seen quite conventionally as secondary and ornamental, is discussed in terms of representing, of giving names. However, symbolism, in Yeats's formulation, is not primarily concerned with designation; the point of symbolism is not only to say "something," either well or badly, but also to enable things to "say" themselves, to give voice. The shift from name to voice, made only tentatively here by Yeats, is crucial. The question of the poet's capacity to designate or name implies a poetics of the proper—of the poet's ability to "see things as they are" and give these things their "fitting" names—names guaranteed by the poet's visionary and linguistic powers. The emphasis is on the capacity of language to sort, classify, and order the real into a stable and durable system of symbolic differences. It is a discourse where stress falls on adequation and the patronym, as the proper name must indeed be appropriate, and the authority behind it recognizable and indivisible.[15]

The figure of the bestowal of voice upon the voiceless, however, opens up two different sets of problems. First of all, rather than the issue being one of attribution of a name or symbolic identity necessary for inscription in discursive networks, the giving of voice implies the bestowal of the capacity to *use* names, to become the source of a discursive instance. This is precisely the issue at hand in most of the works of Beckett with which we will be concerned in this study, particularly the trilogy of novels, *Molloy, Malone Dies,* and *The Unnamable,* and the *Texts for Nothing, Company,* and *Worstward Ho.* Indeed, on a general level, one could say that the difference between the discussion of the common noun "pot" in *Watt,* for example, and the interrogation of pronouns in *The Unnamable* corresponds nicely to the difference between the Yeatsian problematics of "allegory" and "symbolism." In any event, all these later works describe the voice that speaks them as alien, bestowed or imposed, and nonoriginary. The Beckettian "narrators," in this way, could be seen not as representations of the master poet, but as uttering the speech of Yeats's "dumb things" given voices; however, their desire is only to divest themselves of this poisoned gift. The question of the status of this alien and alienating voice thus becomes crucial, and here Yeats's second break with a poetics of adequation takes on its full weight in Beckett. To give voice to something that is *constitutionally* mute, to give a body to that which is incorporeal, are to abandon even the theoretical possibility of the literal, "direct presentation," or the proper, and to enter a poetics whose inaugural gesture is to acknowledge its own figurality, its transgression of the poetics of mimetic or literal immediacy, or even figural adequation. In place of the literal and the proper, we have catachresis and trope. We begin to see why the Beckett "confessional" can never be considered as simple autobiographical or even fictionalized autobiographical "expression." The argument I will pursue in this study is that Beckett's texts tend to present subjectivity as an originary catachresis, and expression as prosopopoeia.

Catachresis, in its most general sense, means any misuse of figural language, as in mixed metaphors, but more specifically, it also means the coining of names for the nameless *by means of the borrowing of other names*. There are two points to be made about catachreses. First of all, they straddle the distinction between literal and figural. For example, "table leg" is clearly "figural" in its use of "leg," but there is no "literal" term for the object designated by that word in English. It may certainly be argued that everyone "knows" what a table leg is, and that accordingly the catachrestical character of the sign in no way impedes reference. This is certainly true enough—the problems posed by catachreses arise not in terms of ordinary language but when it is necessary to distinguish in interpretive contexts between figural uses of language and literal designations. In many metaphors, we "know" what is designated by the figure—"Achilles the lion" does not evoke for the educated reader a beast on all fours. Still, a literary critic of almost any stripe is going to draw distinctions between the phrase "Achilles the lion" and "brave Achilles," to give a trivial example. In terms of these sorts of distinctions, a phrase like "the table stood firmly on its legs" is going to present certain difficulties, as catachresis makes it impossible to decide if the phrase is literal or metaphorical, and thus, to locate the "tenor" or "vehicle" and in consequence any stable signified. Of course, the subversive power of a catachresis comes from the importance of the referent it is meant to designate, and the importance of that referent's literal discernableness and clarity within a chain of meaning. Already we may begin to surmise the possible consequences of catachrestical subjective self-designations, and catachrestical constructions are a central strategy in Beckett's constant positing of figures for an authorial subject whose final literal unveiling is depicted as theoretically impossible, because catachresis renders a terminal point of literality unavailable.

Second of all, and following logically from the above, catachreses foreground the problems of debt, secondarity, and supplementarity in language. In other words, if the term "table leg" can only be understood through implicit reference to the sign "leg," "table leg" becomes in some sense dependent on and posterior to the word "leg," which takes on a kind of priority (just as a metaphor is seen as posterior to the literal meanings of its components). The relationship between "leg" and "table leg" is clearly different from that obtaining between, say, "leg" and "table." One can see the problem catachreses pose for Platonic views of language or any call for a totally sufficient literality, like the Emersonian desire to give something its own name and not that of another. Catachreses manage to infect "literal" designations with the belatedness and alterity of metaphor and figure. This sense of the nonoriginary, of belatedness, secondarity, and debt, is omnipresent in Beckett. One of the major ways he elaborates it is through the massive, albeit discreet, intertextual networks in his texts. Not only do his works often refer to prior texts bearing his signature, but they also create a near-constant echoing sound of allusion, tag, and outright citation. The degree to which Beckett's texts "borrow" their propriety, and open themselves to the otherness of other names, signatures, and works, is only beginning to be explored and will be a recurring issue throughout this study, with a particular focus on Joyce and Dante.

The question of debt is also implicit in Yeats's definition of symbolism, when he stresses that the task is to *give* "dumb things voices, and bodiless things bodies." And this leads to consideration of another central trope in Beckett's poetics—prosopopoeia, the trope of bestowing the capacity to hear or speak upon the dead, inanimate, or absent. Odes and apostrophes are prosopopoeias, as would be Yeats's bestowal of voice upon the mute, or funerary inscriptions in which the deceased is figured as "speaking" the writing on the stone. Beckett makes classic and explicit use of prosopopoeia whenever he has a narrator claim to be speaking from beyond the grave (for example, at the beginning of the story "The Calmative"). In Yeats's symbolist prosopopoeia, the prosopopoeical moment implies gift: it would seem that the poet (or painter as the case may be) lends his voice to that which has none. The possibility of allowing the mute to speak is predicated on the poet's *not* being mute, on a largeness of voice sufficient to give itself over to objects or sensations which speak in a voice or inhabit a verbal body which can only be "symbolic," as it is part of the nature of these objects and sensations to be mute or incorporeal. The poetics of Yeatsian symbolism is depicted as the site of a transfer, and the recognition of an economy of exchange, debt, and gift is shown in Yeats's insistence on the need of symbols and his rejection of any sort of imagistic "direct treatment." But in spite of this, Yeats does seem to maintain an originary plenitude: symbolism takes its origin in the poet's voice.

In Beckett, the problem takes a subtle detour. Certainly, it is a question of giving voice to the voiceless, but now it is the "poet" who is voiceless, the "writer" who is somehow given a voice not his own. In *The Unnamable,* we are told again and again that the "proper" of the agency of speech in the text[16] is silence, thus the speech it utters cannot be its own. That which "speaks" has received not a gift but a punishment, being forced to express that it cannot express, in a speech which gives the lie to its condition. All speech becomes "symbolic," in the Yeatsian sense, in a book like *The Unnamable*. Contrary to certain existentialist readings, there is no "self-expression" to be found in the novel precisely because it is not a self that is doing the expressing, and the expressing fails to represent a prior something one could call a self. In Beckett's trilogy, not only are proper names catachrestical, but even the positing of the authorial or narrative "I" becomes a figural or performative act—a prosopopoeia—rather than the representation of a preexisting, stable reality. It is one thing to state "I am not x," in a traditional introspective search for subjective adequation and proper expression, and quite another to assert "I am not" or, even more, "I am not me." Malone, wondering if the pots in his room are "his" or simply put at his disposal, concludes, "They are not mine, but I say my pots, as I say my bed, my window, as I say me" (252). The problem then is not whether the pots "really belong" to Malone or not—"Malone" here is not even capable of the self-identity that would be prior to any claim of ownership. The first-person pronoun no longer expresses a self in either its plenitude or poverty, but rather becomes itself an "object" which must be endlessly reappropriated for any designation of "proper" attributes to occur. This focus on grammatical appropriation denies the conception of a preexistent subjectivity to be expressed, rendering grammatical construction as a catachrestical act.

The relationship between a thetic "I" and figural language, perhaps not at first blush evident, is crucial.[17] The "figural" per se has never presented a problem for traditional literature or criticism.[18] It is easy to accept that language is largely figural, and to this extent distanced or "improper," and even laud these qualities as constituting literature's "imaginative" or "visionary" core. But it is necessary for this "vision" or "imagination" to be linked and anchored to someone or something, either a referent or a consciousness, which it expresses and represents. If the very proper name or pronoun "I" which sets in motion the figural chain is itself a figure— the catachresis or prosopopoeia which Paul de Man implies it always must be[19]—then a poetics of self-revelation and self-scrutiny, even visionary self-scrutiny, becomes impossible. In other words, the "negative" moments within the "imaginary" or "visionary" literary experience—the hallucination or dedifferentiation caused by figural language—can no longer be recuperated under the aegis of a transcendental subject who could master or at least answer for them. The positing of subjectivity itself becomes one figure in the chain and no longer that chain's origin or destination. Even the aporia that results from the above is denied a direct and unmediated statement—"I don't know" itself becomes a figural proposition. In Beckett, we eventually end up with what could be called an auto-prosopopoeia, in which every thetic statement is presented as borrowed, nonoriginary, indebted, and imposed, although the concept of any exterior, antecedent origin is equally rejected. Not only names, but the most "literal" elements of grammar—pronouns—come to be seen as catachrestical, attempting to carve a space for a subjectivity that can neither outlast the moment of their utterance nor even occupy that moment as it happens. The "dumb thing" is now that which gives the reader the story, in a "speech" which both violates its muteness and fails to express it.

It is this emphasis on violation and inexpressivity which makes Beckett's prose an extremely powerful critique of literary hermeneutic reading. In *The Unnamable* and the *Texts for Nothing*, no subjective presence, either to be revealed or hidden by language, can be found. Current theoretical commonplaces defining subjectivity as an effect of language, rather than its origin or cause, find themselves scrupulously worked through on the most basic textual level of syntactic construction and grammatical continuity in Beckett. It is for this reason that the true importance of Beckett's texts can only be measured by an extremely close reading, which would show how these questions are enacted and staged through writing practice, and not simply by mode of theoretical assertion.

A reading of Beckett's handling of voice seems especially pertinent in the wake of Derrida's analysis of logocentrism, as Beckett appears to mobilize the metaphor of "voice" in his texts precisely to parody its traditional metaphysical investments. In fact, it is around this trope as much as anything that the relevance of "Derridean" approaches becomes apparent. On the rhetorical level, Beckett's manipulation of the figures of voice and speech necessitates a continuation of Paul de Man's thoughts on autobiography and lyric as prosopopoeia, that is to say, as constructed on the figure of a phenomenalized *voice*. For it is in fact this coherent "voice-effect" and all the metaphysical suppositions that it entails which Beckett's postwar prose takes the task of dismantling, either through the dazzling pronominal juggling of *The Unnamable* and the *Texts for Nothing*, or through more deeply embedded structural plays, as in *Molloy, Company,* and *Worstward Ho*. The question of the metaphor of "voice" in Beckett and his way of pressuring the narrative "voice-effect" will receive attention throughout this study, but particularly in chapters 3 and 4, focusing on the trilogy generally and more specifically on *The Unnamable*.

The Cogito and Consciousness

A deconstructive analysis of the "voice" in Beckett inevitably leads to the broader questions of consciousness, self-presence, and subjectivity. As Beckett's prose closes down the space of phenomenal identification based on the representation of a coherent subjectivity, it likewise eliminates the possibility of psychologizing interpretations, or any recourse to the conventional strategies of the introspective tradition. By the power of his staging of the "prosopopoeical" text, Beckett also renders impracticable most of the traditional hermeneutic strategies available for discussing figural language at all, by presenting "consciousness" itself as a "figural" construction with no "literal" underpinning. In the end, one finds no ideality that has been expressed, but only an interminable referential action. Indeed, the term "expression," necessarily implying an exteriorization of a prior interior, is itself inappropriate. One hesitates to speak of "introspection" in terms of works like *The Unnamable* and the *Texts for Nothing, Company,* or *Worstward Ho* because ultimately there is nothing left "inside" to be inspected; the subjective interior upon which introspection is predicated is dismantled.

Beckett works through this problem of subjective interiority through an interrogation of Descartes and the cogito. The cogito's logic of the exclusion of the body, the real, and the sensory from the place of the subject's self-presence and self-knowledge is investigated in many places and registers in Beckett's work. Chapters 2, 3, and 4 will examine some of the cogitolike constructions and distortions found in *Watt* and the trilogy, while chapter 1 will look at Beckett's parody of some of Descartes's most highly invested categorizations as found in the early prose and the poem "Whoroscope." Beckett's concentration on Descartes and post-Cartesian philosophy, often mediated by a psychoanalytic perspective, is the predominant factor that opens his work to issues raised by recent discussions of phenomenology. In fact, Thomas Trezise has brilliantly addressed the grounds of Beckett's implicit critique of Cartesian subjectivity through a discussion of contemporary criticisms of phenomenology. Trezise effectively presents the basis of the Beckettian refusal of subjective interiority when, in a philosophical register and with the help of Deleuze's neologism "effondement," he remarks:

The fundamentally paradoxical character of a subjectivity whose sameness is born in the repetition of its preoriginary difference bespeaks the immemorial *effondement* of separation in an economy where, by reason of the other of separation always already within, subjectivity is always already without . . . the only meaning of the pronoun "I" resides in the sameness *of* its difference, and . . . the allegorical place or space of subjectivity is neither inside nor yet simply outside but in the other of their very separation. (74)

Trezise's fascinating reading of Beckett is largely based on Derrida, particularly the critique of Husserlian subjectivity found in *Speech and Phenomena*. His book is the most convincing work on Beckett to date that uses Derrida to interrogate existentialist and phenomenologist interpretations, while also showing how Beckett's own writing effects this critique to a large extent itself. In this sense, Trezise is crucial in establishing in detail how Beckett might indeed be seen as "self-deconstructive." I hope to build on Trezise's work both on consciousness in Beckett and on the relevance of Derrida for Beckettian criticism, but I will shift the ground slightly, to examine literary precedents for the Derridean and Beckettian readings of consciousness, in particular, Joyce's. Thus, where Trezise used primarily a philosophical lens, I will work more through "literary" analyses and questionings. My argument will be that Joyce's writing practice, and particularly *Finnegans Wake,* is central for both Derrida and Beckett, whose work shares among other things an especially heavy marking by texts from both the "philosophical" and "literary" traditions. The emphasis, then, will be on the implications of Joyce for writing practice, or the mechanics of inscription, more than on philosophical conceptualizations or theorizations concerning language. Joyce's implication of psychoanalytic theory in the linguistic distortions of the *Wake* provided a powerful alternate model to Cartesian framings of subjectivity for Beckett and is central to the joining of psychoanalysis to literature and philosophy evident in his work along with Derrida's. Of course, an emphasis on predecessors leads inevitably to that of followers, to arriving belatedly, to being lost in the wake. Thus, in chapter 5 the *Texts for Nothing* will be proposed as a work that interrogates not only what it means to come after Joyce, to be in his wake, but the entire question of secondarity and response itself.

In addition to a predominantly "literary" focus, in order to respond to the singularity of Beckett's work, the philosophical and the stylistic or rhetorical registers must be merged, as they so often are in the texts he signed—texts which plunder the resources of two literary traditions to stage, rather than discuss, many of the compelling philosophical questions of the last thirty years. A reading that would practice this merging—notable not only in Beckett's texts, but also in Derrida's—is what I hope to offer in the chapters that follow. My focus throughout will be Beckett's handling of the textual construction of subjectivity. By this I mean both Beckett's conceptualization of subjectivity as a text, a deferring and differing economy rather than a referent to be "expressed," *and* his concern with the relationship of subjectivity to the spaces without and within a written, "literary" text. One of the most remarkable ways in which Beckett sets both issues in motion is through his disorienting and violent undermining of the pronominal system and the narrative and linguistic stabilities it strives to guarantee. It is not possible to proceed on our reading of Beckett without a preliminary investigation from linguistic, narratological, and lyric perspectives of pronouns generally and, in particular, the mark that expresses subjectivity in language, the first-person pronoun.

Pronouns, Deixis, and First-Person Utterance

In terms of contemporary theory, by now we are all well aware of the critique of the logocentric pretensions of much first-person discourse, which would ground language as a transparent, mimetic code issuing from a fully present conscious subject who is at once: (1) the guarantor of the univocity of that code's meaning, (2) self-referentially, the content of the meaning that is thus guaranteed, and (3) the ultimate receiver for whom that meaning is made manifest. First-person discourse would be seen as the linguistic expression par excellence in which the substitutive, combinatory, and relational operations of language would be suppressed in favor of a reified, phenomenalized, semantic core of meaning, and in which any interest the text might have is asserted to come from its reflection of the interest of the author who produced it. In opposition, one might quote Marinetti's imperative of 1913, "Destroy the *I* in literature: that is, all psychology" (95), or rally around Mallarmé's assertion: "L'œuvre pure implique la disparition élocutoire du poète, qui cède l'initiative aux mots, par le heurt de leur inégalité mobilisés" (248).[20]

The interest of Beckett's work with regard to these questions is that it seems to carry out a classic logocentric critique by working *through* the first person, rather than by eschewing it. Beckett's first-person texts never support the logocentric claims discussed above, but while rejecting the transcendental pretensions of the authority of the signature, they also reject the dodging of the issue of the origin-effect that a recourse to third-person narration sometimes implies. A shift to the third person perhaps disclaims self-reflexive authority, but it does not do away with the inherent problems of the assumption of the narrative voice. Can we assert that there is indeed a narrative or poetic discourse, or instance of language generally, that is not in some way tethered to the signature effect, to the question of its own "source," "intention," and "reference," even if the text's very purpose is to trouble just these categories? To understand the way Beckett pressures the first person into the position of the breaking point of logocentrism, we need to look at linguistic discussions of pronouns generally and the first person in particular.

Beckett's treatment of pronouns is inextricably linked with the question of "deixis." The "deictic" refers to the capacity of language to signify by showing or pointing, in relation to a specific discursive moment, rather than by naming. Ducrot and Todorov define deictics as "expressions whose referent can only be determined in relation to the interlocutors" (252, translation slightly modified). Thus, "the pronouns of the first and second persons designate, respectively, the person who is speaking and the person spoken to" (252). They then cite three pairs of expressions distinguished only in that the first element in each is deictic: "*here* (the place where the dialogue is occurring)" as against "*there*"; "*yesterday* (the day before the day on which we are speaking)" as against "*the day before*"; and "*at this time* (the time when we are speaking)" as against "*at that time*" (252). As these examples make clear, deictics only gain referential stability (even *fictive* referential stability) through what de Man would call the "phenomenalization" of a "moment" of their utterance. For literature there is one immediate outstanding implication—that deictics like "here" and "now" are completely dependent on a *moment* of utterance, and thus in a certain sense cannot be written, or at least have to be read as if they were not in order for referential certainty to be preserved.[21] Of course, "I" is also a deictic. Anyone can say "I"—"I" refers only to the person saying "I" at a particular moment. More than any other writer, Beckett has investigated the consequences of this for the "I" in written texts, where nobody "says" anything. In linguistic terms, the consequences of the curious temporal construction of the "I" have been analyzed by Emile Benveniste.

It is in his article "The Nature of Pronouns"[22] that Benveniste first points out the entirely deictic referential capabilities of the pronoun. Trying to distinguish the linguistic differences between pronouns and common nouns, Benveniste notes that common nouns refer to "a fixed and 'objective' notion, capable of remaining virtual or of being actualized in a particular object, and which is always identical in the representation it evokes" (*Problems in General Linguistics*, 218, translation modified).[23] In other words, a common noun like "chair" has the same referential capacity regardless of who says it or where it is written. For a pronoun, the situation is different: "But the instances of the use of *I* do not constitute a class of reference since there is no 'object' definable as *I* to which these instances can refer in identical fashion" (218). What then is the "meaning" or "reality" to which a word like "I" or "you" could refer? Benveniste's answer is: "*I* signifies 'the person who is uttering the present instance of the discourse containing *I*'" (218). Subjectivity, then, comes to depend on enunciation — if "I" refers only to the person saying "I" at a particular moment, then the "moment" and the utterance both make possible and are logically prior to subjective designation, rather than being simply the expression of a "moment" at which the subject already happened to find itself. But this "moment of utterance" on which subjective assertion depends is in and of itself not exactly a temporal measure at all. Benveniste points out that the "present moment" implied in the concept of deixis is the "moment" of a deictic sign's instantiation in speech. In other words, the "present" *is in itself* an effect of the "moment" of utterance, rather than a temporal space that receives an utterance as it passes. The questions deixis raises concerning the temporality of subjectivity are explored further in "Subjectivity in Language,"[24] where Benveniste explains, "The 'subjectivity' we are discussing here is the capacity of the speaker to posit himself as 'subject.' . . . 'Ego' is he who *says* 'ego'" (*Problems in General Linguistics*, 224).[25] The ramifications of this somewhat self-evident statement are rather surprising, concerning the referential capacities of the "I." Benveniste is implying here that the "I" no longer refers to a previously existing subjective substance or latency, but rather refers to its own saying, becoming itself the "referent" that it is supposed to signify. "Est 'ego' qui *dit* 'ego'" means "I am the I that I am saying." "I am" is no longer a constative, locutionary phrase, but a constantly renewed performative, referring vertiginously to its own utterance. As shall be seen in chapters 3 and 4, in the trilogy Beckett constantly troubles the already uncertain status of subjective assertions, hovering between constatation and performative, particularly with regard to the presentation of this division in the cogito, in which "I am" both states a prior condition and serves to bring it about through its own assertion. The cogito is the place where Beckett most often addresses the central concern of the relationship between subjective continuity, self-consciousness, and the moment of subjective assertion in language.[26]

The above discussion should begin to show that if autobiographical constructions posit an I talking "of" itself, that "of which" the I talks can have no unproblematic or prior existence to the I that is "talking." Crucial here is the manner in which Benveniste sees "I" as collapsing the distinction between signified and referent, since utterance simultaneously creates that which it represents. Benveniste found this sort of movement to be representative of an entire class of phrases, "performatives," which he was careful to distinguish from Austin's somewhat similar concept. In the course of reproving Austin for diluting the category of "performatives" beyond utility, Benveniste comments on "performative" utterances (like "I promise" or "I apologize") in which "The act is thus identical with the utterance of the act. The signified is identical to the referent. . . . A performative utterance is not performative in that it can modify the situation of an individual, but in that it is *by itself* an act. The utterance *is* the act" (*Problems in General Linguistics*, 236–37).[27] This passage must be read carefully: the word "identical" here means *literally* "identical," not simply "referring to the same object." In this sort of utterance, the signified and the referent do not simply coincide; they are the same object—the sentence in which they are found. Benveniste's "performative" is both performative and constative at once—it names the act which it is by becoming the act which is named. Given the earlier statement "Est 'ego' qui *dit* 'ego,'" the suspicion arises that in terms of "I" once again the referent and signified are identical. To say "I" is both to name and enact. The importance of this for Beckett is found in the manner in which the Beckettian "I" renews itself and rewrites or reutters itself, with a denial of continuity between instantiations. The Beckettian "I" strives for a temporality of self-coincidence, which the prose denies by troubling the grammatical and syntactic structures on which the deictic moment, the guarantee of the continuity of reference of the "I," depends. This is one of the two fundamental methods in Beckett of discrediting the "I" as subjective marker. The other bears a striking similarity to Derrida's critique of Austin's work on performatives, as it consists of the trope of qualifying first-person statements as cited, repeated, or overheard. Particularly in *The Unnamable* and the *Texts for Nothing*, Beckett stresses the "I" as a mark—a mark which can never be saturated by the consciousness or intention it is meant to carry. One can always say "I," but how to invest it with the intention or meaning which makes it my "I" and not someone else's, how to ensure that "I" is said "seriously" and not as if enclosed between quotation marks? Once this difficulty is given sufficient weight, the force of "I" as opposed to "he" or "you" becomes increasingly problematic. "I" no longer cleaves the crucial distance between self and other, but becomes simply one name or designating mark in a series of grammatical options. One can always say "I," but one says it as Malone says "my pots" or "me." The opening lines of *The Unnamable* make this clear: "I, say I. Unbelieving" (291). If one says "I" but is unbelieving, how does one refer to or name that agent of disbelief, or more to the point, how does that agent state the disbelief it entertains, without saying "I"? That is the impossible question the trilogy ends on. The trilogy also, however, ends on "on," the question of going on within its own impossibility. If this question is tied to the first person and subjectivity, it is also linked to the entire range of teleological suppositions regarding "ending" in narratives, of arriving at literary or even syntactic destinations which permit one to *stop* "going on." The question of the "on" in Beckett, of movement without progress, of termination without finality, will be the subject of the reading of the late prose in chapter 6. If the "on" has no destination, however, it is also because the subject, the "I" that "goes on," is denied a place as origin of that movement which goes.

In Beckett, the "I" is not only concerned with talking *of* itself—it is portrayed also as constantly talking *to* itself, insisting that it is listening, overhearing, repeating, citing, and summarizing language originating from an impossible elsewhere. Benveniste is also interesting concerning the way Beckett links the otherness of the "I"'s utterances to the question of address. If first-person discourse is solipsistic in that it is auto-discursively referential, for all that it cannot be considered solipsistically *self-referential*—that is, the expression and representation of a self protected from everything alien, improper, other, or exterior. Rather, it is in certain ways the very discourse that makes evident and enacts the "self"'s own constitutive alterity, through the cleavage introduced by its dialogic structure. As Benveniste points out in "L'appareil formel de l'énonciation,"[28] the moment of the assumption of language by a speaker implies a listener or receiver, even if only hypothetical: "But immediately, as soon as he declares himself speaker and assumes the language, he implants the *other* in front of him, no matter how much actual presence he might attribute to this other. All utterance is implicitly or explicitly allocution, and implies a listener."[29] The consequence of this is that dialogue, or exchange, rather than the emission of a "monologic" utterance, becomes the fundamental structure of enunciation. That is to say, rather than conceiving of dialogue as a complex variety of utterance, where there are two speakers instead of one, Benveniste argues that monologue "should be posited, despite the appearances, as a variety of dialogue, which is the fundamental structure. The 'monologue' is an interiorized dialogue, formulated in an 'inner language,' between a self who speaks and a self who listens."[30] This automatic division of the "self" or *moi* that the assumption of the first person necessitates finds an incredibly complex elaboration in Beckett, usually figured by the trope of listening—one cannot say "I" without hearing oneself say "I," but that which hears can never be identical with the "I" that is said. Hearing oneself talk can be the consummate figure of im-mediate subjective self-presence, but in Beckett the totality of the divorce between the "I" that speaks and the one that "hears" is such that the hearer cannot even be sure if it is, in fact, he who is speaking. As Beckett's late work implies, talking provides a company whose substantiality, rather than irreality, renders it unsettling.

Blanchot, Neutrality, and Desire

No discussion of Beckett's refusal of subjectivity and the "I" can ignore Maurice Blanchot's thoughts on this issue. Blanchot's work on the "neutre" or the "il" has provided one of the most powerful nonexistentialist or phenomenological theories for addressing Beckett's handling of subjectivity and was itself to a certain extent inspired by Beckett's works. Blanchot makes clear that when he writes of the "il," or "third person," he is not dealing *literally* with pronouns: "I will not hark back to 'the use of personal pronouns in the novel.' . . . I think we must go further back."[31] Rather, Blanchot seems to be discussing the moment when the author's language, and thus his or her subjectivity, are no longer her or his own: "What speaks in him is the fact that, in one way or another, he is no longer himself; he isn't anyone anymore," and later, "The third person is myself become no one, my interlocutor turned alien; it is my no longer being able, where I am, to address myself and the inability of whoever addresses me to say 'I'; it is his not being himself."[32] Such lines are certainly evocative of the trilogy: "I shall say I no more," says Malone (283), making a promise which, as we shall see, he can neither break nor keep. And to "say I no more" in Beckett is always double, meaning on the one hand no longer to utter the "I," to have become something other, but also on the other hand ceaselessly and obsessively to repeat "I no more"—that is, for the subject constantly to proclaim its impending disappearance, in a proclamation which must inevitably cast the event into the future. In line with the Beckettian problematic, Blanchot makes clear that his argument must not be mistaken as a call for the perfection of omniscient detachment, but still, it is difficult to accept that the "neutre" is entirely neutral. Blanchot is extremely provocative when he argues that the "il" opens the space where:

L'autre parle. Mais quand l'autre parle, personne ne parle, car l'autre, qu'il faut se garder d'honorer d'une majuscule qui le fixerait dans un substantif de majesté, comme s'il avait quelque présence substantielle, voire unique, n'est précisément jamais seulement l'autre, il n'est plutôt ni l'un ni l'autre, et le neutre qui le marque le retire des deux, comme de l'unité, l'établissant toujours au-dehors du terme, de l'acte ou du sujet où il prétend s'offrir. (*Entretien*, 564–65)

[The other speaks. But when the other is speaking, no one speaks because the other, which we must refrain from honoring with a capital letter that would determine it by way of a majestic substantive, as though it had some substantial or even unique presence, is precisely never simply the other. The other is neither the one nor the other, and the neutral that indicates it withdraws it from both, as it does from unity, always establishing it outside the term, the act, or the subject through which it claims to offer itself. (*Infinite Conversation*, 385)]

This presentation is quite useful, provided one reads "personne ne parle" as meaning no full subject, working from a plenitude of intention and consciousness, is speaking. However, when Blanchot writes, shortly above the last passage cited, "Ce qui se raconte n'est raconté par personne: elle parle au neutre" (*Entretien*, 564) ["What is being recounted is not being recounted by anyone: it speaks in the neutral" (*Infinite Conversation*, 384)], we must guard against the temptation of an "absolute" language, similar to the omniscience derided by Blanchot above, which would present and manifest itself from nowhere, with no effect of signature or source. For in this sense, language is *never* neutral, but constructed of differences which are also referential. This is seen in Blanchot's own terminology: in English we could call the neutral the "it," but Blanchot's designation of the "neutre" as the "il" already inscribes the system of gender oppositions into the mark of the neuter itself, the very element that is supposed to trouble all systems of oppositions through the establishment of the "ni l'un ni l'autre." Could we, could Blanchot, conceive of the "elle, le neutre," or for that matter, the "ça, le neutre"? These considerations perhaps belong to another discussion, but in any case, the neutral, already, is not neutral. We cannot say that "what is recounted is not recounted by anyone" if we imagine the place of the telling as some vast "neutral" space, somehow invested with language but yet beyond differentiation. We could say, however, that "what is recounted is recounted by no one," provided that we offer a detailed analysis of the constitution of a linguistic no one, itself inscribed in many varying differential relationships to assertions of subjectivity. This could in no way entail a foreclosure of the issues of gender, temporality, and location in regard to this "no one," because all of these distinctions are *already* inscribed in the structure of language.

One of the great paradoxes of *The Unnamable,* for example, is that although in many ways it seems the perfect model of Blanchot's "neutre," all the same it retains highly determinate relations to inscriptions of gender and also to the specificities of different languages, nationalities, and geographies. The insertion of English words into the French version is well known (along with the obvious presence of Irish proper names), and the English text likewise carries clear historical and geographical markers, like the site of the story attached to the name "Mahood," which "takes place" on rue Brancion in Paris, in front of the now destroyed equine slaughterhouse of the rue Vaugirard. In addition to the near-constant presence of a sexual and scatological register in Beckett, the careful abrasion of such highly invested imagoes of identification as nationality, native language, and the nuclear family makes clear that psychoanalytic models of subjective alterity are just as crucial for a reading of Beckett as linguistic and philosophical ones, even if the psychoanalytic intertexts are less clearly foregrounded in the postwar prose than in *Murphy* and *Watt.* When Blanchot writes of "l'autre qui parle," his warning against "honoring it with a capital letter" seems a dig at Lacan. Be that as it may, the alterity that speaks in Beckett's texts is also that of an inscrutable desire, which cannot be understood or even recognized by that which speaks it and which it speaks. We can agree with Blanchot that Beckett will show us "je devenu personne," but that which replaces the "je" ("replaces" is not entirely accurate—it is never clear that there was an original "je" to be replaced) is not a desireless, bodiless, transhistorical "no one." On the contrary, we are constantly reminded that "ataraxy," or perfect philosophical indifference, has not been achieved, and the "no one" that is (not) speaking is riven by desires and drives which pain precisely by being not its/his own. Thus, the double task that presents itself is to examine Blanchottian "neutrality" in Beckett but without forgetting the role of desire as motor of utterance, and to engage in psychoanalytic approaches without reducing the "neutral" to a mere symptom. The first chapter, then, will look at Beckett's own collapsing of philosophical and psychoanalytic discourse as seen in his early fiction and poetry and his work on Descartes. One of the issues around which the two discourses come most clearly together is the proper name, specifically the *M* and *W* names ubiquitous in Beckett's works. It is around this question that we shall begin.

1. "Will in Overplus"
A Graphic Look at Beckett's W/horoscopes

Samuel Beckett's comment that he chose the name of "Murphy" for the protagonist of his first novel because "it was the most common surname in Ireland"[1] has, not surprisingly, become a classic point of reference in Beckett criticism. Not only does the remark present two equally biting evaluations of the Irish—first, that Murphy is their typical representative; second, that he is not—it also opens an entire field of questions concerning nomination and onomastics which have been central to Beckett's work throughout his writings. For proper names, as opposed to common nouns, function precisely according to their singularity—if everybody had the same name, in effect no one would have any name, as the name would no longer serve to distinguish one individual from another. To the extent that a proper name is common or shared (and Murphy, we are reminded, has no first name), it fails to be a name. In the case of Murphy, the epigone of failure, this seems entirely appropriate—the ubiquity of his name renders him entirely ungrounded in the symbolic system of nomination. But the moment we make this assumption, we are immediately caught in a double bind. For as soon as we identify the name "Murphy" as the name that fails to name, the antiname, we begin to consider it precisely as the name that names this failure, the name of the antiname. "Murphy," by its very institution as the antiname, the failed name, becomes by the same token the perfect, transcendental name, the name that names its own failure to name. Because the name "Murphy" is capable of instigating the effect of anonymity, as soon as it becomes the figure of the anonymity of which it partakes, it is paradoxically perfectly appropriate and distinctive. And this figural moment is, in this case, extratextual. That is to say, it is only Beckett's comments on the motivation of the choice of the name "Murphy" which thrust it into its maddening *Watt*-like dialectic, rendering it appropriate by its very lack of propriety, which final appropriateness seems disappointingly inappropriate with regard to the thematics of *Murphy*. This kind of dialectic is literally interminable, for we can continue by positing that the most fitting irony of all is that the name does fit, that it fails to fail, after which we may assert that this sort of recuperation of failure (here posing as success) is just the sort of metaphysical economics *Murphy* argues against, thus the name is not fitting, which quality, of course, would render it perfectly fitting, *ad infinitum*.

The point here—one which will remain crucial for Beckett through the trilogy and beyond—is that if "anonymity" is left nameless, it cannot be thematized, and once given a name or figure, it becomes the opposite of the effect it is invoked to create to the very extent that it succeeds in creating it. As Beckett wrote in *Watt*, "the only way one can speak of nothing is to speak of it as though it were something" (77). The "as though" points to the necessarily figural nature of all such representations, and over the course of his work, Beckett increasingly casts the problem of anonymity, or namelessness, in terms of catachresis, or the "borrowing" of names which remain provisional, "other," figural, and improper with respect to what they designate. This can be seen in the obvious intertextual overlap and serial interreference of the chain of Beckett character names beginning with *M,* or its dialectical inverse, *W,* to wit, Murphy, Watt, Mercier, Molloy, Moran, Malone, Macmann, Mahood, Worm. The final result of Beckett's investigation of catachresis is the production of the unname "the unnamable," which, rather than being the ultimate name in the Beckettian series of overlapping and indistinct "characters" is instead the marker of the narrative space where nominational effects—even catachrestical nominational effects—are no longer allowed an even provisionally stable inscription. But it is indeed the existence of this catachrestical structure in Beckett's work that adds another level of irony to Beckett's remark (admittedly made in private correspondence) concerning his choice of the name "Murphy," as it passes over in complete silence the clearly overdetermined role of the *M* and the *W* in Beckett's nominative choices. The sense of overlap, indistinction, and displaced reference created between Beckett's "characters" is effected not only through the numerous intertextual allusions within Beckett's prose and his constant narrative jumbling of voices, but also through the blatant and explicit seriality of the *W* and *M* names listed above. And if we consider not only Beckett's "character" names, but also the titles of his works, the list of *M* and *W* names extends back to his first published poem, "Whoroscope," through *More Pricks than Kicks* and "Waiting for Godot," and ends with his last "novella," *Worstward Ho.* "Murphy" may be the most common name in Ireland, but it also fits into a foregrounded series of names and titles which generates a significatory structure of its own.

"Whoroscope" seems a particularly fruitful place to begin an inquiry concerning the role and function of the *M* and *W* in Beckett's work, for if it marks the first appearance of the *W/M* siglum, it also shows most clearly its gratuitous, overdetermined structure, in two different ways: first of all, the *W* in "Whoroscope" is clearly extraneous and nonessential—an addition attached to an already existing, entire word; second, it is silent. These two qualities are complementary. To create the pun on "whore/horo," the *W* can only be attached because it is silent, but as it is silent, it is never entirely "there" in any single, discrete manifestation, but creates its effects in two different ways. First, rather than being simply an addition, it is also a subtraction, removing the integrity of the *phonic* sign "horoscope" by contaminating it with an obscene meaning that no pronunciation of the word, no matter how meticulous, can protect against. On the other hand, the graphic space of the written text allows precisely the differentiation that the graphic addition of the *W* subsequently destroys for spoken utterance. The *W* in "Whoroscope," then, is really neither a phonic nor a graphic presence or sign in the classical sense—it functions rather as an agency which motivates and reaffirms the differential and substitutive structure of language which makes such puns and slippages both possible and inevitable. But the superfluous *W* in and of itself cannot be posited as a bearer of either some sort of proper phonic or graphic meaning, as its punning structure depends on its being both phonetically silent when the "word" "whoroscope" is read *and* graphically imagined when the "word" "w/horoscope" is heard. Just as the *W* is initially extraneous to the word "horoscope," and read as an addition, so even with regard to its own functioning within this structure, it never fully "presents" itself semiotically, remaining silent when it is literally, materially given, and imposing itself onto the phonic signifier which in no way presents it or manifests it at all.

Given this structure, two things become apparent with regard to certain larger issues of Beckett's textual practice. First of all, any naive valorization of silence in Beckett's works as either a finality free from the travail of signification or as an originary moment not yet divided by the unstoppable noise of language must be avoided. This is not to say that Beckett's work does not occasionally thematize these possibilities, but rather to assert that if Beckett sometimes evinces a nostalgia for silence it is because in his textual practice silence is already no longer silent, no longer the beyond or outside of signification, but already implicated in the semiotic structure itself. For Beckett, "silence" is never the opposite or negative of "speech," but part of a continuum with it, its "spaces" between words and phrases, phonemes and graphemes, as semiotically charged as the marks themselves.[2] This is perhaps emblematized by the silent work of the *W* of "Whoroscope," but it is also seen in Beckett's habitual troubling of all "silent" moments of finality or closure through repetitive structures. The clearest example of this might be the last pages of *The Unnamable,* which seem less to end than to stop, offering less the quiet of a conclusion than a rhythmic pause before a postulated reprise. The frank intertextuality of Beckett's fiction only heightens (albeit retroactively) the effect of interruption. And even as early as *Murphy,* the discussions of figure and ground thematize the semiotic function of the apparently "formless" in any designation of "form." For Beckett, silence is no more proper, no more capable of a plenitude of absence, than is "speech" capable of achieving a self-identical moment of single meaning and completed expression which would make a following silence practicable.

Second, we should guard against atomistic phonemic or graphic interpretations of the *W/M* trace. As the preceding analysis has shown, the *W* of "Whoroscope" functions, as it were, both silently when inscribed as a grapheme and "invisibly" in the aural register, while calling all the more attention to its place in the Beckettian catalog by its very superfluity. For this reason, Leslie Hill's recent linkage of the phoneme /m/ to both the signifier "mother" or *maman* and to a thematically corresponding physical "sucking motion with the lips . . . said to imitate the sound of the infant at the breast" (114) seems to me suspect. He cites (in French) the famous passage from *Molloy* in which Molloy, speaking of his mother, writes that he called her "Mag" because "la lettre g abolissait la syllabe ma, et pour ainsi dire crachait dessus" (25).[3] Hill goes on to argue that "the phoneme /m/ seems to mark a desire for fusion or inclusion," which he contrasts with the "glottal sound" of the /g/ in "Mag," in turn described as "an expulsion of air animated by the sphincters at the rear of the throat . . . echoing a coughing movement of expectoration" (114). Although it is undeniable that Beckett's *M* carries resonances of "mother" and of that assuredly primal mother, Mary, let us remember that this *M* is first of all emphasized as name or title and second is thrown into a repetitive series along with the "inverted" *W*. To argue that the *M* functions as the mark of a phoneme which is in itself the metonymy of an infantile desire would imply a properly paragrammatic reading of the phoneme /m/'s occurrence in words and phrases generally, outside of proper names and titles. Moreover, this purely phonemic identification fails to account for the capacity of the *W* to evoke and displace the whole series of *M* names, or for the inevitable displacement of *M* onto *W*. Here one sees the possibility, perhaps, of a cryptonymic reading, in Abraham and Torok's sense, in which the *W* would through inversion signify the *M*, but the logical consequence of this would be the acknowledgment of the /m/'s capacity to signify in the absence of its phonemic voicing. That is to say, it would be functioning as the mark of its own severance from a psycho/physiological need (assuming the initial link is admitted), not as its recapitulation or reenactment. The "phoneticist" reading would have to assert that since the *W* of "Whoroscope" has no phonetic register at all, it bears no relation to the series of *M* names. If on the contrary we admit that the *W* by its *graphic* inversion of the letter *M* can call up resonances of the phoneme /m/, even when the *W* in question is not a phonetic character at all, we are clearly outside the realm of the onomatopoeics of sucking.

Finally, let us look closely at the passage under analysis: Beckett is indeed quite clear that it is the letter *g* that abolishes or, "pour ainsi dire," spits on the syllable "Ma." Hill argues that it is the coughing movement of the throat, similar to that of expectoration, in the formation of the sound /g/ which makes it "spit" on the syllable "Ma." But Molloy does not specify what it is about the sound, or even whether it is the *sound* of *g*, which gives it this power. His word is *lettre*. And the *letter g*, regardless of any deep psychological or developmental significance which one might like to lend it phonetically, certainly does transform the "Ma" of Maman and Marie into the Mag of Mary Magdalen, a dialectical figure indeed with regard to the Christian exemplar of maternity who is Mary. And as the "Mag" passage makes clear, it is a dialectic that is at issue:

> And I called her Mag because for me, without my knowing why, the letter g abolished the syllable Ma, and as it were spat on it, better than any other letter would have done. And at the same time I satisfied a deep and doubtless unacknowledged need, the need to have a Ma, that

is a mother, and to proclaim it, audibly. For before you say mag you say ma, inevitably. (17)

The relation between the *M* and the *G*, then, seems not to represent, as Hill argues, "the difference between attraction and repulsion, between embracing the mother and rejecting her, between the mother's kiss and her violence, between oral inclusion and anal expulsion, fusion and separation" (115), but rather the temporality of saying by unsaying, of Freudian negation in which the appended "no" permits the conscious articulation of repressed material. In this structure there is no clear opposition between "embracing" and "rejecting," "inclusion" and "expulsion," "fusion" and "separation," but both sides of each pole are enacted in the same motion. The mother must first be articulated in order to be denied, especially if part or even most of the pleasure of the denial is this preliminary articulation necessary to it. But if these movements of rejection, expulsion, and separation rely on the positing of logically prior moments of embracing, inclusion, and fusion which in themselves are pleasurable, note that these moments and their pleasure can only be tolerated when posed as a threat or consciously admitted when conjured up as objects of repudiation. Attraction and repulsion are no longer in diametric competition against each other, representing separate, conflicting feelings, each with its own phonemic representative, but rather form components of a single movement, in which the pleasure of defilement comes largely from its emphatic proximity to or even creation of that which is to be physically expelled—a pleasure protected by its representation as a denial, heightened by its fugitive nature, and whose repetition is structurally ensured. There is pleasure both in fusion and separation, but it is only through the second that the pleasure of either can be experienced. The true power of "Mag" is not that it abolishes "Ma" but, on the contrary, that it allows "Ma" to be uttered and proclaimed—"Mag" *protects* "Ma," graphically writing the dynamics of expulsion as a movement precisely of fusion and incorporation, as the very substitute for the word "Ma" is shown to contain that word within it.[4] And in the movement from Ma to Mag it certainly is a question of fusion, or even infusion, as the whole of Molloy's encounters with his mother or maternal figures is cast largely in the shadow of *À la recherche du temps perdu,* in which it is precisely the madeleine which allows the narrator a fusion with and perhaps incorporation of the female sexuality of his mother, grandmother, and aunt.[5] The two poles Mother/Mary and Magdalen operate in both texts, the "Mag" or Magdalen "abolishing" the

mother/Virgin precisely by representing the sexual attraction both generated and prohibited with respect to her. This is the logic of Proust's
collapsing of the real orality and symbolic incorporation of the sacrament
onto the figure of Mary Magdalen, who is *already* the carnal aspect, the
"incarnation" of the virgin as object of adoration.

The traditional Christian parsing of femininity between Mary and
Mary Magdalen, the virgin mother and the prostitute, is oddly mirrored
in Beckett's *M/W* marker, in which the *M* is expressly associated with the
mother, and the first appearance of the *W* creates a pun on "whore." If we
have previously discussed the semiotic structure of the pun in "Whoroscope," we should perhaps now turn to the thematic networks this structure correspondingly brings into play, as the pun of the title "Whoroscope," when critically considered at all, is usually seen as the gratuitous
itself: a juvenile wordplay whose humor comes from its apposition of the
highly serious subject of the philosophy of Descartes with the obscene
word "whore." Not surprisingly, the pun has several more precise and
complex functions than that.

First of all, in Beckett's poem the idea of the horoscope is already largely
motivated by etymological considerations. Beckett composed his poem
for submission to a contest which had called for poems on the subject of
time (Harvey, 3). In this context, "horoscope" means not only a star chart,
but also carries its etymological sense of hour-watching, of the observation of time and its passage (*horo/skopos*). With respect to this meaning,
as Beckett's notes to the poem make clear, Descartes's "horoscope," or device for measuring time, is the ripeness of a hen's egg, which Descartes
preferred between eight and ten days of age: "The shuttle of a ripening
egg combs the warp of his days" (*Collected Poems,* 5).[6] Time is measured
in terms of gestation and reproduction, but the end of the cycle is not the
appearance of a new generation, but rather abortion and ingestion:

> Are you ripe at last,
> my slim pale double-breasted turd?
> How rich she smells,
> this abortion of a fledgling!
> (lines 84–87)

"Whoroscope," with its various references to paternity in terms of Descartes's proof of the existence of God, and filiality in terms of his borrowing from Saint Augustine (see lines 72–83), conceives of procreation not

as the creation of new life which would in some way preserve, extend, and figure its procreators, but as a limited investment in the fabrication of nourishment for the living. Time is not measured as a cyclical passing from generation to generation, youth to age, in which parents make way for maturing children who will symbolically extend them through yet another generation, but rather as a maniacal arrestation on the part of the dominant generation of all that threatens to supplant or outlast it with an ensuing cannibalization that ensures that the younger generation will *literally* and *materially* extend its "parents." The humor is that Beckett pits Descartes against chickens, but the anxiety of mortality is first thematized by the very title, which alludes to Descartes's aversion to having his fate foretold, then extended in the account of the death of Descartes's daughter (lines 31–35), and ends only with the final lines which tell the story of Descartes's antipathy for and distrust of the physician who either treated him during his mortal illness or killed him with the mortal treatment of bleeding ("Oh Weulles spare the blood of a Frank," line 94).[7]

If, leaving "horoscope," we try to imagine on the other hand what sort of thing could be represented by the neologism "whoroscope," we might imagine a device for looking at prostitutes. And if the thematics of voyeurism and prostitution are not evoked in the poem "Whoroscope" or its notes, they are certainly not far off in Beckett's oeuvre. The story "Walking Out" (another *W*) in the roughly contemporaneous *More Pricks than Kicks* tells, among other things, the story of protagonist Belacqua Shuah's desire to procure a "cicisbeo," or surrogate lover, for his fiancée, and culminates with his being beaten upon his discovery in an act of voyeurism. The motif of voyeurism and punishment is clearly indebted to the Phoenix Park incident of *Finnegans Wake,* and if the *Wake* coins "Waterloo" as a term of reference for the girls' pee in the park, we should remember that "Belacqua," while certainly a reference to Dante's slothful purgatorial figure, can also be "etymologized" in perfectly Wakeian fashion into "pretty water." A whole series of graphematic exchanges seems to be in operation, as "Whoroscope," with its overemphasized *W,* takes us to "Walking Out," which by thematizing voyeurism leads us to the *Wake* and "Waterloo" and the subsequent reading of "Belacqua" as "pretty water." Finally, we should note that the *character* Belacqua's initials—B. S.—bear a relationship to those of its author in some ways analogous to that which an *M* might entertain with "Whoroscope"'s *W.* In this case, the pertinent *M* would be that which inaugurates the name Murphy, who replaces

Belacqua Shuah as protagonist in Beckett's next work of fiction. *Murphy*, in addition to presenting a character who is a prostitute, Celia, also gives an explicit reading and extension of the poem "Whoroscope."

"Whoroscope" is from the start a poem concerned with and constructed through intertextuality and the breaking of boundaries generally. Beckett's abrupt selection, translation, and condensation of Descartes's writings and Adrien Baillet's *La vie de M. Descartes* are more reminiscent of much of Pound's work in the *Cantos* than of *The Waste Land*, a poem to which it is more usually compared. For both Pound and Beckett, the work at hand is less a scholarly or historical analysis of a given subject than a labor of specifically *textual* appropriation, accomplished through narrative excision, paraphrase, and translation. Neither Pound nor Beckett works primarily toward a reconstruction of given historical subjects, personages, or ideologies—methodologically, both are much more absorbed in the reelaboration, reorganization, and juxtaposition of specifically linguistic, textual elements. The poem's inscrutability not only mirrors what Descartes wished upon his own stars, but causes the poem to point constantly outside itself to the source information that would make legible its own transitions. It is crucial to note that the bits of information given in the poem are themselves presented as incomplete, as fragments—not only does the poem "itself" not include its own "meaning," it fails even to complete internally its own system of reference. This situation of self-exteriority is made evident and rendered literal by the addition of the not especially explanatory "notes" Beckett composed for the poem, causing it to include in its own self-articulation as poem the "nonpoetic" outside represented by the notes. Textually, it contains within "itself" that which it is not (the notes) while failing to be structurally the container of its own reference (thus the notes' necessity). No wonder the poem circles the questions of reproduction, legitimacy, and abortion, and is read in a text—*Murphy*—that never mentions it by name. Or does it? Perhaps in *Murphy*, people are discussing it all the time.

In the first chapter of *Murphy*, Celia interrupts Murphy's rocking-chair reveries with a phone call announcing, simply, "I have it" (8). *What* she has, for what appears to be the sake of narrative suspense, we are not told. Chapter 2 consists of Celia's interview with her grandfather, Mr. Kelly, in which she details Murphy's aversion to work and her insistence that he find some. Murphy has ceded, she explains, but has written her that, "as there was no possibility of his [Murphy] finding in himself any reason for work taking one form rather than another, would she kindly procure a corpus of incentives based on the only system outside his own in which he felt the least confidence, that of the heavenly bodies. In Berwick Market there was a swami who cast excellent nativities for sixpence" (22–23). Abandoning the free indirect style, shortly after this Celia has the following exchange with Mr. Kelly:

> "And now I ring him up," concluded Celia, "to tell him I have it, and he tries to choke me off."
> "It?" said Mr. Kelly.
> "What he told me to get," said Celia.
> "Are you afraid to call it by its name?" said Mr. Kelly. (23)

The word that Celia the prostitute is "afraid" to utter is of course "horoscope," and her aversion will be repeated in the novel. Thus, when she finally presents the document to Murphy, it is again with the laconic phrase "what you told me to get" (31). Later, in exasperation with Murphy's self-servingly slothful interpretation of his theme, Celia protests:

> "You tell me to get you this . . . this . . ."
> "Corpus of deterrents," said Murphy. (34)

Once again, she cannot bring herself to name it. But the pun on "whoroscope" has consequences which go beyond Celia's speech impediment. In terms of the narrative, the horoscope is one of the most important elements of the entire novel, governing many of Murphy's actions and decisions and, more important, his own interpretations of them and their consequences. The question to be asked is to what extent Murphy and *Murphy* are then both governed not only by destiny and the stars but also by the "whoroscope" and voyeurism or, more important, by the structure of substitutionality and displacement established between the two.

To start with, in light of this discussion, Celia's own name begins to carry its full weight. She is not "heavenly" in any metaphorical sense at all, but her name continues the superposition of time and the "whore" as objects of scrutiny that was inaugurated in "Whoroscope." And we should remember the mechanics of Murphy's first encounter with Celia. Murphy's eyes first fall on Celia when he is in the process of shifting his gaze back and forth between the June star chart and the "brightness of the firmament" (14). Celia represents both an interruption of and replacement for Murphy's scrutiny of the skies—at the end of the encounter, "they walked off happily arm-in-arm, leaving the star chart for June lying in the gutter" (15). It would be easy to say here that Murphy abandons his contemplation of the heavenly bodies for the heavenly body of Celia, in a movement from passivity to activity, contemplation to action, mental to physical, et cetera. However, we should remember that what gets left in the gutter is not the stars, but the star chart. Celia doesn't only replace the stars as the object of contemplation — though she does do that — she also displaces and troubles the *act* of contemplation itself. For Murphy is not only looking at the firmament — he is also gazing at the document that reads it. In this sense, Murphy is engaged in a kind of reading himself. His abandonment of his *text* to the gutter for what we are told is "a striking case of love requited" (16) maps the whole episode over Dante's Paolo and Francesca ("Quel giorno più non vi leggemmo avante")[8] and inscribes it in the dynamics of identification and repetition emblematized by the latter. Celia represents not an alternative to Murphy's narcissistic scrutiny of the skies — narcissistic in that his interest in them lies in his viewing them as a text of his own life, of himself — but its continuation. In Murphy's dialectic, Celia is one stop on the path that begins with the firmament and ends with Mr. Endon, in which all acts of scrutiny are investments in self-scrutiny, and where all objects derive their interest from narcissistic projection.[9]

Celia, then, is a substitute not so much of an object of interpretation as of an act of interpretation, an oscillation between the firmament and the text which both reads the former and is made legible by its light. Does the horoscope, the June star chart, give a mapping of celestial Celia, or is Celia herself the text of the stars' meaning? The question, perhaps, should not be posed in those terms. Celia seems rather a figure of the stars' own textuality, of the narcissistic and therefore erotic investment in their scrutiny and interpretation. In "Whoroscope," the hour of his nativity, the seal of his coming into being, is precisely what Descartes, the abortion eater, the thinker hunched over the impression of his own existence, keeps for himself. In chapter 2 of *Murphy*, then, the play on Celia and the celestial, horoscope and whoroscope, certainly implies that the "corpus of incentives" based on the "system" of "heavenly bodies" is not only the nativity but Celia's own body — and this is literally the case as she has threatened to leave Murphy if he doesn't find work. The figural physicality lent to "corpus" and "heavenly bodies" seems extended when Murphy states that the latter constitutes "the only system outside his own in which he felt the least confidence" — "system" here coming to signify not only the implied "philosophical" or "cosmological" but also the circulatory system — Murphy's topic of discussion with Neary in the book's opening pages.[10] That is to say, he will quit his mental and physical solipsism only for (and only in the hopes of yet greater solipsistic returns) Celia's heavenly body (itself, etymologically, something of a redundancy) and Suk's horoscope. The play on "w/horoscope" eroticizes the entire theme of the nativity, the moment of birth containing the life's secret, but also the thematics of observation and reading or interpretation. "Mercury," Murphy declares, is the "god of thieves, planet *par excellence* and mine" (31), neglecting to mention that he is also the god of commerce and business, ostensibly Murphy's concern here, and of communication and interpretation. And if Celia's name links her to the stars, if Murphy abandons the star chart of June for her company, we should think back on the strange list of measurements of Celia's physical attributes which introduces her without comment and begins chapter 2. This is, with its orderly progression and precise mathematical notation, a map or chart of the physical positions and dimensions of her "heavenly body," or, in other words, a whoroscope. Mercury seems to have stolen the referent implied by the neologism of the poem's title and deposited it into the novel *Murphy*. Thus, in the novel both the title and the "referent" of "Whoroscope" are namelessly reproduced out of the abortive poem.

If the play of "w/horoscope" maps stargazing onto voyeurism and reads the "heavenly bodies" as erotic objects of (self-)delectation, it also pushes the ubiquitous *W* and thus its inversion, the *M,* up into the skies, into relation with astronomy and astrology. If one asks, as one might, not "what is the 'referent' of the neologism 'whoroscope'?" but "where would there be a *W* in a horoscope?" the answer is, in Joyce's *Ulysses.* In Stephen Dedalus's famous discussion of Shakespeare's *Hamlet* is found the following passage, which considers the circumstances of the Bard's birth:

> What's in a name? That is what we ask ourselves in childhood when we write the name that we are told is ours. A star, a daystar, a firedrake, rose at his birth. It shone by day in the heavens alone, brighter than Venus in the night, and by night it shone over delta in Cassiopeia, the recumbent constellation which is the signature of his initial among the stars. (172)

Stephen's figure is based on the unelaborated fact that the constellation Cassiopeia designs the shape of the letter *W* (or *M,* depending on how you look at it), thus, it is "the signature of his initial among the stars." Cassiopeia also presents an instance where the relational, spatial differentiation between *M* and *W* is not articulated—both letters equally figuring and figured by it. The imprint of the *W* and the *M,* the mark of signature Beckett so often leaves in his work through titles and names, can perhaps be read as the imprint of Cassiopeia, itself mentioned by Joyce precisely in terms of the name and the signature: "the *signature* of his initial among the stars" (my emphasis). This initial and the name it inaugurates receive considerable attention both in Shakespeare's work and Joyce's commentary upon it. The passage cited above came in the midst of a discussion of how Shakespeare embedded his own first name in his plays and played on the signification embedded within his name in the sonnets. Is the *M/W* in Beckett the mark of the appropriation of an astral signature? Is Beckett citing and claiming the name, author, and authority behind the mark, or is he citing (and displacing) Joyce's whole discussion of how marks are claimed and appropriated as signatures? Is Beckett appropriating the Bard's signature or a discussion of the dynamics of appropriation? Perhaps Beckett here is acting as *Mercury*, stealing and reversing the *W* in the skies that is rightfully Shakespeare's.

Once Joyce puts into motion the play on "Will" as sexual organ and the question of the embedded name and its signatory mark among the stars, the proliferation of signification even "within" *Ulysses* is enormous. Cassiopeia as a *geometric* figure signs not only "Will" but the Mulligan, Molly, Milly, Martha, McIntosh, and MacDowell that one finds in the book, to say nothing of the apparently pseudonymous sailor "Murphy" encountered in the cabmen's shelter. As "Will" becomes the mark in *Ulysses* of the possibility of slippage between proper name and common noun (seen also, but in reverse, in "McIntosh," in which a common noun designating an article of clothing metonymizes itself into a proper name), embedded signatures, and auto-reference, the book's celebrated final words need to be reexamined. "I will Yes" seems to carry among its resonances, within the book's own foregrounded polysemia, "I am Shakespeare, Yes" (if we consider Stephen's discussion of how Shakespeare used his first name to create effects of self-reference), "I am the phallus, Yes" (if we consider Shakespeare's own play on his name), and "This is my signature, Yes" (if we consider "will" as the site of the discussion of the signature—this would be analogous to Flaubert's "Emma, c'est moi").

Beckett's repeated use of the *form* of Cassiopeia as a kind of signature to cite his master's own figuration of Cassiopeia as the signature of a certain form or letter is all the more appropriate as Joyce uses the figure of Cassiopeia as Shakespeare's mark to create his own relations of filiation. In "Ithaca," as Stephen and Bloom look at the skies, we find listed among their considerations:

the appearance of a star (1st magnitude) of exceeding brilliancy domi-
nating by night and day (a new luminous sun generated by the collision
and amalgamation in incandescence of two nonluminous exsuns) about
the period of the birth of William Shakespeare over delta in the recum-
bent neversetting constellation of Cassiopeia . . . and of other stars of
(presumably) similar origin which had (effectively or presumably) appeared in and disappeared from the constellation of Andromeda about
the period of the birth of Stephen Dedalus. . . . (575)

Shakespeare's star is in Cassiopeia, Stephen's stars, in Andromeda: in
Greek mythology, Andromeda is usually considered to be Cassiopeia's
daughter.

To put the *W* into "horoscope," then, is to write oneself into a whole
series of inscriptions concerning names, signatures, and filiations, and thus
also citations, repetitions, and inscriptions. It is to cite, allude to, and repeat a gesture of citation, allusion, and repetition. If the letters *M* and *W*
can figure Cassiopeia, just as Cassiopeia figures *W* and by extension "Will"
and "Will Shakespeare" in Joyce—and also figure this figuration—then
Cassiopeia can also figure the "whore" who is in some way astralized in
this complex series of displacements. After Murphy's departure to his job
at the mental hospital, Celia increasingly takes to sitting naked in Murphy's rocker, in which she could "lie down in the paradisial innocence of
days and places and things and people" (149). This is perhaps the Celestial Celia's assumption of the heavens she names, as the literal meaning of
Cassiopeia is "the lady in the chair."

Beckett's *M/W*, from its inception in "Whoroscope," is always inscribed
as the surplus, the gratuitous, the appended, but what it adds on is not so
much a signature, or an instance of signature, like a hieroglyph or a clue
to be decoded, but the problematics of the effects of the signature, naming, and names, of which it is the intertextual mark. We cannot eliminate
it or remove its effects by finding the "referent," phonetic or not, or "sig-
nator" beneath it. Yet in one of Freud's case histories, specifically, that of
the "Wolf *M*an," there is also a *W*, which is likewise treated not as a signifier of identity or key to its revelation, but precisely as the gratuitous,
the extraneous, that which has not to be explained, but removed for the
inscription of identity to be revealed. Here is the passage:

"I had a dream," he [the "Wolf Man"] said, "of a man tearing off the
wings of an *Espe*."—"*Espe?*" I asked; "what do you mean by that?"—

"You know; that insect with yellow stripes on its body, that stings." — I could now put him right: "So what you mean is a *Wespe* [wasp]." — "Is it called a *Wespe?* I really thought it was called an *Espe.*" (Like so many other people, he used his difficulties with a foreign language as a screen for symptomatic acts.) "But *Espe,* why, that's myself: S. P." (which were his initials). (Freud, *Three Case Histories,* 287)

The threat for Freud, for Joyce's Bloom, for Beckett, is certainly not that one will have the *W* of will in overplus. Perhaps the role of the famous "will-lessness" of apathy in Beckett's work needs to be reexamined in this light. Meanwhile, we have already discussed how the initials of Belacqua Shuah, read across the *M/W,* bring S. B. into play. But who is S. B.? In *Watt,* Beckett's second novel, the question of the construction of such a potential identity (perhaps hinted at by the narrator's name of "Sam") is explicitly linked to just the elements that Freud points to in bracketing the Wolf Man's *W:* the structures of language and culture, along with their attendant fantasmatic screens of native belonging and foreign estrangement, which provide the material through which identifications and thus subjectivity take shape. "Whoroscope" and the early prose provide the first instance of a reading of Descartes which will prove crucial for Beckett, linking Descartes's concerns with certainty, doubt, and subjective existence to those of the obsessional, and the process of philosophical self-scrutiny to a narcissistic erotics. *Watt* continues Beckett's Cartesian investigations, but shifts them into an anthropological register, putting to thorough examination the methods of ritual, but also desacralizing the rites of method.

2. "Ways of Being We"

The Subject as Method, Method as
Ritual in *Watt*

Beckett's mystifying second novel, *Watt,* seems to have generated two main lines of critical approach. One influential trend points to the mock-Cartesian elements of the novel and reads it as a critique of rationalist epistemological pretensions regarding both hermeneutics and problem solving. As Thomas Cousineau writes, "Critics have tended to treat *Watt* as an allegory in which human beings' rationalistic pretensions are ridiculed."[1] Many critics have pointed out, for example, that Watt's absurd speculations concerning Mr Knott's knowledge and approval of the arrangements concerning the preparation and ingestion of his food, along with the suppositions regarding the dog and the Lynches, wholly follow Descartes's four crucial epistemological precepts from the *Discours de la méthode:*

> Le premier était de ne recevoir jamais aucune chose pour vraie, que je ne la connusse évidemment être telle: c'est-à-dire d'éviter soigneusement la précipitation et la prévention. . . .
>
> Le second, de diviser chacune des difficultés que j'examinerais, en autant de parcelles qu'il se pourrait et qu'il serait requis pour les mieux résoudre.
>
> Le troisième, de conduire par ordre mes pensées, en commençant par les objets les plus simples et les plus aisés à connaître, pour monter peu à peu, comme par degrés, jusques à la connaissance des plus

composés; et supposant même de l'ordre entre ceux qui ne se précèdent point naturellement les uns les autres.

Et le dernier, de faire partout des dénombrements si entiers, et des revues si générales, que je fusse assuré de ne rien omettre. (46)

[The first was never to accept anything as true that I did not know to be evidently so: that is to say, carefully to avoid precipitancy and prejudice. . . .

The second, to divide each of the difficulties that I was examining into as many parts as might be possible and necessary in order best to solve it.

The third, to conduct my thoughts in an orderly way, beginning with the simplest objects and the easiest to know, in order to climb gradually, as by degrees, as far as the knowledge of the most complex, and even supposing some order among those objects which do not precede each other naturally.

And the last, everywhere to make such complete enumerations and such general reviews that I would be sure to have omitted nothing. (*Discourse*, 41)]

No reader who has staggered through the serial lists of Mr Knott's displacements of his furniture or changes in appearance would dream of reproaching Watt, or the narrator, Sam, with having ignored Descartes's final precept. However, these "antirationalist" readings seem to suffer from two major inadequacies. First of all, they often end up privileging, by contrast, an implied intuitionism that the novel's devastatingly systematic strategies of estrangement and doubt throw into equal disrepute. Second, they tend to overlook the clear specificity of the sort of conundrums that arouse Watt's "failed rationalism": they virtually always are linked to symbolic exchange and social practice—habits, custom, ritual, art, and language. There is little phenomenological anxiety concerning the attempt to grasp the true nature of a "thing" as such, but rather affective eruptions and hallucinations concerning the cultural economies that produce, inscribe, and retain meaning. As Watt attempts to penetrate the meaning of his duties at the Knott household, or the picture in Erskine's room, or the word "pot," the book's metaphysical investigations are linked to a kind of practical anthropology in a manner quite foreign to the sort of pseudo-Cartesian philosophizing that runs rampant in the trilogy or the *Texts for Nothing*, for example.

Perhaps in response to these limitations, more recently another school of criticism has arisen, which despite significant divergences of emphasis tends to be in accord in its consistent stressing of the issue of the foreign, the artificial, the unnatural, and the unknown. Thus, Watt's obsessive and convoluted hermeneutic enterprises tend to be taken less as a global critique of rationalism than as reactions to the violently incomprehensible customs and undivulged mysteries of the Knott household, while the novel's stylistic dislocations are seen as reinforcing this problematic by providing a systematic estrangement of the reader from the conventions of the realist novel and narrative fiction generally. Once this basic framework is established, its implications are then allegorized in a variety of ways. To list a few recent examples, Knott's household has been taken for an allegory of the realm of human experience in its entirety, skeptically seen as epistemologically unknowable, as the site of a systematic breaking down of the familiar patriarchal structures of filiation and symbolic reproduction, and, more mystically, as a crystallized centering of the circumference of nothingness which habitually brackets our petty acts of interpretation in the world as we live it. The wrenching away of the English from its usual syntactical forms and the plethora of gallicisms, in turn, are also often read biographically as an effect of Beckett's long sojourn in France and isolation from other English speakers during his wartime hiding in Rousillon, and thus as a harbinger of his subsequent shift into French as a literary language following his completion of the novel.[2]

I, too, shall read the novel largely in this light—as a transition from Ireland to France and English to French, and stylistically, a transition from the solid mock realism of *Murphy* and the early stories into the extremities of plotlessness and characterlessness found in the trilogy and *Texts for Nothing*. The novel stands firmly between the learned, arch wit of *Murphy* and the more austere syntactical and grammatical demolitions conducted in the trilogy, while its approach to character and narrative conventions pull further away from realism than the previous novel, while stopping short of the trilogy's near-total evacuation of these props. But if both biography and authorial "development" amply justify a focus on such concerns, more important than this is the fact that the narrative of the novel itself, such as it is, with its constant emphasis on demarcations, limits, thresholds, boundaries, and arrivals and departures, already displays a continual obsession with the issue of transition, regardless of the context of the book within Beckett's biography and œuvre.

As for Beckett's impending personal and linguistic transitions, we should note that not long after the novel was completed, Beckett wrote a short, little-known piece which also explicitly raised the question of the foreign and cultural difference, in the entirely literal context of Franco-Irish postwar cooperation. By June 10, 1946, Beckett had written a text titled "The Capital of the Ruins," intended for broadcast over the airwaves of Radio Éireann, which detailed his experiences as a volunteer in the Irish Red Cross Hospital in Saint-Lô, Normandy, where he had worked from August 1945 to January 1946.[3] He wrote the text to defend the enterprise against Irish criticism of its lack of facilities and poor working conditions, which by implication were criticisms of the French elements of the staff and administration. Coming in the immediate aftermath of World War II and following Beckett's experiences in the *résistance* and subsequently in hiding in the Rousillon, it is also one of Beckett's first statements of the postwar sense of physical and moral desolation of which his drama would be taken as a major expression in the fifties. But if the text is devoted largely to portraying the devastation of the city of Saint-Lô, "bombed out of existence in one night" (*As the Story Was Told*, 25),[4] it also gives a fair amount of space to questions of cultural appurtenance and cultural difference—issues clearly of interest to Beckett at this time. Indeed, Beckett asserts that the final importance of the project is to be found elsewhere than in the concrete medical aid brought by the Irish: "And yet the whole enterprise turned from the beginning on the establishing of a relation in the light of which the therapeutic relation faded to the merest of pretexts" (22–23). Beckett claims that what was "important" was rather "the occasional glimpse obtained, by us in them and, who knows, by them in us (for they are an imaginative people), of that smile at the human conditions as little to be extinguished by bombs as to be broadened by the elixirs of Burroughs and Welcome" (23). Behind Beckett's characteristically caustic view of the Irish, one finds an uncharacteristically optimistic, reassuringly humanist rhetoric in this passage. It is, however, subjected to an immediate correction which I would like to quote in full:

> It would not be seemly, in a retiring and indeed retired storekeeper, to describe the obstacles encountered in this connection, and the forms, often grotesque, devised for them by the combined energies of the home and visiting temperaments. It must be supposed that they were not insurmountable, since they have long ceased to be of much account. When I reflect now on the recurrent problems of what, with all proper modesty, might be called the heroic period, on one in particular so arduous and elusive that it literally ceased to be formulable, I sus-

pect that our pains were those inherent in the simple and necessary and yet so unattainable proposition that their way of being we, was not our way and that our way of being they, was not their way. It is only fair to say that many of us had never been abroad before. (24–25)

Beckett's articulation of cultural difference, contained in the "so unattainable proposition" that "their way of being we, was not our way and that our way of being they, was not their way" deserves careful reading. Obviously, Beckett is not laying claim to any naive notion of insuperable cultural difference—he is not saying "their ways were not our ways." Nor does he write, "Their ways of being they were not our ways of being we," which would imply that although culture may be arbitrary, after a certain point unsurpassable limits become established. We must also avoid even a more sophisticated potential paraphrase which might affirm, "They tried to be like us and we tried to be like them, but both our ways failed to achieve their objects." Such a proposition would imply a "natural" or at least naturalized Irishness and Frenchness, which each foreign party attempts to approximate through artifice, a "way" which can never be more than an affectation. In other words, the French way of being Irish would not be the same as "really" being Irish, nor would the Irish way of being French be the same as simply being French. But Beckett rejects this also. For in Beckett's formulation there is no *unmediated* cultural appurtenance at all—he does not even claim that "they" were not "we" and that "we" were not "they." Beckett acknowledges that they *had a way* of being we; they *were* we, in a way. And again, this does not mean that they were we, *in a way,* while we were simply we, for we were *also* we "in a way": "their way of being we was not our *way.*" Thus, if they are not *simply* "we," for that matter, neither are we: our "weness" is just as constructed as their attempt to be "like us." Meanwhile, they are not simply "they" either, for they also have a *way* of being they. We see now why this "simple and necessary" proposition is also "unattainable," for if one follows its rigorous logic we arrive at a point where the law of noncontradiction is clearly violated: "they" both are *and* are not "we"—they are "we" in that Beckett's grammar places "their" claims to "weness" and "our" claims to "weness" in exact, indistinguishable parallel. But "they" are not "we" in that a difference is introduced between "their way" of being ourselves and "our way" of being ourselves. Beckett's delicate rhetoric here recognizes cultural identity as a construct and thus theoretically nonexclusionary for foreigners. But more importantly, being a construct, cultural identity is

also on one level just as much an artifice, a "way" of behaving, react-
ing, and constructing reality for those who are defined or who define
themselves as within as for those who are defined or define themselves as
without. Beckett refuses all rhetoric which might pose a "native" culture as
being natural or naturalized in a manner which would place a "foreigner"
in an irremediable relationship to it of exteriority, mediation, and artifice.
Yet Beckett *also* rejects any appeal to nonhistorical, nonculturally specific
criteria of "universal human values," which can so easily serve to erase
the distinct specificities and very real divergences that collectively constitute "universal" human culture and history. Strictly speaking, there are no
"theys," but every "we" has its "way." An unattainable proposition indeed.

Thus, "The Capital of the Ruins" invites meditation on the construction of subjectivity through cultural ritual—the "ways" through which
one becomes what one is. And *Watt* is largely an investigation of ritual,
whether it be the mysterious, guiding rituals of the Knott establishment,
or those surrounding the meetings and discussions of Sam and Watt, or
the increasingly ritualistic use of serial repetition as a stylistic device in
the narration. But the rhetoric of "The Capital of the Ruins" also offers
a means of reconciling the "anthropological" school of criticism with the
metaphysical one, if we examine the novel's use of Cartesian thought in
its light. For if Descartes largely ignores questions of culture and cultural
difference, his concern is nevertheless nothing other than *how* the subject
constructs and recognizes itself as such. For Descartes, of course, neither
immediate certainty nor a priori subjective presence is ever a given, and
even the most fundamental of all intuitive notions—the sense of one's
own existence—is seen by Descartes to be in fact constructed through
the logical and linguistic practice of the cogito. In this sense, the cogito,
chief among Descartes's *méthodes,* itself may legitimately be seen as a "way
of being oneself"—a radical way which through its profound skepticism
regarding all externality seems to annul any possibility of a "we," while
simultaneously rendering plural every individual subject through its logical exigence that one witness oneself.[5] Thus, linking Beckett's emphasis on
the "way" to Descartes's *méthode, Watt* may be seen as Beckett's attempt to
write the necessarily repetitive, performative, skeptical ritual of the cogito
and the individual over the performative, repetitive, group rituals and rites
by which a "culture" enacts itself.

Beckett's attempt to think this juncture between culture and subjectivity, between subjective singularity and a cultural plurality which must
in some way precede it, inevitably leads him to Freud and psychoanaly-

sis.[6] For if *Watt* is evidently concerned with ritual and "method" (in the Cartesian sense and more generally), it is also equally concerned with law, transgression, and taboo, and the elaboration of the rites and prohibitions of the Knott household (whose proprietor's name simultaneously invokes the law's prohibitions and the necessary vacancy of the symbolic space that anchors them) seems resonant with echoes of Freud's reading of ritual in *Totem and Taboo*. For *Watt* not only superimposes cultural practice over Cartesian "method," it also draws the latter into relation with the repetitive personal rituals of obsessional neurotics. Yet the novel's rendering of taboo is oddly vacuous, in that it never allows the extrapolation of the unconscious impulses which, according to Freud, taboo laws are established to counter. A large part of the novel's difficulty derives from its voiding of the libidinal energy that such a taboo structure should generate (in stark contrast to both halves of *Molloy,* for example). The book is neither a simple critique of Cartesian "rationalism" nor an anthropological inquiry into cultural practice, patriarchy, and the foundation of law, but rather an attempt to think subjectivity as ritual, ritual as method, and method as neurosis, in a chain which would refuse to label neurosis as simply a rhetorical response to desire. *Watt*'s elaborate staging of what could be called culture shock, in that Watt's crises are so often linked to his utter estrangement from and incomprehension of the rituals it is his task to perform, is thus not an affirmation of the inscrutability of the foreign, nor simply an assertion of the inherent "foreigness" of all culture as compared to some sort of "naturalness" of the individual which could preexist it. The novel deconstructs the opposition individual/culture, allowing no clear boundary between culture shock and what could be called "subject shock": indeed, for Descartes the "shock" is produced by the culture of the real. Throughout the novel, the point of convergence where questions of subjective introspection dissolve into allegories of cultural inscription is language, and it is there that our reading must begin.

Many critics have noticed the prevalence of gallicisms in the novel, and speculation abounds as to whether their presence is due to an intentional authorial choice or unconscious linguistic interference from the French. Is Beckett then suffering from the interference endemic to those who immerse themselves in a foreign code, or is he commenting on it? That the inclusion of the gallicisms indicates at least in part a deliberate decision is evident from the obvious foregrounding Beckett provides for many of them, as we shall see. They also tend to be concentrated in certain sections of the novel, most notably the early discussion between Hackett, Nixon, and Tetty, and Arsene's parting speech to Watt. Indeed, at one point, Arsene seems to catch himself committing one: "Where was I? The change. In what did it consist? It is hard to say. Something slipped. There I was, warm and bright, smoking my tobacco-pipe, watching the warm bright wall, when suddenly somewhere some little thing slipped, some little tiny thing. Gliss—iss—iss—STOP! I trust I make myself clear" (42–43). Arsene is apparently on the verge here of replacing "slip" with the French "glisser," thus what is slipping is in fact the word "to slip." The "change" Arsene is discussing when "slip" slips is that from his prior feeling at Knott's that "he [i.e., Arsene] may abide, as he is, where he is, and that where he is may abide about him, as it is" (41) to this other condition, which Arsene is unable to define more precisely than in the following terms: "What was changed, and how? What was changed, if my information is correct, was the sentiment that a change, other than a change of degree, had taken place" (44). Typically, Arsene never manages to bring these meditations to any conclusion, deliberately changing the subject with the announcement that he has "information of a practical nature to impart" (45). But prior to this, he clearly depicts the effects of this undefined change as a *dépaysement* from the comfortable fit between himself and the Knott residence where he was abiding:

> The sun on the wall, since I was looking at the sun on the wall at the time, underwent an instantaneous and I venture to say radical change of appearance. It was the same sun and the same wall, or so little older that the difference may safely be disregarded, but so changed that I felt I had been transported, without my having remarked it, to some quite different yard, and to some quite different season, in an unfamiliar country. (43–44)

The rhetorical chain here is relatively clear: this radical change is both figured as a transportation to an "unfamiliar country" and referred to as a "slip," while this act of designation itself instigates a linguistic slip into the language of another country, sliding into "glisser." What happens, then, is that the act of *naming* the "slip" repeats and reproduces it. So the language of Arsene would seem not only to represent but also to symptomatically reenact what it recounts. Such a conception, however, only delivers half of the complexity of the passage. For the "slip" represented by Arsene's linguistic shift is not just a repetition of but also the *model for* Arsene's previous slip, as it is only in terms of transportation to an "unfamiliar country" that the latter can be understood. In this sense, linguistic interference, or what might be termed "cultural" interference generally becomes the model for all subjective "qualitative changes," and not just a species within their genus. Group identity and cultural economy is thus rhetorically posited as *prior* to any sort of individual subjectivity which would subsequently extend itself toward a group. The mediation between the group structures and the subject's self-positing seems to be effected in this passage through a further slip of the "tongue." Let us consider some of Arsene's early comments concerning the dawning of the recognition that this "change" has taken place. Speaking of the uncanny day when, although feeling better than ever, the servant of Knott is nevertheless led to ask himself, "Am I not a little out of sorts, to-day?" (42), Arsene goes on to claim: "But that is a terrible day (to look back on), the day when the horror of what has happened reduces him to the ignoble expedient of inspecting his tongue in a mirror, his tongue never so rosy, in a breath never so sweet" (42). In the immediate context of the passage, the phrase would seem to imply the servant's desire to check himself for symptoms of illness, but in the larger context of the disorder Arsene sketches, this "tongue" must also be read in its Gallic nuance as "language," so intimately tied to Arsene's unnamable catastrophe. And indeed, *Watt* certainly gives us one of the greatest spectacles we have of an author "inspecting his tongue in a mirror," as it were, not least of all in section 3 where Watt narrates to Sam in what could be seen as *mirrored* inversions of words, sentences, and paragraphs.[7] To examine one's tongue in a mirror would thus mean not simply to produce an adequate representation of it, but to work through a representation which necessarily doubles by reversing. Beckett's "mirror" is not at all the perfectly transparent medium of representation, but rather one which reveals by doubling and extending the original in an uncannily inverted fashion, thus highlighting and estranging the structure of articulations of the original which had come to be naturalized. Arsene's following speech is filled with somewhat understated gallicisms: "ordure" (46), "luxurious" for "lustful" (49), "defunct" for "deceased" and "Daltonic" for "color-blind" in the space of two lines (51), and "collation" and "imprevisible" in the same sentence (53), to name a few. The relationship of these "slips" to the something that "slipped" is left unelaborated, although the evocation discussed above of the sense of transportation to an unfamiliar country cannot but color our reading of them. However, in order to continue our examination of gallicisms in the context of the inspection of the tongue, we must turn to the verbal perpetrations of Tetty Nixon.

The discussion surrounding Tetty Nixon's burlesque account of the birth of her son, Larry, and the history of Watt foregrounds gallicisms even more clearly than does Arsene's speech. There is at the least a Gallic inflection in Hackett's use of "antecedents" (22) to designate Watt's past, and Nixon's term "facultative stop" (19) for a tram stop serviced only if requested by a passenger is a clear transposition of the French. But Tetty's gallicisms are different—they are not based on the choice of a false cognate, as in the examples given above, but are rather phonetic transpositions of French terms, which do not respect the regular morphological structures of English appropriations of Latinate words.[8] Thus, describing the sudden onset of labor pains, she says, "No trace of this dollar appeared on my face" (13), where "dollar" would appear to be her pronunciation of the French *douleur,* or "pain." A few lines later, she refers to a risqué repartee as "Not too osy" (14). Hackett, at a loss, asks, "Not too what?" Mr Nixon replies, "Osy. . . . You know, not too osy" (14). "Osy" here would seem to be an assimilation of the French *osé.* But one cannot claim that Tetty's speech is simply denatured by the invasion of foreign terms, for prior to her notable gallicisms, Tetty demonstrates a sort of aphasia which it is impossible to attribute to the interference of a foreign code. As Tetty recounts the fateful night of Larry's delivery in the midst of a dinner party, we find the following exchange:

> The first mouthful of duck had barely passed my lips, said Tetty, when Larry leaped in my wom.
> Your what? said Mr Hackett.
> My wom, said Tetty.
> You know, said Goff, her woom.
> How embarrassing for you, said Mr Hackett. (13)

This phonetic disturbance "within" the "mother tongue" is a harbinger of much that is to follow in the novel. First of all, it introduces the structural convolutions of the English language which comprise so much of the burden of part 3, and which Beckett investigates more systematically, more methodically in the Cartesian sense, than any other author has ever done. Second of all, this insistence on Tetty's error in contrast to the gallicisms that follow seems to warn against a reading that would interpret these structural convolutions and breakdowns as the result of an incursion of the "foreign" that would in some way damage the integrity of a given code. The damage is already operative from the "inside," and note that these linguistic disturbances within the "mother tongue" take place in the context of a discussion of maternity, and thus in the context of that other notable system of differences, which is kinship structure. On the one hand, Beckett parallels linguistic structures, whether syntactic, discursive, or phonetic, to family and kinship structures, and in *Watt*, disturbance in one register tends to mirror disturbance in another. This is why the novel disallows a separation of Cartesian skepticism or epistemological investigation from questions of cultural and social practice and kinship organization. The interrogation of patriarchal structures epitomized by the Knott household is written into the interrogation of linguistic structures we have been examining, and both investigations are conducted through the mode of estrangement. On the other hand, any idea of naturalness which might be associated with the "mother tongue" is implicitly challenged not only by Tetty's aphasia, but also by the wholly uncanny story of maternity she recounts. Larry is delivered in three minutes flat single-handedly by the mother herself while his father and friends play billiards downstairs. The umbilical cord, we are told, was severed by the mother's teeth, she "not having a scissors to her hand" (14). Thus, if linguistic law and patriarchal law are clearly put parallel in the book, we should resist all recourse to any concept of the maternal or the natural to which these laws would be opposed. Rather, in *Watt* both the "maternal" and the "natural" are necessarily seen as effects created and dominated by these very structures.

The novel itself expounds the idea that concepts, categories, and oppositions are not simply descriptive terms that maintain a relationship of adequation with the real, but rather products of structures which the relationship to the real provokes. Indeed, the "real" itself is also paradoxically described as one of these effects. This problematic is treated most explicitly in the episode involving the Galls, father and son, who come to tune Mr Knott's piano. The passage, one of the most widely discussed in the novel, is quite rightly described by Leslie Hill as "paradigmatic" (20). Indeed, the narrator tells us it is a model for many of Watt's "experiences" in his early days at the Knott household. Hill goes on to read the episode in the light of filial relations, stressing that which pertains between the Galls and the memory they induce in Watt of his father's legs and trousers. This leads to a broader discussion of Knott as symbolic father. Critics also often discuss the role of music in the novel, additionally raised by the picture of the piano in the "addenda," and finally, mention is usually made of the way the passage's discussion of memory establishes Watt as a generally "unreliable" narrator.[9] However, the major point of focus tends to be the status of this passage as the novel's most detailed exploration of the relationship between experience, immediacy, memory, and linguistic construction, questions that recur incessantly in *Watt*. Certainly, as a theory of Watt's need to narrativize and construct meaning, it provides the thread that will bind all the subsequent episodes: indeed, it leads directly to the famous discussion of the "pot," which, in turn, is immediately followed by the long episode recounting Knott's dietary habits, the need for a dog to dispose of his leftovers, and the hallucinatory Lynch family. Now, what must be emphasized is that the concerns raised by these two later episodes are entirely extensions of the problems caused by the "memory" of the Galls. A full forty-five pages after the beginning of the section on the Galls, the story of the Lynches concludes with a declaration on precisely what was at stake in the previous saga also. For Watt has no conviction at all concerning the veracity of the elaborate myth he has constructed around the Lynches: "Not that for a moment Watt supposed that he had penetrated the forces at play, in this particular instance, or even perceived the forms that they upheaved, or obtained the least useful information concerning himself, or Mr Knott, for he did not. But he had turned, little by little, a disturbance into words, he had made a pillow of old words, for a head. Little by little, and not without labour" (117). What is established in the sequence of these three central passages—the Galls, the pot, and the Lynches—is a link between, respectively, linguistic constructions of memory and meaning, the referential tie implied by any semiotic act, and kinship and family structures. The "pillow of old words" is composed of a familial narrative, and the construction of reference is embodied in the story of the father and son. The point of this is not that some Oedipalized structure forms a "primal" content of all subjectivity but rather that there is profound complicity between subjective self-scrutiny and kinship structures inasmuch as the former insists on an emphasis on the question of origin which only the latter can answer. It is through the concatenation of these passages that Beckett achieves his linkage of Cartesian dogma to questions of filiation and thus of Cartesian method to Freud's view of obsessional ritual. Obsessional ritual leads to taboo and finally to the investigations of patriarchy conducted through the figure of Knott.

The incident of the Galls, like that of the Lynches, involves disposing of "disturbances" by transferring them into language or "foisting a meaning there where no meaning appeared" (77), not in the sense of determining a metaphysical signification but merely through the construction of the simplest temporal narrative. Thus, we learn that in fact the "incident of the Galls" might in reality have had nothing to do with either a piano, tuners, or a father and son, and that this might simply be the "meaning"

Watt arrived at to disperse his phantoms: "For to explain had always been to exorcise, for Watt" (78). And this explanation might very well be pure fabulation:

> Watt spoke of it [the incident] as involving, in the original, the Galls and the piano, but he was obliged to do this, even if the original had nothing to do with the Galls and the piano. For even if the Galls and the piano were long posterior to the phenomena destined to become them, Watt was obliged to think, and speak, of the incident, even at the moment of its taking place, as the incident of the Galls and the piano, if he was to think and speak of it at all. (79)

Moreover, we are told that Watt's fabulations tend to wear out and necessitate new ones to take their place, themselves to be at times replaced in turn by previous constructions which have recovered their power to convince. It is due to such considerations that "one is sometimes tempted to wonder, with reference to two or even three incidents related by Watt as separate and distinct, if they are not in reality the same incident, variously interpreted" (78). Thus, concerning what "really happened" in the incident of the Galls, we know absolutely nothing, but only how at one particular moment Watt linguistically and conceptually "exorcised" it. We do not know if this was the original exorcism, the only one, or simply the latest of a long series. As this incident is the type of the majority of those which occurred at the Knott household, strictly speaking we have no idea if any of the events therein should be taken as anything other than Watt's fabulation. Such a skeptical reading would give us a very different novel, consisting of the early episode of Hackett and the Nixons, Sam's account of meeting Watt in part 3, perhaps the departure at the train station, and then a long, interpolated narrative with the status of a fable. This reading would produce a work in line with *Company,* or the problems raised by Moran's disavowal of his narrative in *Molloy,* which is far from the optic in which *Watt* is usually read.

In any case, the incident of the Galls, the discussion of the pot, and the story of the Lynches all emphasize linguistic narrative as a means of constructing "reality" and memory, not as a means of representing them or depicting them. The manners in which this form of construction is itself arbitrarily structured and subject to disturbance are foregrounded in many ways: largely by the way the book permits rhyme schemes and sentence structure to generate slots and oppositions which are then filled by a semantic content which comes to seem increasingly random, irrelevant, and, in practical terms, increasingly difficult to convert into ideational content given the density of the repetitive linguistic mass that vehiculates it. But as we have seen, the book also stresses very early on such structural disturbances as aphasia and interlinguistic interference, such as gallicisms. This being the case, it seems worth pondering the proper name of the piano tuners: given our gallicisms, what does it mean for the Galls to come to tune the piano? After our awkward gallicisms, do we finally have the arrival of the Galls in person, and not just their linguistic forerunners?[10] After all, their task of "tuning the piano" can be read in highly allegorical fashion: they have come to tune the literary instrument, language, so clearly off key in the novel up to this point. Such an allegory has at least two clear applications. First of all, it replicates one of the central, founding myths of early Anglo-American modernism: that a turn to French literature was necessary to achieve a cleaner, clearer, harder, "modern" literary language. Such thinking is prevalent in Eliot, in Joyce's admiration and emulation of Flaubert, and most of all in Pound's critical writings. And it may be argued that it is only with *Watt* that Beckett manages his difficult break with the modernist trend these writers represent, which is much more clearly in evidence in his earlier prose and poetry. The Galls then would represent a paradigm that Beckett here is rejecting.[11] However, this episode could also be seen as a comment on Beckett's own subsequent shift into French as language of composition and a reinscription of his filial position within a different symbolic structure (thus the Galls "father and son"). But before embarking on a heroic reading of the shift into French as the choice of the proper, well-tuned instrument, the move away from a suffocating, castrating maternal language into a phallicized, instrumentalized, distant paternal one, or a move away from the language bearing the patriarchal inscription of the patronym into a neutral space of auto-engenderment,[12] we should remember that the episode of the Galls is constantly stressed as a *fantasy*, as "foisting a meaning there where no meaning appeared" (77). Thus, the story could also be taken as a warning against all forms of critical linguistic exoticism, that is, the assertion that a shift from one specific linguistic structure to another can free one from the bounds of structure generally, or the symmetrical claim: that all linguistic structure distances one from the purity of a real beyond expression.

The episode of the Galls can also be taken as an allegory of allegorization generally, that is, of the need to foist meaning where there is none. But this does not lead to a global critique of hermeneutics and a privileging of the literal and the proper, for the pages on the Galls make it quite clear that the construction of any literal or proper is *already* an allegorization in this sense. The literalist readings of Beckett would be the most mystified of all. Beyond this sort of "allegory," all is unnamable, but not in the sense of being ineffable or beyond the illusory grasp of linguistic mediation. On the other side of cultural graphematic constructions is something which seems much less the "real" of traditional Western metaphysics, to which language can only point and approximate, than the real as evoked by Lacan. Speaking of Watt's occasional failures to foist meanings in the manner of the Galls story, Sam tells us:

> As to giving an example of the second event, namely the failure, that is clearly quite out of the question. For there we have to do with events that resisted all Watt's efforts to saddle them with meaning, and a formula, so that he could neither think of them, nor speak of them, but only suffer them, when they recurred, though it seems probable that they recurred no more, at the period of Watt's revelation, to me, but were as though they had never been. (78–79)

It is important to note here Beckett's distance from both phenomenology and logical positivism. For the events that resist being saddled with meaning or formula have no phenomenological status at all and cannot be considered events or objects as such—as the passage tells us, they are literally unthinkable. Being unthinkable, they cannot be considered in the light of Wittgenstein's language games either, in which words or counters are exchanged for prelinguistic entities. The sort of narrativization of which the Galls story forms the example has all the characteristics of an obsessional ritual or rite, being repeated, modified, and, when need be, reinvented in a ceaseless effort to keep a potential suffering at bay. Indeed, the opposition of meaning, no matter how gratuitous, to suffering is one upon which all critics of the novel would do well to dwell. If Watt is dominated by the pleasure principle, his suffering cannot be said to originate with the distance between language and a "real"—indeed, it is the possibility of such a difference which provides his occasional salvation, and his rituals are less motivated by a desire to comprehend or represent the real than to create a real whose laws provide repose. And this "exorcism" through explanation would seem to hold good for Watt's fabulation generally, being the archetype of most of his experience at Knott's: "For the incident of the Galls father and son was the first and type of many"

(76). Thus, the general process for which the Galls provide the model and which is also the model for most processes generally undertaken by Watt, might be called *gallicization*—that is, the need to foist a meaning where there is none through the creation of a ritual narrative.

Thus, staying within the Gallic register we may begin to see how the novel reads Descartes—not only as the author of a narrative of rituals, the precepts, but also as the philosopher who takes as his foundation a ritual narrative, that is, the cogito. Already in "Whoroscope," as we have seen, Beckett had read Descartes in terms of ritual and superstition, such as those surrounding the preparation of his omelettes and his fear of fortune tellers. And indeed, Descartes's own investigations in the *Discours* and especially the *Méditations* teeter precariously between the need to recognize meaninglessness on the one hand, and the need to abrogate or name it, on the other. In this connection, God is the name given to the fact that rationally, reason cannot be established as equivalent to truth. According to Descartes, in addition to things that can be proven, we must accept as true also those which defy logical proof but are intuitively obvious. Yet for Descartes, the only assumption which permits us to accept as true the suprarational intuitive would be the existence of a perfect God, disinclined to deceive us in our innermost impressions: "Car, premièrement, cela même que j'ai tantôt pris pour une règle, à savoir que les choses que nous concevons très clairement et très distinctement, sont toutes vraies, n'est assuré qu'à cause que Dieu est ou existe, et qu'il est un être parfait, et que tout ce qui est en nous vient de lui" (67) [For, firstly, even the rule which I stated above that I held, namely, that the things we grasp very clearly and very distinctly are all true, is assured only because God is or exists, and because he is a perfect Being, and because everything that is in us comes from him (*Discourse,* 58)]. Descartes offers the above to argue specifically that only the hypothesis of the Deity allows us to have faith in our ability to distinguish dreaming from waking life, for while we dream we often have the impression of being awake, and at no particular moment can we be rationally or phenomenologically certain we are not within some particular dream, with its own particular false reality. Now this distinction between reality and hallucinatory or oneiric perception is one which, the Galls episode teaches us, Watt has no desire to make—all that matters for him is the imperative that there be a meaning; its ontological status is of no real concern. But there is another Cartesian proof of the existence of God that is perhaps also in play here. In "Whoroscope" Beckett sums it up in the following lines:

I'm a bold boy I know
so I'm not my son
(even if I were a concierge)
nor Joachim my father's
but the chip of a perfect block that's neither old nor new,
the lonely petal of a great high bright rosê.

(lines 78–83)

In the notes, Beckett explicates this passage with the phrase, "He proves God by exhaustion" (*Collected Poems*, 6). Beckett is here referring to Descartes's assertion that his own existence is proof of the existence of God. Descartes reasons that he did not bring himself into existence, for were he "l'auteur de mon existence" (211) [the author of my birth and existence (*Discourse*, 127)], he would be endowed with every perfection, being his own cause and therefore independent of all externality. As he is instead, in Beckett's Irishism, a far from perfect "bold boy," another answer must be hazarded. The obvious answer, that his parents created him, is not a final answer, because of course his parents could not have brought themselves into existence either, and thus another step back must be taken. As living things cannot create themselves ex nihilo, moving backward genealogically one is obliged to finally assert the existence of a first cause, that is, God (by exhaustion). However, in Descartes's argument in this section of the third meditation, the conclusion is not only that God is the ultimate engenderer, but also that he leaves his mark on his creation, "comme la marque de l'ouvrier empreinte sur son ouvrage" (215) [like the mark that the workman imprints on his work (*Discourse*, 130)]. Descartes goes on to claim that this mark of resemblance to God is known by the individual through the same mechanism by which the individual knows itself: "Je conçois cette ressemblance (dans laquelle l'idée de Dieu se trouve contenue) par la même faculté par laquelle je me conçois moi-même; c'est-à-dire lorsque je fais réflexion sur moi" (215) [I perceive this likeness, in which the idea of God is contained, by means of the same faculty by which I apprehend myself; that is to say that, when I reflect upon myself (*Discourse*, 130)]. The Galls, who appear as father and son, are perhaps an evocation of this exhaustive link; that "There was no family likeness between the two, as far as Watt could make out" (70), is perhaps Beckett's ironic nod at the idea of the creator's imprint left on the creation. But in any event, the implication of this passage from the *Méditations* and Descartes's accompanying argument that not only is God the ultimate engenderer but that he reengenders each being in every separable moment of its existence is that the cogito serves not only to prove my existence but simultaneously and by the same token to inscribe me in a filial position in a fully elaborated kinship structure.

Indeed, despite the cogito's apparent logical austerity, its status as proof is untenable without this inscription: "[I]l est nécessaire que Dieu soit l'auteur de mon existence; car tout le temps de ma vie peut être divisé en une infinité de parties, chacune desquelles ne dépend en aucune façon des autres, et ainsi de ce qu'un peu auparavant j'ai été, il ne s'ensuit pas que je doive maintenant être, si ce n'est qu'en ce moment quelque cause me produise, et me crée" (211–12) [God is necessarily the author of my existence. For the whole time of my life may be divided into an infinity of parts, each of which depends in no way on the others; and thus, it does not follow that because I existed a little earlier, I must exist now, unless at this moment some cause produces and creates me anew (*Discourse*, 127)]. Thus, subjective ritual comes to be both dependent on and productive of progenitory myth, which links the Cartesian rituals of self-recognition or subjective assertion to those Freud describes in *Totem and Taboo*, equally concerned with subjective construction through kinship structuration. Likewise, this moves us from the Galls dyad to the sprawling Lynches.

Although *Totem and Taboo* is most notorious for its mythic account of Oedipal violence and desire, the burden of the book is in fact more occupied by discussing how kinship structures are built through relation to a totem animal. Freud argues that it is through a shared relation to the same totem animal that any particular group establishes its identity. Moreover, it is this identity and *not* that established by the nuclear family which will be the model of all group identities, including national, to follow. This contradiction is only one of appearance, however, because the totem itself represents a father figure, transformed into animal shape. The general prohibition on killing or eating one's totem animal echoes the prohibition on parricide, whereas the ritual eating of the totem animal on festival days serves two purposes: first, it enables the identification with the totem animal to be reinforced through a literalized incorporation, and second, it gives expression to the other pole of the ambivalent relation to the father, that is, the homicidal one. But following Freud's logic, it is not the "real" tribal father who is projected into the totem, but rather the relationship of paternity itself is only constructed by the mapping of the totemic relationship onto it. The relevance of all this for *Watt* lies in the book's emphasis on taboo rituals and the erection of the bizarre and absent patriarchal icon with the name of Mr Knott. Much of the book's discussion of taboo centers precisely on culinary ritual: in what seems a condensed parody of *Totem and Taboo,* the elaborate prohibitions regarding Mr Knott's eating habits and leftovers lead to the absurd and lengthy investigations of the kinship structure of the Lynch family. The Lynches, joint custodians of the sacred dog appointed the task of eating Knott's remains, also provide us with a totem animal. Watt's relationship to his duties is also clearly governed by taboo law, that is, not an internalized sense of right and wrong pertaining to conscious intention, but a "superstitious" belief that the failure to observe certain regulations and rituals will have disastrous consequences, regardless of the intentions surrounding their observance. An example of this is found in Watt's uncharacteristic transgression consisting of his refusal to actually watch the dog eat Knott's leftovers. We are told that this refusal "might have been supposed to have the gravest consequences, both for Watt and for Mr Knott's establishment" (115) and that indeed "Watt expected something of this kind" (115). We learn that Watt's course of action was determined by his insurmountable hatred of dogs, despite his fear of its consequences. These consequences, however, fail to appear:

> As it was, nothing happened, but all went on, as before, apparently. No punishment fell on Watt, no thunderbolt, and Mr Knott's establishment swam on, through the unruffled nights and days, with all its customary serenity. And this was a great source of wonder, to Watt, that he had infringed, with impunity, such a venerable tradition, or institution. But he was not so foolish as to found in this a principle of conduct, or a precedent of rebelliousness, ho no, for Watt was only too willing to do as he was told, and as custom required, at all times. And when he was forced to transgress, as in the matter of witnessing the dog's meal, then he was at pains to transgress in such a way, and to surround his transgression with such precautions, such delicacies, that it was almost as though he had not transgressed at all. And perhaps this was counted to him for grace. And he stilled the wonder the trouble in his mind, by reflecting that if he went unpunished for the moment, he would not perhaps always go unpunished, and that if the hurt to Mr Knott's establishment did not at once appear, it would perhaps one day appear, a little bruise at first, and then a bigger, and then a bigger still, until, growing, growing, it blackened the entire body. (115–16)

The above should give pause to the many naively "Oedipal" readings to which *Watt* has been subjected. What this remarkable passage establishes is not Watt's resentment of the paternal principle or its laws, but rather his anxiety at the potential fragility of these laws themselves. Watt does not fear punishment, but rather that he will not be punished. For this sort of reason, we should hesitate to read Knott simply as an emblem of paternal or patriarchal despotism. For Knott, as his name might imply, is not simply the source of the system, although he does seem to be the knot which ties it together. And the novel does not give us the drama of the son's embattled assertion of his subjectivity in the face of oppressive paternal authority, but rather anxiety at the potential breakdown of a social signifying structure in which the father is no more than a marker, thus, "not." Not the primal father who dominates his subservient sons, Knott far more closely resembles the sort of tribal chiefs discussed by Freud, who by the fact of their very sacredness are *more* bound by taboo law than their subjects.[13] As Freud explains, since the totemic ruler is divinely linked to the well being of his subjects (being intimately tied to the elements, for example), it is crucial that he be protected from any mishap which might find a cosmic reflection. These protections are often violently restrictive. Such a structure once again represents for Freud a compromise formation in which the primal ambivalence toward the ruler may be expressed: on the one hand, taboo laws protect, honor, and isolate him. On the other, they can eventually become so restrictive and violent that they come to resemble the murderous act that they are established to defend against. A detail from Freud which seems particularly relevant to *Watt* is that "the principal part [in taboos concerning kings and priests] is played in them by restrictions upon freedom of movement and upon diet" (45–46), both of which are prominent in the rituals surrounding Knott's care and behavior. Freud then quotes a list of prohibitions from Frazer concerning the Flamen Dialis of ancient Rome, which for the very rhythm of the list of nots, in addition to its content, is evocative of Beckett's novel: "He 'might not ride or even touch a horse, nor see an army under arms, nor wear a ring which was not broken, nor have a knot on any part of his garments; . . . he might not touch wheaten flour or leavened bread; he might not touch or even name a goat, a dog, raw meat, beans, and ivy' " (46).[14] In addition to the knot, the dog, and the prohibition on naming, the broken ring also has its place in the novel, being depicted in the picture in Erskine's room.

Thus, the novel's emphatic Oedipal nods must be answered not in terms of the boy-child's desire for the mother, which finds itself blocked by the "Not!" of the Father's commandment. The figure of the mother is largely absent from the novel, as desire is from Watt, while Knott, like one of Freud's tribal chiefs, is as powerless as his subjects. Rather, Beckett's interrogation of the patriarchal economy seems more concerned with its function in determining subjective identifications, positionings, and group identities. Of course, the question of desire cannot be separated from the process of identification, but as we saw above, the anxiety of the novel is centered not on castration, or the paternal punishment of the son's desire, but rather on the fragility of the laws which give the son his "place" in the symbolic economy.[15]

Thus, if Knott seems in some ways to be invulnerable, abiding impassively the serial replacements of his rotating servants, he is by no means beyond the laws they enforce. Indeed, Knott's apparent omnipotence is, in fact, but a reflection of the most imperious need of all: "For except, one, not to need, and, two, a witness to his not needing, Knott needed nothing, as far as Watt could see" (202). The need to need nothing is precisely the need that can never be met, as every abolition of need becomes no more than a reinforcement of its law. In order to finally achieve the state of needing nothing, one would also have to reach the state where one no longer needed to need nothing, which would then open the door to all the needs one wished to exclude. So Knott is also the tie that doubly binds.[16] Thus, just as Watt must witness, so must Mr Knott be witnessed—neither are free from or within their places in this arrangement which looks less like Hegel's master/slave dialectic than Freud's description of an "organized" group. In his "Group Psychology and the Analysis of the Ego," Freud begins by summarizing accounts of how the behavior of groups tends to reduce or cancel the intelligence, moral inhibitions, and critical functions of the individuals which comprise them. But following W. McDougall, Freud also discusses what he calls "organized" groups, which on the contrary allow for greater achievements than those undertaken by individuals alone. Of the five necessary conditions for the formation of an organized group, four are strikingly present in the Knott household, the third being the only conspicuous absence:

The first and fundamental condition is that there should be some degree of continuity of existence in the group. This may be either material or formal: material, if the same individuals persist in the group for some time; *and formal, if there is developed within the group a system of fixed positions which are occupied by a succession of individuals.*

The second condition is that in the individual member of the group some definite idea should be formed of the nature, composition, functions and capacities of the group, so that from this he may develop an emotional relation to the group as a whole.

The third is that the group should be brought into interaction (perhaps in the form of rivalry) with other groups similar to it but differing from it in many respects.

The fourth is that the group should possess traditions, customs and habits, *and especially such as determine the relations of its members to one another.*

The fifth is that the group should have a definite structure, expressed in the specialization and differentiation of the functions of its constituents. (*Civilization, Society and Religion*, 114–15, my emphasis)

This sort of organized group is held together not so much by the libidinal ties between its members nor by those between the members and their leader, but rather by an identification with an abstracted concept of the group itself—a group which should continue beyond the lives and scope of the individuals who comprise it at any given moment. Watt's fixations are less on the other servants or even Mr Knott than on the customs and rituals that constitute the household. And as Watt's speculations concerning Knott's consciousness of and responsibility for his feeding arrangements indicate, there is no necessity that Knott be taken as the origin, source, or inventor of these customs, although his structuring role within them is crucial. Like the Cartesian God, Knott becomes a necessary hypothesis for the functioning of a series of repeated rituals that create subjective identifications. The sense in the novel that prohibitions and rituals are due to arbitrary custom rather than the whim of an individual source of power and desire is reinforced by the way Watt seems to inherit them— although we are told that Erskine did spend some time explaining to Watt his duties (85), the perpetuation of the enduring structures of the Knott household, despite the frequent changes of not wholly articulate servants, seems to lend the customs a regulating power of their own. The laws of the household are inherited and assumed like social custom, like the divergent cultural manners that form the "ways of being we," and, of course, also like the structures of language, which present themselves as the laws of the signifying combinations through which the subject can be constructed. It is precisely these laws which begin to dissolve for Watt in the famous "pot" passage.

This amply discussed passage describes the dissolution of semantic links for Watt, so that the object or concept of a pot no longer completely corresponds to the word that signifies it: "Looking at a pot, for example, or thinking of a pot, at one of Mr Knott's pots, of one of Mr Knott's pots, it was in vain that Watt said, Pot, pot" (81). What Watt suffers here is quite properly an estrangement from the seeming naturalness of linguistic structures. Contrary to many other sections of the novel, this passage presents us with no aphasia. For example, Watt does not find himself unable to recall a word that would signify "pot," nor does he hear the word "pot" without remembering what it signifies, as in classical cases of aphasia. On the contrary, he clearly remembers the law that binds the signifier to the signified but is forced to make the detour of an appeal to this law for his understanding to function. Jakobson defines similarity aphasia as an atrophy of the metalinguistic function: "The aphasic defect in the 'capacity of naming' is properly a loss of metalanguage" (104). But for Watt the situation is the inverse: only metalinguistic verification allows him to keep his faith in semantic links that no longer ring either true or false for him. As many critics point out, this is the situation in which one finds oneself when learning a foreign language, in which the links between signifier and signified have yet to be reinforced by repetition, use, and context and are established only by the copula of the bilingual dictionary. But what is lost for Watt here is neither linguistic binding, in the sense of an aphasic, nor lexical anchoring, in the sense of someone operating in a foreign language. We are told:

> And Watt preferred on the whole having to do with things of which he did not know the name, though this too was painful to Watt, to having to do with things of which the known name, the proven name, was not the name, any more, for him. For he could always hope, of a thing of which he had never known the name, that he would learn the name, some day, and so be tranquillized. But he could not look forward to this in the case of a thing of which the true name had ceased, suddenly, or gradually, to be the true name for Watt. (81–82)

Thus, in the case of a foreign language, Watt would be willing to apply the new name, as arbitrary and denatured as it might seem. But what has happened here is that an undeniable, recognizable, and "proven" name continues to *function,* but ceases to seem "*proper.*" What Watt has lost is the literal, having entered a world where the word, though recognizable, seems a catachresis—a figure or substitute name for something which is really "something else." Watt is clear on this throughout: one can call it a "pot"; others will call it a "pot"; if I call it a "pot" others will understand me, but "pot" is not the right word. That Watt extends his worries about this phenomenon to the word "man" is not coincidental, as in the trilogy all subjective auto-designation and identification will come to be seen as catachrestical. In *Watt*, however, the end of the proper means the end of the natural, the end of the internalization of the identification which allows us to oppose a "we" to a "they," although it could be argued that such a *distinction* is still possible, based on the difference between those who know what "pot" is supposed (in the literal sense) to mean in the system of English and those who do not. Thus, there is a clear analogy between the episode of the Galls and the question of the pot. As we have seen, the Galls story is less a memory than an attempt to saddle the meaningless with a meaning or a formula, to prevent its constant haunting return. In the later passage, the word "pot" would be seen as just such a saddle, which for Watt begins to fray. Beckett's criticism of language here is in no way that language fails to represent the real in its plenitude (the lack and distance inherent in the mediating sign), nor that language falsifies through its distorting figural additions (the spillage or the excess of the mediating sign with regard to the signification before which it should withdraw). Rather, the real in its plenitude is itself structured by language in the large sense, including the marks that are assembled to constitute memory, in a movement which seems to precede the distinction between true and false, relying more on the pleasure principle and its distinction between suffering and its other. And this is where Descartes's "method" finally meets Watt's pseudo-linguistics, pseudo-anthropology, and obsessional rituals, because for Descartes it is the real itself that is radically foreign and consequently threatening to subjective constitution, as seen in his radical exclusion of it from the interiority of the subject. Indeed, the cogito may be seen as an obsessive ritual defense mechanism against the incursions of all that the ego has rejected as outside it: not only the sense perceptions by which the real penetrates, but also and significantly the body and the drives it registers.

It is in the trilogy, the short stories, and the *Texts for Nothing* that this retreat from the question of collectivity and its relation to that of the construction of all intrasubjectivity will be carried out. The singularity of *Watt* in Beckett's oeuvre lies precisely in its interrogation of group or communal structures, and the mechanisms by which the sense of belonging or estrangement is built. In the works composed during the famous "siege in the room," these questions will have largely disappeared through a sort of phenomenological reduction of all that they presuppose. Thus, *Watt* also marks the transition between Beckett's humorous investigations of Irish manners and morals in the early prose and the more atemporal, severe later work.[17] So, having looked extensively at examples of foreignness in the novel, and the encounter with that which presents itself as the foreign, I would like to close by examining a very little studied passage.

Surely one of the most remarkable of the many tirades in Beckett's work is the "short statement" (39) that Arsene delivers to Watt when the latter arrives to take his place in the Knott establishment. Arsene's rant exceeds twenty pages, and in its descriptions of the eating habits of the hypothetical maid Mary, the list of ancestors, and the account of the sequences of Mr Knott's servants and their replacements, it provides an early example of the many mathematical permutations and serial lists that are the novel's most salient stylistic trait. But critics have paid rather little attention to some of the less immediately striking passages that discuss what Knott's household will mean for Watt.[18] Speaking of the sense of peace the new arrival at Knott's must feel, Arsene describes it in these terms:

> But he being what he has become, and the place being what it was made, the fit is perfect. And he knows this. No. Let us remain calm. He feels it. The sensations, the premonitions of harmony are irrefragable, of imminent harmony, when all outside him will be he, the flowers the flowers that he is among him, the sky the sky that he is above him, the earth trodden the earth treading, and all sound his echo. When in a word he will be in his midst at last, after so many tedious years spent clinging to the perimeter. These first impressions, so hardly won, are undoubtedly delicious. What a feeling of security! They are transports that few are spared, nature is so exceedingly accommodating, on the one hand, and man, on the other. With what sudden colours past trials and errors glow, seen in their new, their true perspective, mere stepping-stones to this! Haw! All is repaid, amply repaid. For he has arrived. He even ventures to remove his hat, and set down his bags, without misgiving. Think of that! He removes his hat without misgiving, he unbuttons his coat and sits down, proffered all pure and open to the long joys of being himself, like a basin to a vomit. (40–41)

The passage, with its emphasis on journey and arrival, clearly evokes a return from exile or banishment, but that from which the servant has been banished is himself—in rhetoric prefiguring the pronominal torsion of the trilogy, Arsene states, "When in a word he will be in his midst at last." As we have seen, this is hardly the experience that awaits Watt. Yet this scene of homecoming, already bracketed by the inevitable expulsion which Arsene lives here in Watt's place, is a sort of narcissistic arrival, a perfection of projection and fusion where the issue of the foreign disappears as the boundary between what one is and what one is not is annihilated: "when all outside him will be he, the flowers the flowers that he is among him, the sky the sky that he is above him, the earth trodden the earth treading, and all sound his echo." This destruction of the threshold between the inner and the outer—that is, this destruction of the central organizing concept of the Cartesian system—is an element to which Arsene explicitly returns: "For my—how shall I say?—my personal system was so distended at the period of which I speak that the distinction between what was inside it and what was outside it was not at all easy to draw" (43). Arsene's implication here is that bliss comes not when the external world simply *corresponds* to the internal, as in the case of "natural" belonging or identification, but rather when the external world no longer maintains any externality at all—to come home in this sense means to *be* the home one comes to, and the joy of "being oneself" is the joy precisely of being *both* the basin and the vomit. In this context, some of Freud's remarks from "Instincts and their Vicissitudes" seem quite apt. After asserting that the ego originally hates the external world for introducing stimuli it cannot control, Freud writes: "At the very beginning, it seems, the external world, objects, and what is hated are identical." Then Freud describes the fate of the external objects that, despite their extraneity, provide pleasure: "If later on an object turns out to be a source of pleasure, it is loved, but it is also incorporated into the ego; so that for the purified pleasure-ego once again objects coincide with what is extraneous and hated" (*On Metapsychology*, 134). Freud thus describes the ego as working by tautology: what is hated *must* be categorized as belonging to the outside; if anything is loved, its exteriority is simply denied through identification. Arsene's ideal of total narcissistic identification would serve to neutralize the world of objects entirely. One must think the pun on "Knot" in this sense also—a site which is not, or a site where that which one is not, is not.

But such a schema implies that to be banished *from* oneself is, in fact, identical to being banished *within* oneself; the sense of exile from oneself derives from one's own awareness of the boundary between the internal and the external. It is, then, the existence of objects that leads to the banishment. This odd contradiction—that it is, in fact, the existence of an outside which divides the subject from itself—is what leads Beckett to Descartes, for whom the subject can only be defined through the suspension of the external. This, as we shall see in the following chapters, is the proposition that the trilogy refuses, enacting the utter rejection of all the appropriative assumptions, linguistic and philosophic, that allow Descartes to postulate subjective self-presence in the ideal absence of an external world. But *Watt*, on the contrary, depicts such a hypothetical self-presence as necessarily constitutive of its own lack. To arrive at the sort of self-delimitation which constantly eludes the trilogy's "voices" is here defined as banishment, as subtraction from a world always irredeemably other, while, as the trilogy will make clear, to be both the traveler and the home, both earth trodden and the treading earth, both the basin and vomit, is to be originally doubled, and in consequence no less divided. On the one hand, then, subjective and objective self-presence create a remainder that cannot be managed, on the other, self-integrity is banishment.

The great irony of *Watt*, however, is found in the enormous distance between this vision of total harmony, reflection and fusion proffered between "haws!" by Arsene, and the absurdly arbitrary, ritualistic duties Watt is obliged to carry out, with no sense of their meaning or utility. As we have seen, Watt submits to the peculiarities of the functioning of the Knott household as to a law—questions of utility, desirability or significance cannot even be raised. Although Watt seems to enjoy the utter alienation of his service, it is certainly a far cry from the sort of bliss that Arsene had evoked. We seem to move from total narcissistic boundless unity and identification to the violent exteriority of the inherited, arbitrary law. But this is perhaps a contradiction in appearance only, for Arsene's vision goes beyond that of desire instantly gratified, providing instead a schema in which desire is automatically preempted, as the spacing or difference necessary for its establishment is denied. In both cases, objects, or that which is hated, have been removed from play—in one case, through the refusal to recognize separation, internalizing everything, in the other, through a structure of prohibitions in which libidinal investment in the structure replaces investment in the objects and actions this structure prohibits. This shift enables the structure itself to break its link from a repressed unconscious and to become truly arbitrary in the sense that Saussurian linguistics speaks of the arbitrariness of the signifier. Thus custom and ritual are logically prior to desire, and if they inevitably serve to create it, they cannot be said to represent it in the sense that a sign is classically seen to represent a logically prior referent. But what could be called Watt's hypercathexis of custom and ritual seems to create an economy where linguistic law goes lax and enters the motivated relationship to the unconscious that the taboo rituals do not here present. Both Arsene's evocation of complete narcissistic extension and Watt's experience of total egoistic effacement before an internalized ego ideal serve to short-circuit the tension that Beckett will explore in the trilogy—that of the ego's self-apperception. This, of course, leads to Beckett's further investigations of the cogito, but the crucial difference between Beckett and Descartes is that if for Descartes the cogito is logically prior to the hypothesis of the relationship with a possible other, for Beckett the mechanics of identification in the formation of the subject lead him into a sort of temporal aporia, or even anachrony, as we shall see in the following chapters.[19] And the privileged figure for this dialectic in Beckett will be that of *voice,* which inextricably links the Cartesian question of the subject's self-apperception to the alterity of the interlocutor and shared social structure that Descartes attempts to provisionally bracket. Thus, it is to the question of voice that we must turn in the next chapter.

3. "Distant Music"

Origin, Voice, and Narrative

in the Trilogy

One of the most basic questions raised by Beckett's trilogy of novels, *Molloy, Malone Dies,* and *The Unnamable,* is quite simply that of the origin and authority of the narratives we are given to read, and the language in which we are given to read them. This problem is perhaps not immediately evident at the outset, but it will become the explicit theme of *The Unnamable,* with its litany of disavowals and abdications of responsibility for the utterances it presents. Indeed, the relationships between origin, source, reference, and language obsess Beckett's fiction from the trilogy right through the final texts, although earlier on in the trilogy the issue is presented less by means of the direct questionings found in *The Unnamable, Company,* and *Worstward Ho,* for example, than through the implications of certain structural and narratological economies. These issues are crucial to the structure of the trilogy as a whole, assuming it is a whole, because the first-person *disavowals* of utterance in *The Unnamable* are balanced by a great number of assertions of forthright literality—assertions that can be used to oppose the "voice" of *The Unnamable* to the "personae" represented by the characters of the earlier novels. Interpretations of *The Unnamable* seem to divide between readings which posit it as the final presentation of the trilogy's ultimate voice, now laid bare, and those which rather tend to see it as an ultimate arrival into Blanchottian neutrality. The archeological balances the teleological in this debate. Before entering it, then, it might be wise to look at how the trilogy discusses origins and destinations, especially as the "characters" in the trilogy tend to depict the "destinations" of their journeys as an arrival at some sort of point of origin for themselves. Is the origin something Beckett's texts allow us to arrive at? Let us begin by looking at *Molloy*.

Within *Molloy*, the issue of origin and reference is foregrounded by the obvious parallels between Moran's journey and Molloy's: to list only the most salient resemblances, both stories tell of long bicycle trips in search of persons who are never encountered (in Molloy's case, his mother; in Moran's case, Molloy); both narrators suffer from progressive physical incapacitation, notably, a stiffening of the knees; both spend protracted stays in a forest, in which each commits a brutal murder; and both finally arrive at the destination where we find them at their stories' beginnings and where accounts of their experiences are demanded by vaguely defined "others." The obvious repetitive overlap between Molloy and Moran naturally invites critical speculation as to the relationship between the two stories and the two "characters," speculations that historically have almost always aimed at establishing chronological priority between the two halves of the novel and logical, causal, and figural priority in terms of the events recounted and the "characters" presented. As we shall see, these speculations enact a desire for origin—and destination—that the books of the trilogy increasingly foreground, parody, and problematize.

If the similarities of the two sections of *Molloy* have led critics to notice that the book in many ways consists of the same story told twice, certain instructive problems arise when one attempts to construct a determinate narrative structure around the fact of these repetitions. One common strategy has been to assert that the similarities between the two halves of *Molloy* can be explained by the assumption that Molloy and Moran are in fact the same "character." Within this framework, the key question becomes that of temporality: if Molloy and Moran are the "same person," how does one account for their differences in name, condition, family status, and perspective, to say nothing of the differences in the "events" they recount? One common move is to argue that *Molloy* inverts a chronology in which Moran is Molloy at an earlier point in his life.[1] From this angle, one could argue that Moran's explicit purpose in his journey—to find Molloy—is at some undefined point fulfilled, as Moran, through his progressive psychic disintegration, in fact, finds Molloy inside himself. In this argument, the story of Moran is precisely the story of the *origin* or source of the sensibility that produces the narrative we read under the signature of Molloy. Conversely, Molloy is often privileged for his distance from the consideration of social niceties and moral duties which torments Moran, and for what some critics take to be a more "authentic" relationship to his desires and drives. Extending this line of thought, the "Molloy" seething beneath the Moran exterior becomes the underlying cause or source of Moran's disaggregation. Of course, these two interpretations are in fact mirror images, and no matter the subtlety with which these readings are conducted, they are inextricably bound to a hermeneutics of causality, primacy, and determination. The novel, however, gives ample reason to suspect that this kind of hermeneutics is precisely what its dynamics have been constructed to bring into question. Both stories in *Molloy* foreground and parody just this sort of interpretive quest and the assumptions that go with it. After all, Moran is himself a "detective" of some sort, one whose task is to "find" Molloy—a task identical to that taken up by the critic who would argue that Moran is Molloy in embryo. The critic who asserts that Moran is in fact and unbeknownst to himself Molloy has become in turn and with equal ignorance a double of Moran. Similarly, the desire for origin implicit in Molloy's search for his mother requires no elaboration. The concatenation of these two stories should perhaps make the reader question what is at stake in her or his journey of interpretation.

If, however, we proceed with the argument that *Molloy* inverts the sequence of the stories it tells, a number of other problems will also present themselves. To begin with, the assertion that Moran is an earlier version of Molloy fails to explain why the chronology would be reversed in the book. A greater problem, however, is that this solution fails to address the issue to which it was meant to respond: that of the similarities between the events of the two different narratives. For this reading asserts that the two different narratives *do* in fact recount two different sets of events. But if this is the case, the similarities between the two stories remain entirely coincidental (as they would if one assumed that Moran and Molloy were two different characters telling two different stories) or would need to be explained through the hypothesis of some sort of conjecture concerning a "repetition compulsion" on the part of the "character" Molloy/Moran. That is to say, even if Moran and Molloy are thought to be the same person at different moments, there is no reason for the structural particularities of the two journeys to mirror each other. Logically, in this case one would be led to expect wildly differing sets of events, told by two uncannily similar *subjectivities.* Instead, we seem to be given two uncannily similar sets of events, told by subjectivities, which, given this narrative repetition, are uncannily *dissimilar.*

In fact, the widespread critical attempts to arrange the two narratives of *Molloy* into some sort of chronological order seem to be a displacement of the problem, as within a hermeneutic logic of interpretation, the repetitions between the two narratives would lead less to the conclusion that we are dealing with two sets of events, whose similarities consist in that they "happened to" and are recounted by the "same person," than that we are dealing with the *same* events, recounted from two different perspectives. And here is where Beckett's use of first-person narration becomes essential. If both halves of *Molloy* were recounted in the third person, with the first narrative referring to a character named Molloy and the second to one named Moran, the temptation would indeed be great to assume that we were dealing with the same "events" recounted from vastly differing, contradictory perspectives. This would give us something that could be thought of as a twentieth-century version of *The Ring and the Book,* in which the discrepancies between the narrations would probably have to be accounted for by recourse to psychoanalytical concepts of psychosis and paranoia. Nevertheless, it would ground the narrative in the possibility of a recuperation of the ontological basis on which the narrations were constructed, through careful collation of the stories and astute analysis of the narrators' unconscious desires, conscious motivations, and predominant structures of psychic distortion. What seems intolerable is to identify the "events" as being identical but to locate these discrepancies within the consciousness of the same subject, and this is one of the things the device of first-person narration in *Molloy* seems to demand. One could argue that the identification of Molloy with Moran and their collapsing into a single character does exactly this, but let us remember that the catastrophic *metamorphosis* this model proposes, either from Moran to Molloy or Molloy to Moran, creates a de facto division into entities which can only be treated as two distinct and separate subjectivities.[2] It is not coincidental that Beckett's text refuses us this catastrophe, leaving us with other, more troubling possibilities, which need to be examined.

Assuming that Moran and Molloy are the "same character," we have an image of utter dispossession from consciousness of one's own memories, experiences, and even name. As Molloy, and to a lesser degree, Moran, often comment on their aporetic relationships to just such a dispossession, this is indeed an inviting interpretation. On the other hand, yet analogously, we could argue for an uncanny inversion of *The Ring and the Book* structure—not a group of witnesses arguing for the accuracy of their testimonies concerning events seen, but two "protagonists" each arguing in good faith that he is not only the witness, but also the subject of the events recounted. In this sense, we have two characters,.Moran and Molloy, each recounting a single story as his own, and this mirrors nicely the narration in *The Unnamable,* where the narrating "I" insists precisely that he is *not* the subject of the stories "he" tells in the first person. In either case, on the level of "character," what is forgotten is the relationship not only to one's "own" memories and experience, but to the boundaries of the space of realist narrative, which permits the existence of characters as such. Beckett lets the characters themselves enact the forgetting of their own conditions of possibility. Thus Molloy writes, "Yes, there were times when I forgot not only who I was, but that I was, forgot to be" (49). The oddity of this passage, and its humor, is due once again to the positioning of the first-person pronoun. A completely different sort of problem would be posed by a sentence reading, "There were times when I forgot not only who he was, but that he was" (we could imagine Moran saying this about Molloy). The doubling of the first-person pronoun carefully attacks not the subject's capacity to know objects with certainty, but its capacity to know, by the experience of its very aporia, that it is a subject. It undermines the grounds of Descartes's massive recuperation of skepticism in the service of certainty.[3] Note that in Descartes, as in *The Unnamable,* "it's the fault of the pronouns" (404). Neither, "I think, therefore she is," nor "She thinks, therefore I am," make the cogito's case. Nor for that matter would "He thinks, therefore he is," uttered from my perspective. On the level of pronoun and narrative, Beckett will constantly put into play the necessity of the doubling of the first-person pronoun which the cogito implies.

In terms of narrative, then, what is erased is even the conception of some sort of certainty of uniformity of event, which could be "reconstructed" through a prismatic analysis of the two narrations. And along with the evaporation of this certainty also disappears the concept of subjectivity itself as site or ground of meaning or reference. To see exactly how this works, we need to look at the final passage of part 2 of *Molloy,* when Moran, in typically scrupulous fashion, extends his autobiographical narrative right up to the moment of its own composition. Moran had begun his report with the words: "It is midnight. The rain is beating on the windows" (92). He ends it with these: "Then I went back into the house and wrote, It is midnight. The rain is beating on the windows. It was not midnight. It was not raining" (176). Molloy's narrative abandons all hope of explaining how it came to be written—he professes utter ignorance as to how he was transported from the ditch at the edge of the forest into his mother's room. Moran, on the other hand, promises to end his story only at its arrival at the absolute present of the moment of its own narration, and this he does indeed do: he *did* in fact write "It is midnight. The rain is beating on the windows." Those *are* the words that begin his report. However, as his final words inform us, those words do not accurately state the circumstances of their inscription, and this causes us to doubt the accuracy of the entire narrative which has led up to the disclaimer.

The paradox for the reader is that only by nevertheless assuming that the narrative is for the most part accurate can we credit the final assertion, "It was not midnight. It was not raining," which had originally called into question the report's credibility. As has been noted before,[4] this structure represents a variation on the Cretan paradox (the Cretan says, "All Cretans are liars"), and if its conception is not altogether new, its narratological implications for the first-person narration of Moran are. For this paradox prevents the temporality of what is narrated from ever eventually catching up to and coinciding with the temporality of the narration. That is to say, if we start with the very simple distinction between the Moran who recounts the story and the Moran who is recounted, the report offers a model which would end with the narrated Moran sitting down at his desk and lifting his pen with the hand of the narrating Moran. This moment of the abolition of difference between the narrating Moran and the narrated Moran is what the text refuses. The report's final words are indeed "written" by the Moran who up to that point had been the narrated character, yet the import of his words, disclaiming as they do the accuracy of Moran-narrator's statement, is precisely that the narrator had in some way previously been written by him. Beckett's aporetic move simultaneously refuses to bestow upon what is narrated a mythic status as referential source in two senses: first, as the ontologically prior history which is subsequently "expressed," and second, as the story which explicitly recounts the events (Youdi's request for a report) that brought the narrative act itself into being. Beckett thus refuses all the traditional ways in which the narrated content is figured as the ultimate referent and cause of the narrative, that is to say, as the narrative's *origin,* since the narrative is qualified as a fiction. The tour de force is Beckett's simultaneous refusal to shift the burden of the origin onto a "narrator," who could be posited as subjective source of the narration, reliable or not (either case would give us the classic psychological realist study—one could take Ford Madox Ford's *The Good Soldier* as an example of the latter possibility). This is accomplished by placing that narrator *within* the fiction. The prosopopoeia of the deictic moment in which the "I" tells its story is retroactively obliterated. In this way, Beckett knocks over the two poles of reference—first, the "referent" consisting of a tale's "real events," and second, the "ideal meaning," conscious or not, of a subject's inventing—and makes clear the insurmountable deferral of any ultimate subjective position, implicit in virtually all autobiographical structures. In other words, if the "I" is in some way invalidated as source of enunciation, it does not recede here before some sort of impersonal or neutral "he" or "it," but rather before what can only be *another* "I," an impossible, supplemental "I." Let us look at an example of this.

In the case of Dante's *Commedia*, we have a long tradition of distinguishing the attitudes and judgments of "Dante-poet," who is recounting his story, from those of "Dante-pilgrim," who is traversing Hell, Purgatory, and Paradise. The irony implicit in the occasional divergences of views and responses between the poet and the pilgrim has become a commonplace of Dante criticism and is undeniable. More problematic is the common critical practice of curbing the irony against the figure of Dante-poet, for Dante-poet—the man who sits down to write the experiences he "had" as pilgrim—is, of course, no less a "fictional character" than the pilgrim himself, being, in fact, that pilgrim at a fictionalized "later date." This obvious fact allows us, even forces us, to hypothesize a new "figure"—"Dante-author," the "real," "historical" Dante, who spent a good part of his life elaborating and defining the two characters, "Dante-pilgrim" and "Dante-poet." Once we begin working with Dante-author, however, we add another level to our ironic structure, as Dante-author provides us with a perspective from which the views and opinions of Dante-poet concerning Dante-pilgrim could *themselves* be implicitly ironized. In other words, Dante-author could be seen as critically, sometimes ironically, representing two "characters": both the pilgrim who traverses the eternal realms *and* the poet who retrospectively attempts to assess and recount his own experiences. So far, so good. The problem comes when we ask what is to stop us from imagining some sort of "arche-Dante-author," from whose perspective one could examine "ironically" the implicit position of the implied author who would establish an ironic oscillation between Dante-poet and Dante-pilgrim?

Obviously, once we enter this structure, there is no possibility of assigning it a terminal point: one can always move a step farther back, unless one is willing to grant an empirical grounding to what de Man has helped us to see as the prosopopoeia of the narrative moment and narrative subjectivity. Even in the case of a less avowedly "fictional" work, for example, Rousseau's *Confessions,* where the proper name, the signature, the contemporary legal structure, and the nature of the events recounted bind the narrative voice to an empirical subject and to empirical events in a manner not found in the *Commedia,* we still find the need, in our psychoanalytic or even deconstructive readings, of placing the narrative voice *within* the fiction. More than this, we are forced to realize that the agency of that placement is itself already "within" the text also.

The importance of these considerations with regard to the trilogy becomes clear when we look at the way *Molloy* spills into *Malone Dies,* and the way *Malone Dies* is picked up in *The Unnamable.* For the figure of Malone, writing his tale of Macmann, so similar, it would seem, to his own story, retrospectively offers another model for understanding the oddly similar, repetitive narratives of Molloy and Moran: that of two drafts of the same, apparently autobiographical tale. When *The Unnamable* comes along, containing Malone and the others, the assumption can be made that Malone's story was itself a draft, in a way, of the story of a figure who would write a book like *Molloy.* In other words, Malone's odd thoughts and queries as he lies in bed, waiting to die, could be taken as representing the kind of life or thoughts perhaps entertained by a presumed "author" of *Molloy.* By focusing on the figure of the author, then, *Malone Dies* would be seen as offering another sort of story of the origin of *Molloy.* Following this line of reasoning, *The Unnamable* would be seen to refuse fictionalization, substitutes, pseudonyms, surrogates, and "delegates," to use Beckett's term, and to unveil the ultimate author finally speaking freely, frankly, and literally of "himself," or at least speaking freely, frankly, and literally of the impossibility of speaking of himself. The contradiction inherent in the latter possibility begins to show the poverty of this sort of logic with regard to the trilogy, but for the moment let us stress that following this reading, the trilogy is seen as presenting stories within stories within stories, of which the ultimate container and source is a single voice or subjective instance, often referred to as "the unnamable." The doubling, ironic structure is given a resting place.[5]

I would like to argue, however, that one of the most interesting and important aspects of Beckett's trilogy is precisely its refusal to accept the possibility of any such moment of propriety of utterance, reference, or intention. This is due not only to Beckett's sense of the unconscious—

though this surely plays a major role—but even more fundamentally to his refusal of the temporality of a present moment in which a subject could seize itself. This, I think, is evident not only in Beckett's treatment of the entire question of narration as seen throughout the trilogy, but also within the not so strict limits of the book called *The Unnamable*.

Within the argument that *The Unnamable* represents a break from the "fictions" of the earlier novels and their imposed or false proper names— that is, an abandonment of the figural personae encapsulated by the long string of proper names and an acceptance of autobiographical literality—a necessary assumption is that the book is narrated by a single, unitary narrator. When this assumption is made, that narrator is usually called "The Unnamable." However, this assumption in and of itself already raises a great deal of problems and rests on inferences which are far from self-evident. To designate something as "unnamable" implies not only that the thing or "person" in question does not have a name, in other words, is anonymous, but also that it *cannot* have a name, cannot be named. To assume there is such a substance, or "voice," in the book *The Unnamable* and to refer to it as "The Unnamable" is already to violate the conditions under which the text tells us this phenomenon may be discussed.[6] *Perhaps* such a violation is necessary, even programmed by the text, but even if this is the case, the implications and the economy of such a violation would need to be addressed. And any investigation of this question should recognize the way the prose of *The Unnamable* refuses not only the stability of reference offered by the proper name, but even that of the entire pronominal system with its built-in deictic distinctions between who is speaking and who is being spoken of. How can one posit a "character" called "The Unnamable" when the voice through which it apparently speaks ceaselessly asserts that it is not its own voice, that it is speaking someone else, that someone else is speaking it, that it is not itself? Could we somehow locate and definitively delimit some sort of character, essence, perspective, subjectivity, or voice in *The Unnamable,* there would be, of course, nothing to stop us from calling it, paradoxically, "The Unnamable," or even Molloy, Moran, Malone, or anything else we wanted, for example, Basil, Worm, or Mahood. The point is, in this case it would be *namable*.

If the concept of "unnamability," however, is of relevance here, it is precisely because what we will have to call provisionally and under erasure "the effect of narration" in *The Unnamable* does not delimit or totalize itself in a way that would make it susceptible to nominational effects. Rather than being the consummate name in the trilogy's long series, the "unnamable" is not a name at all, but the marker of a space which refuses nominational effects. In terms of the trilogy, a distinction needs to be made between the unnamable and the ineffable. The ineffable is that which cannot *be expressed*—in the trilogy, unnamability raises the issue of that which cannot *express,* and in this way must be brought into direct relation with Beckett's statement in the "Three Dialogues" regarding, "The expression that there is nothing to express, nothing with which to express, nothing from which to express, no power to express, no desire to express, together with the obligation to express" (*Disjecta,* 139). That is to say, an ineffable being may speak in full authority—it cannot, *properly,* be spoken of. The effect of narration in *The Unnamable,* however, not only has no name by which "it" could be referred to, or refer to itself, but in addition *it cannot even refer "itself" through the use of a pronoun.* That is why Beckett's prose so relentlessly attacks the implicit deixis of the implicit "I" which lurks behind any utterance, no matter how "neutral." The effect of narration in *The Unnamable* could not even *hypothetically* speak "in its own name." In reference to the mark *différance,* Derrida comments that if " '[t]here is no name for it,' " it is not due to an effect of ineffability: "This unnameable is not an ineffable Being which no name could approach: God, for example" (*Margins,* 26). Rather, Derrida continues, "This unnameable is the play which makes possible nominal effects, the relatively unitary and atomic structures that are called names, the chains of subsitutions of names in which, for example, the nominal effect *différance* is itself *enmeshed,* carried off, reinscribed, just as a false entry or a false exit is still part of the game, a function of the system" (26–27) [Cet innomable est le jeu qui fait qu'il y a des effets nominaux, des structures relativement unitaires ou atomiques qu'on appelle noms, des chaînes de substitutions de noms, et dans lesquelles, par exemple, l'effet nominal <<différance>> est lui-même *entraîné,* emporté, réinscrit, comme une fausse entrée ou une fausse sortie est encore partie du jeu, fonction du système (*Marges,* 28)].[7] Beckett, too, offers an overdetermined chain of substitutions of names, precisely, that of the proper names beginning with *M* or *W* which swell the trilogy along with the rest of his work, and Beckett's "unnamable" is also, I shall argue, the space where the possibility of nominational effects, of the proper name, even catachrestical or provisional, is examined.[8]

As it is an examination of nomination, an investigation of names, and not their transcendence or surpassing which is at stake in *The Unnamable,* I cannot agree with David Watson's argument that the rejection of proper names is only a first step in an ultimate rejection of language as a "false" representation of subjectivity. Watson begins with a poststructuralist critique of realism, and argues that Beckett's text "must reject the claim that language can ever achieve knowledge of that supposed extra-linguistic presence which is the fixed subject, the subject which is already there to 'be known'" (32–33). However, Watson goes on to argue that the consequence of this is that the "Beckett text must logically insist on a rejection of the status of the narrative voice as a locus of identity: the voice which speaks is as false, as *mensongère,* as that which it talks about, since it can only appear in words" (33). Watson is right to insist that Beckett breaks with the kind of realism that would privilege a prelinguistic referent, and I agree (and have argued) that Beckett is sensitive to the reference-effect as a production of language. One would think, however, that Watson's argument on that issue would invalidate his subsequent assertion that the voice is false because "it can only appear in words," an assumption which seems to implicitly rehabilitate the extralinguistic subjective referent that Watson had disqualified. Once we abandon that "supposed extra-linguistic presence which is the fixed subject," we cannot argue that it is the semiotic constitution of the voice that renders it "false," as opposed to a "true" subject which it fails to express.[9] On the contrary, we have gone beyond (as Watson suggests) a discourse of subjectivity based on the oppositions of true and false and expression and expressed. The rejection of the proper name, then, should not be seen simply as a rejection of the "false," "linguistic," or "figural" in favor of a "literal" truth, although this logic, in fact, is behind many other readings of the question of "unnamability" in relation to proper names.

For example, Leslie Hill argues that in Beckett there is a major drive to free oneself of the "name prescribed by others at birth," which represents "the alienation of a name which does not belong to whoever is obliged to bear it, or which fails to represent, or misrepresents the flesh on which it is written. To accept the name inscribed by others is to be born under an assumed name, and therefore not to live but die, just as to be buried under a false name is not to die at all, but to live on as a restless ghost" (105–6). The implication here that the refusal of nomination reflects a greater fidelity of the speaker and its flesh to themselves—already implying the possibility of a "speaker" separate from and prior to naming—seems to be heartily rejected by the dynamics of *The Unnamable.* Names are not problematic in the text because they are foreign, imposed, or "paternal" (Hill, 117),[10] but rather because they fail to offer the stability or security the nominative system promises. Beckett is not interested in the "true name," but rather in the mechanics by which any name may be appropriated or referentially circumscribed into what Derrida calls "relatively stable, unitary, atomic structures." By opposing a "paternal" name in Beckett to a "maternal" body (117), Hill runs the risk of psychologizing what Beckett poses as a philosophical problem.[11] My view is much closer to that expressed by Stephen Connor, when he writes, "*The Unnamable* in fact names a difference, names the movement whereby names are conferred and abolished in sequence, 'I,' 'Basil,' 'Mahood' and 'Worm,' each standing in a problematic and mixed relationship of identity and variation with what comes before" (40). *The Unnamable,* then, does not deliver the spectacle of the final putting off of "masks," but rather investigates the mechanics by which "masks" could even be put on, or names assumed. It does this by linguistically examining the processes of identification and appropriation, and ends at a point where the necessary "I" of a sentence like "I am in my mother's room" (7) or "my" of a sentence like "My name is Moran, Jacques" (92) seem no more necessarily proper or authentic than the nominational, pseudo-nominational, and referential acts they make possible.

The very first lines of *The Unnamable* present this dilemma through their treatment of the first-person pronoun: "I, say I. Unbelieving" (291). As it will be over and over again, here the "I" is simultaneously asserted and effaced, in a double bind that this study will attempt to stay within: that of the necessity of denying the grammatical propriety of the pronoun by a movement that inevitably also affirms it. That is to say, to say "I," disbelieve it, be the "I" that disbelieves the "I," and therefore not be that "I." No impersonality or neutrality ever takes the place of this "I," nor does any unspeakable, ineffable alterity before which speech could recede, yet the "I" never takes its own place either. Obviously, this syntactic and grammatical double bind bears an extraordinary resemblance to the narrative double bind of Moran's "report," in which only by remaining "within" the report's narration can we reach the point which irreparably fissures and disclaims that very interior on which the validity of the fissure was based. Thus, *The Unnamable* raises on the level of syntax and grammar the same questions that Moran's report raised on the level of narrative structure: those of the source or origin and those of the source of the source's rejection. Therefore, the real stakes of *The Unnamable*'s universally recognized stylistic brilliance and ingenuity can only be gauged by a close reading that would follow with precision the logic of the constructions of the simultaneous affirmations and denials of the novel's acknowledged "aporetics."

Such a reading will be conducted in the following chapter, but before a like project can be undertaken, a preliminary question must be addressed: that of "voices" and "voice" in their roles in the trilogy as narrative and narrational sources. The "characters" in the trilogy hear things they call "voices" throughout, and the voices they hear are central to the formation of the narratives they speak and write. However, the "narrators" of the trilogy find a constant difficulty in identifying the origin of these voices that they hear, that is, of deciding if the voices which and with which they speak are their "own." In this way, the word "voice" becomes in the trilogy the central term for the phenomenon of interest here—that of the appearance of "language" in the apparent absence of any unequivocal productive source, secure intentional motor, or unquestionable, ideal meaning—because these voices do get "spoken" and in the end may very well be what narrates the tales in which their own appearance is recounted. Moran, at least, explicitly states that it was "the voice" that caused him to write his report:

> I have spoken of a voice telling me things. I was getting to know it better now, to understand what it wanted. It did not use the words that Moran had been taught when he was little and that he in his turn had taught to his little one. So that at first I did not know what it wanted. But in the end I understood this language. I understood it, I understand it, all wrong perhaps. That is not what matters. It told me to write the report. (175–76) [12]

In *The Unnamable,* the problems of distinguishing such a "voice" from that or those which we as readers are exposed to in the shape of the written text we are given to read becomes an even greater question. *The Unnamable* first mentions the voice in these terms:

> Let us then assume nothing, neither that I move, nor that I don't, it's safer, since the thing is unimportant, and pass on to those that are. Namely? This voice that speaks, knowing that it lies, indifferent to what it says, too old perhaps and too abased ever to succeed in saying the words that would be its last, knowing itself useless and its uselessness in vain, not listening to itself but to the silence that it breaks and whence perhaps one day will come stealing the long clear sigh of advent and farewell, is it one? I'll ask no more questions, there are no more questions, I know none any more. It issues from me, it fills me, it clamours against my walls, it is not mine, I can't stop it, I can't prevent it, from tearing me, racking me, assailing me. (307)

In this passage, it would seem that "this voice that speaks" is precisely the voice that has recounted all of the novel that we have "heard" up to this point. It is, in fact, the very voice that suggested we "pass on" to more important things. This extraordinary passage then gives us de facto a "new" narrator, although the voice with which this other subjectivity would distance itself from the previous narration is also the voice which is being repudiated. This leaves us, as readers, in a similar position to that which the voice will describe as its "own" a few pages later, when, as Basil is rechristened Mahood, the voice clarifies its absolute inability to know if "it" is speaking of "itself," speaking of "someone else" (in this case, Mahood), if "someone else" is speaking of it, or if someone else is speaking of someone else whenever "it" speaks:

> Then my voice, the voice, would say, That's an idea, now I'll tell one of Mahood's stories, I need a rest. . . . But it would not be my voice, not even in part. That is how it would be done. Or quietly, stealthily, the story would begin, as if nothing had happened and I still the teller and the told. . . . But now, is it I now, I on me? (309–10)

If it is not "I on me," we must ask ourselves, how has that question been able to be asked by the text, and who has asked it?[13]

Obviously, in the trilogy, the motif of the voice, in its constant alterity and inscrutability, functions very differently from that so often analyzed by Derrida, in which it is the guarantor of the full presence of the intention, source, and meaning of the speech which it utters. It is no doubt largely due to the logocentric investments in the concept of voice in Western metaphysics that Beckett's handling of it in the trilogy is so powerful and disturbing. Indeed, the "voices" of the trilogy are everything but a logocentric guarantee and manifestation of subjective self-presence. In fact, the trilogy hints in several passages that the term "voice," the very agency that is meant to fix and anchor meaning, reference, and trope, itself straddles the distinction between the literal and the figural. In the passage cited above, we should note three different resonances of the final question, "is it one?" This can mean, first of all, is this voice actually a voice; second of all, is this voice *one,* that is, a single voice, rather than an abstraction made from many voices; and finally, is this voice "one" in the sense of being a unitary, self-identical source of meaning? Later on, the *figural* nature of the term "voices" is clearly stated: "But it's entirely a matter of voices, no other metaphor is appropriate" (325). But even if (especially if) "voices" is a metaphor, we must still inquire as to why it is the only one which is "appropriate."[14] And for this, we must look not only at the well-known and well-studied role of speaking in Beckett, but also at the equally prevalent but less discussed role of hearing and listening in the trilogy.

For Beckett, as for Descartes, consciousness, subjectivity, and certainty are intimately tied to the temporality of language and propositional statements. In the second *Méditation,* reviewing the cogito, Descartes writes the following:

> De sorte qu'après y avoir bien pensé, et avoir soigneusement examiné toutes choses, enfin il faut conclure, et tenir pour constant, que cette proposition, *je suis, j'existe,* est nécessairement vraie, toutes les fois que je la prononce ou que je la conçois en mon esprit. (*Discours,* 180–81)

> [So that, after having thought carefully about it, and having scrupulously examined everything, one must then, in conclusion, take as assured that the proposition: *I am, I exist,* is necessarily true, every time I express it or conceive of it in my mind. (*Discourse,* 103)]

The key point here is that the validity of "cette proposition" holds only at the moment that it is being said or thought: "toutes les fois que je la prononce ou que je la conçois en mon esprit." This is the obvious consequence of Descartes's proof, in that if it is only the fact of my thinking that proves my being, in order to prove that I am, I must prove that I think, and I must prove that I think precisely by thinking, by producing an *act* of thinking. In Descartes, this act is portrayed as necessarily linguistic: I think "I think," and at that moment I know that I am. The fact that the cogito as act only has validity at and for the moment in which it is *enacted* seems to be acknowledged later in the second *Méditation,* when Descartes writes, "*je suis, j'existe,* cela est certain. Mais combien de temps? à savoir autant de temps que je pense; car peut-être se pourrait-il faire si je cessais de penser, que je cesserais en même temps d'être, ou d'exister" (*Discours,* 183) [*I am, I exist:* that is certain; but for how long? For as long as I think, for it might perhaps happen, if I ceased to think, that I would at the same time cease to be or to exist (*Discourse,* 105)]. As Derrida has pointed out in "Cogito and the History of Madness" (*Writing,* 31–63), one of the key unthought cruxes in Descartes is the complexity of the relationship between the precise instant of thought, by which and only at which the cogito has validity, and the necessity of temporalizing the fact of this instant of thought in a linguistic structure—the sole structure capable of presenting the consequences of this instant in a recognizable form which can allow it to function as evidence or proof. For Descartes, one proves one's existence not only by thinking, but also by being able to think "I think," that is, by thinking linguistically. In the Cartesian system, certitude comes from the capacity to *recognize that one has thought,* to think one's own thinking in a movement of linguistic temporality. One thinks. One thinks, "I think," and one knows that one is. Consciousness, for Descartes, consists of speaking, of *producing* language. In the Cartesian system, sense impressions, dreams, hallucinations, and errors of reasoning happen *to* a consciousness that cannot, logically, achieve a state of absolute certitude regarding these externalities.[15] But this consciousness can be sure that it, in fact, has existence prior to all these, by its very capacity to question itself as to their validity. Consciousness cannot be certain of what is happening or has happened to it, but it can be certain that it itself has *always already happened,* is independent of the "events" it debates and considers.

In the trilogy, however, this a priori consciousness is consistently denied. Rather than remaining the constant support of any aporetic debate concerning the existence or characteristics of all that is external to it, or even concerning its own past or history, consciousness *itself* becomes paradoxically one of the externals that must logically presuppose a *prior* and separate consciousness. For Beckett, consciousness starts not with *speaking,* but with *hearing.* We have seen how in Descartes the cogito must be read to a certain extent as "I speak, therefore I am." The Beckettian cogito would be, "I hear, therefore I am." This is already implicit in Descartes— one must hear oneself at the moment of one's speaking in order to convince oneself—but for Descartes the originary moment is that of the realization of thought in language. For Beckett, the originary moment is that of the perception of audible matter—matter which the trilogy's narrators often cannot assimilate or understand as language and certainly cannot identify as having come from "within." Consciousness is what happens to the subject, is an event which the subject suffers.

The linkage of thinking, consciousness, being, and hearing is made repeatedly throughout the trilogy. Among the most interesting examples of this is the speculation in *The Unnamable* concerning Worm's existence as "a pure ear." The most explicit, however, comes shortly after Molloy writes of a "small voice" at Lousse's, advising him to leave. In terms proleptic of Moran's final comments on his voice, Molloy writes:

> And I was afraid . . . of wearing out the small voice saying, Get out of here, Molloy, take your crutches and get out of here and which I had

taken so long to understand, for I had been hearing it for a long time. And perhaps I understood it all wrong, but I understood it and that was the novelty. (59)

Not long afterwards, Molloy more precisely defines this constant, often incomprehensible rustling noise as, if not his own thought, at least that which is attended to in the process of "thinking": "At last I began to think, that is to say to listen harder" (61). Unlike in Descartes, where one thinks, and hears oneself think, and therefore is, in Beckett, thinking cannot be "heard" because thinking *is itself* hearing. Can one hear oneself hear? And if thinking is an *act* of hearing, not the object of what one "hears," what does one hear when one thinks? This is a real question in Beckett, whose answer is provisional and catachrestical: voices—"no other metaphor is appropriate."

Given what is at stake in the Beckettian notion of hearing and voices, we should listen closely to the first place in the trilogy where we are presented with an example of this kind of hearing as thinking. It appears early on in *Molloy,* while a policeman, who has espied Molloy "resting," is escorting him back to the police station. Molloy writes that during their journey:

I seemed to hear, at a certain moment, a distant music. I stopped, the better to listen. Go on, he said. Listen, I said. Get on, he said. I wasn't allowed to listen to the music. It might have drawn a crowd. He gave me a shove. I had been touched, oh not my skin, but none the less my skin had felt it, it had felt a man's hard fist, through its coverings. While still putting my best foot foremost I gave myself up to that golden moment, as if I had been someone else. (21)

This "music" would seem to be the "small voice" that Molloy only comes to understand at Lousse's—let us remember that he tells us he "had been hearing it for a long time" (59). The phrase "distant music," in relation to this murmuring, seems crucial for a variety of reasons. First of all, the word "music" imparts a quality of asemanticity to this audible matter, on which the trilogy constantly focuses. In Descartes, language and meaning seem identical—in hearing one's speech one inevitably hears one's meaning, one's thought. There is no necessity of an interpretive detour or mediation. What one "hears" in Beckett is simply sound—the question of deciding if it has a meaning, and what that meaning might be, remains a constant one for the "characters." Molloy: "And perhaps I understood it all wrong, but I understood it and that was the novelty" (59). Moran: "But in the end I understood this language. I understood it, I understand it, all wrong perhaps. That is not what matters" (176). Molloy and Moran are both in a way translators, translators of "themselves," perhaps, just as the narration-effects in *The Unnamable* often assert themselves to be a kind of loudspeaker, voicing speech which is not theirs. If "music" designates an asemantic (although not asemiotic) quality of the "voices," conjointly the adjective "distant" implies the alterity of this sound which must be attended to with the utmost concentration. The very concept of listening to oneself within the possibility of not hearing, of failing to achieve an auditive self-apperception, already troubles any definition of intrasubjectivity as ideal interiority. In fact, the different topographies of the "voices" sketched in the trilogy and the concomitant troubling of the relationship between hearing and the heard serve to obfuscate distinctions between introjection and projection, and the implicit dichotomy such distinctions rely on of the without and the within.

However, the reader of the English text of the trilogy may very well be led, when reading the phrase "distant music," to imitate Molloy and hear a distant music himself or herself: that sounded in Joyce's story, "The Dead." On a literal level, of course, the events recounted in "The Dead" center around the theme of music and the annual concert the "Misses Morkan" are hosting. But the phrase "distant music" refers, oddly enough, not to an aural, but to a visual phenomenon. Gabriel Conroy stands "in the gloom of the hall" (Joyce, *Dubliners,* 210), unseen, watching his wife Gretta listen to music that he himself cannot clearly hear:

> He stood in the gloom of the hall, trying to catch the air that the voice was singing and gazing up at his wife. There was grace and mystery in her attitude as if she were a symbol of something. He asked himself what is a woman standing on the stairs in the shadow, listening to distant music, a symbol of. If he were a painter he would paint her in that attitude. . . . *Distant Music* he would call the picture if he were a painter. (210)

Already we have a mechanics of translation perhaps not without parallel in Beckett. Here the "translation" is sensory and intersubjective—the distance of the music renders it inaudible to Gabriel, but the auditory is translated into the visual as the quality of the music is rendered to Gabriel by the aspect of his wife as she listens to it. A sensory exchange, then, is paralleled by an intersubjective exchange. In addition, in this passage,

Gabriel, "unseen," voyeuristically hears by *seeing,* and the question of audible or linguistic constructions of imaginary specularity (perhaps the flip side of Gabriel's move here) is frequently worked through in Beckett by consideration of the myth of Narcissus and Echo.[16] The phrase "distant music," then, is already heavily charged in this passage with issues of relevance to Beckett: it represents a hypothetical title, and thus the problem of the proper name and naming; the question of symbolism, and thus also the concept of the figural; erotic intersubjectivity and voyeurism, and thus the construction of objects of desire; and finally the relationship between this kind of intersubjectivity and the issue of translation, exchange, and transposition of the senses. The phrase will be repeated in this story so obsessed with (unsuccessful) repetition, in an equally charged context. Pondering an old love letter he had once written to Gretta, Gabriel reflects, "Like distant music these words that he had written years before were borne towards him from the past" (214).

It is hard to know what status to accord Beckett's echo of Joyce's echoing phrase. If it is indeed a deliberate allusion, it is clearly underplayed, yet Beckett had certainly heard the Joycean music before. References to Joyce abound in the trilogy, ranging from Molloy's own name, which would seem to establish a kinship between his monologue and Molly Bloom's, to the description of Sapo as a "little cloud" (190, 194), echoing the *Dubliners* story of the same name, to Mrs. Lousse's Circe-esque characteristics, to Molloy's assertion, shortly before the "distant music" scene, that "I don't diffuse the perfumes of Araby myself" (19), to name only a few. As Barbara Reich Gluck has noted, the final passage of "The Dead" itself was the object of an explicit parody in Beckett's early story, "A Wet Night." "The Dead" ends like this:

> Yes, the newspapers were right: snow was general all over Ireland. It was falling on every part of the dark central plain, on the treeless hills, falling softly upon the Bog of Allen and, farther westward, softly falling into the dark mutinous Shannon waves. (Joyce, *Dubliners,* 223)

Just before the end of "A Wet Night," we have:

> But the wind had dropped, as it so often does in Dublin when all the respectable men and women whom it delights to annoy have gone to bed, and the rain fell in a uniform untroubled manner. It fell upon the bay, the littoral, the mountains and the plains, and notably upon the Central Bog it fell with a rather desolate uniformity. (*More Pricks,* 82–83)

Meanwhile, John Harrington has convincingly shown the debt of Beckett's early story, "A Case in a Thousand," to "A Painful Case" from *Dubliners*.[17] And even restricting ourselves to the operation of the phrase "distant music" within "The Dead," our speculations are furthered by the fact that it already raises the questions of citation and repetition which an intertextual reference would imply. First of all, the phrase "distant music," at the moment at which Gabriel Conroy formulates it, is *already itself* an allusion and a reformulation. Earlier in the story, we learn that he had written in a review of Browning: "'One feels that one is listening to a thought-tormented music'" (Joyce, *Dubliners*, 192). Contemplating the image of his wife, the "thought-tormented" will be replaced by "distant." So the phrase "distant music" *already* contains a distance from itself, in the way it alludes to another phrase, just as it is distant from itself in Beckett by its echo of Joyce. And if Gabriel pilfers the "music" for the title of his imaginary painting, he will likewise borrow the adjectival segment of the phrase in his long speech toasting the Morkan sisters: "But we are living in a sceptical and, if I may use the phrase, a thought-tormented age" (Joyce, *Dubliners*, 203). If "distant music," then, in its very functioning in "The Dead" shows itself to be a citation, an allusion to another phrase, we should also remember that Gabriel additionally unambiguously designates it as the name of the persistence of language and signs in the memory: "Like distant music these words that he had written years before were borne towards him from the past" (214). It is worth quoting just what these words from the past are: "'Why is it that words like these seem to me so dull and cold? Is it because there is no word tender enough to be your name?'" (214).

If we take the phrase "distant music" in *Molloy* seriously as one that, should we stop and listen, will make us hear Joyce, we find that in "The Dead" the phrase first of all functions through allusion (to "thought-tormented music") and second of all is used to name the mnemonic properties of language which allow it to rise up intact from other contexts, as the phrase "distant music" seems to do in *Molloy*. The picture of Molloy getting punched by the policeman when he stops to listen seems a parody of the portrait Gabriel would like to paint of Gretta. Moreover, the linkage in the trilogy between listening, music, and thought, which we have begun to discuss above, takes us back to the other of Gabriel's title, that is, "thought-tormented music." When the trilogy's thought-tormented characters listen and think, it is otherness they hear. Molloy seems to signal this when he closes his description of the listening by writing, "I gave myself up to that golden moment, as if I had been someone else" (21).

Molloy's "as if I had been someone else" is key. Throughout the trilogy, stories of "others" are told "as if" they belonged to oneself, and most explicitly in *Malone Dies,* the possibility is raised of telling one's own story "as if" it were someone else's. The possibility of the "own" on which this distinction depends will not survive the trilogy. In *The Unnamable* we find, "I have to speak in a certain way, with warmth perhaps, all is possible, first of the creature I am not, as if I were he, and then, as if I were he, of the creature I am" (335). Intertextuality, then, becomes another figure of the otherness and lack of propriety of the voices to which the trilogy attends, and with which the "characters" paradoxically assert their "own" subjectivity. To the extent that thinking is figured as listening, it is also necessarily repetition and citation. Beckett's characters don't "produce" thought as much as interpret, translate, and repeat the "thought" to which they are subject. In its simple, literal meaning, "distant music" implies both the alterity and asemanticity of what is heard, but in addition, as an echo of Joyce, the phrase also would enact the economy of repetition, citation, and secondary replication implicit in the conceptualization of thinking as hearing. To isolate these two words in Beckett as a highly elaborated conscious allusion to a node of problems in Joyce might seem farfetched, and indeed it is. Yet the trilogy's constant effort to present speech as citation, thought as the overheard, necessarily begs the question of origin and alterity in such a manner that it becomes somewhat problematic to allow the author's conscious intention to fully govern the entire textual scene, as the intentional bournes of linguistic acts, and their identity as singular, self-contained events, are precisely what Beckett is putting into question. Or to put it another way, the structural *possibility* of this allusion, its virtual reality, so to speak, is in and of itself illustrative of the implications of the classic Beckettian representation of speech and thought. As *The Unnamable* ceaselessly emphasizes, for Beckett to speak is to repeat, to cite, and the key issue is the process and implications of the appropriation of what is cited. The agency of the act of appropriation on a grammatical level, as *The Unnamable* and the *Texts for Nothing* insist, is the distinction between the first-person pronoun and the second and third. But the citational schema already destroys any possibility of expression as the totalized outpouring of a fully present, interior self-consciousness, regardless of appropriative maneuvers and gestures. The echo of Joyce, then, serves to posit the *reader* as a hearer and overhearer, placing him or her in a situation somewhat parallel both to that of Molloy and the voyeuristic Gabriel. The reader is forced to share Molloy's concern with "understanding" voices, along with his aporia concerning the locus of their origin, and Gabriel's with symbol and trope, as intertextuality shows most graphically the possibility of language to subsist and function as *signs,* divorced from and independent of an "original" motivating meaning or context. This is how thinking almost always functions for Beckett's characters, their "own" thought needing to be interpreted as if emitted by "another." Beckett's characters must always traverse the sign, even in terms of intrasubjective understanding. The moment of originary expression is always an echo.

To speak one's desire in another's language, to speak another's desire in one's own—these two possibilities circle the investigations of appropriation, citation, and authority carried out in the trilogy, and end in a questioning of the possibility of the propriety of desire. That the other's language is sometimes Joyce's is not without consequence, inscribing Joyce into a Dantesque relation of paternity to Beckett, and allowing Beckett to usurp Joyce's authority precisely through the humble act of deferring to it by simply seconding and repeating it. One may wonder about the relationship between the unassuming, ironically dubbed *Gabriel* Conroy, whose task is to deliver the annual, stereotyped, conventional valedictory address to the three childless women, and *Molloy*'s Gaber, Youdi's apocalyptic messenger. In any case, for Gabriel "distant music" is the sound of (written) marks repeating themselves, marks in fact that claimed the poverty of representation in the face of the ineffable: "'Why is it that words like these seem to me so dull and cold? Is it because there is no word tender enough to be your *name?*' Like distant music these words he had written years before were borne towards him from the past" (Joyce, *Dubliners,* 214, my emphasis). Molloy, for his part, shortly after hearing his "distant music" is led to the police station, where he has a minor revelation: "And suddenly I remembered my name, Molloy. My name is Molloy, I cried, all of a sudden, now I remember" (22–23).

Beckett's repetition of the Joycean phrase "distant music" in relation to thinking, consciousness, and memory might be seen as illustrative of the trilogy's repeated assertion that not only is consciousness repetition and citation, and therefore secondary, but also that there never is nor *was* any original or primary to be repeated. This is seen in the fact that the phrase "distant music" in Joyce was already an allusion, and a name for the process of the citation of signs. "Distant music," even within "The Dead," remains at a distance from its own articulation. At the moment when Molloy cocks his head toward the famous Beckettian "interiority," the text disrupts its own boundary, its own "inwardness," in a manner more usually associated with Joyce or Pound.

An obvious objection can be made, however, to counter my general claim that the operation of the phrase "distant music" moves against any attempt to find at the trilogy's end either some final point or originary moment of interiority, authenticity, or self-present consciousness. This objection would be quite simply that the particularity of this allusion works only within (and without) the *English* text of *Molloy,* being, on the level of material reproduction of the graphic mark (the level on which the mechanics of this citation operate) wholly absent from the French *Molloy.* Following this reasoning, either I am entirely misled concerning the implications of this echo, or one is forced to conclude that the English and French versions of the trilogy, although both authorized, are in fact very different books. This objection is wholly valid; however, it only serves to reinforce my point, as the relationship between the two texts in the two languages echoes and duplicates the features of the trilogy's textuality discussed above. That is to say, the two texts double and repeat each other, obviously, across the two languages, but equally obviously, not without the introduction of unavoidable differences due to the different linguistic structures, along with wholly avoidable differences (for example, the French *Molloy* opens with Molloy's contemplation of the walkers labeled A and B, in English they are A and C), due apparently to the author's whim.[18] Yet *both* versions are equally authorized and equally "valid"—one cannot prefer the French as the "original," as the translation was composed by the author, and in his native tongue, no less. Nor can one prefer the English as the later or final revision, as the "original" French was allowed continued publication without the incorporation of many of the changes introduced into the English text. As there is no way to collate the two texts into some sort of Ur-text that would reconcile the two, nor a means to privilege one text over the other, in a very real sense one is constantly forced to read the text *against itself.* At any moment, working from either language, one is always potentially performing an exegesis which the other, parallel text would disallow in its own textuality. The Beckettian bilingual texts, then, are never present to themselves—one always works in the absence of the text's full self-articulation, often in the face of an unavoidable surplus of self-contradiction.[19] That Beckett's texts are double in this way means that there is never an authorized, single phenomenal *moment* of text that presents itself for exegesis. In a manner with striking parallels to his treatment of character, narrative, and subjectivity, Beckett's *literal* double inscription of his works denies a unified, originary surface of interpretation, just as the texts in their significations deny an originary moment of consciousness or source of meaning. For the simplest of structural reasons, then, in addition to the more elaborate philosophical and linguistic ones, the Beckettian text(s) can never be read in its (their) plenitude. They unwrite and overwrite their own plenitude. The music will remain distant, and we, too, should give ourselves up to that golden moment, in our necessity of reading *Molloy* as if it were something else, as if it were *Molloy*.

4. "I Sum Up"

Temporality, Subjectivity,
and Cogitation in *The Unnamable*

According to Beckett's drafts, the original title for the novel that became *Malone meurt* was *L'Absent*.[1] If the name was rejected as title of the book, its traces still remain in the text of the trilogy, although somewhat displaced. Toward the very end of *The Unnamable*, we find buried the phrase "I am the absentee again" (413) [Me voilà l'absent (*L'Innomable*, 210)], and indeed, one of the inescapable directions the book seems to take is toward a phrase such as "I am absent." For if the book constantly emphasizes the absence of any ultimate subjective source, essence, or locus, it also paradoxically insists on the subject's urgent need to witness, testify to, and perhaps sign this absence. This witnessing, of course, necessitates the erasure of the very absence it is meant to establish. A mediated account of subjective impossibility will not be accepted—the subject has to *say* its own inexistence. Thus, the sentence that must be said is unsayable. This double bind of relentless subjective scrutiny of subjective nonbeing, found in many of Beckett's works, but seen most clearly in *The Unnamable,* mirrors and has perhaps even programmed some of the major divisions in and frustrations of Beckettian criticism. On the one hand, it is difficult to accept the phenomenological and existentialist interpretations of *The Unnamable* as scrutiny and expression of inner subjective experience in all its purity, as Beckett's work constantly puts into question the categories of experience, interiority, and self-presence to which this criticism appeals.[2]

On the other hand, interpretations that claim to follow Blanchot and insist on the "neutral" character of Beckett's work often seem to miss the violence of the repeated subjective insistence of this supposed neutrality. The existentialists and phenomenologists are right to focus on the subjectivity effect Beckett stresses, even if he does so only for the purpose of disqualifying it. Let us not forget that if subjectivity is impossible for Beckett, no less impossible is its elimination.

From the need to witness and proclaim one's own inexistence and the dual impossibility this entails comes the nightmarish aspects of the Cartesian cogito for Beckett: the very fact of thinking "I am not" proves that I am, yet should I cease thinking, how could I testify to this fact? The cogito depends on the self-reflexive moment at which thinking and thinking that one thinks are simultaneous—as we saw in the previous chapter, it is, in fact, this simultaneity which necessitates the constant repetition of the cogito in its function as proof. The phrase, "I am absent," however, could never be achieved in a temporality of simultaneity: its very articulation undoes its claims. The absence and the witnessing can *never* coincide—thus in Beckett the methodical repetition is not that of a moment whose own finitude demands its eternal reproduction, but rather the oscillation of two movements each of which always necessitates its own subsequent invalidation by the other and which can never achieve together a moment of finality or resolution. This is quite evident in the novel's final "I can't go on, I'll go on," which presents this oscillation in one of its most reduced forms. *The Unnamable* is in this sense also the interminable.

Of course, in the end Beckett didn't choose to name *Malone Meurt* "L'Absent," but he did choose to name *The Unnamable* with a title that denies nominative choice itself, while inevitably also affirming it. The acceptance of contradiction inherent in naming something "unnamable" in itself might indicate an attempt to move away from oppositional, binary logic, such as that of the double bind of witnessing absence. In fact, the shift from "L'Absent" to *L'Innomable*, from ontology, matter, and presence, to naming, law, and signification, I think can legitimately be seen as a shift from a binary oppositional structure of presence and absence into a differential, or supplemental schema. And this shift is crucial, for the end result of Beckett's prose is a subject which, if never present, is equally never absent, a subject which cannot be done away with. The yearning toward presence and the yearning toward absence are identical in *The Unnamable:* only at the moment that the subject can seize itself may it do away with itself. When this self cannot be delimited, there will always be risk of remainder. Beckett provides us with a *double* double bind. On the one hand, the "I" which proclaims its own inexistence invalidates its statement simply by making it. On the other, it is the very inexistence of the "I" as totality, as essence, as namable, which forces its continual rearticulation as pronoun, or more precisely, as the space between pronominal marker and reference. Unnamability, in its economy, goes beyond the traditional topos for speaking one's absence (one which Beckett employs abundantly) — that of speaking from beyond the grave. Thus, it goes beyond prosopopoeia in the traditional sense, as no totalized absence is posited to be replaced. *The Unnamable*'s subject cannot die, one could say, because it cannot properly (in all senses of the word) get born. But it cannot die. So if there is no question of any ultimate negation, it is because there is not even the possibility of an affirmation which could eventually be negated. There can be no silence. Yet let us not forget: it is an "I" which tells us this.

The question of this "I," or of subjectivity and its relation to language, expression, consciousness, and meaning is ubiquitous in *The Unnamable*. Literally turning the form of the soliloquy inside out, the book refuses every imaginable literary or metaphysical convention concerning interiority, sincerity, and mimetic representation of consciousness in the Western tradition. To inventory the book's methods would imply a virtual doubling of the text. In this chapter, we will focus on three major recurrent motifs through which the book poses these questions. First is the relationship between what initially appears as a "voice" and what it refers to as "mannikins" or "delegates" — the name-bearing "characters" of the trilogy. Crucial here is the way the voice toys with but ultimately subverts a conception of "itself" as creator or author of the delegates and characters — a conception that would posit it as logically prior, literal as opposed to their figures, the signified that they represent, et cetera. As I have already suggested, the first-person pronoun in *The Unnamable* becomes just as figural, just as improper as the catachrestical "names" of the trilogy. But as *The Unnamable* moves from the serial replacement and supplementation of strings of proper names to their abandonment, the second point to be examined is the status of the pronoun as opposed to the proper name. This will lead to discussion of the question of appropriation, that is, the construction of the "proper" as opposed to the figural, and thus the mechanics of enunciation and deixis with regard to pronouns. Finally, we must continue our look at "hearing" as the privileged figure of the concept of subjective appropriation that Beckett puts forward, as he replaces some sort of originary "authentic" voice by the citing and appropriation of a murmuring which must initially be overheard.

An ultimate disappearance of the "I," something *The Unnamable* continually strives for in full ironic acceptance of its impossibility, is first seriously posited and worked through in relation to the pronominal network in *Malone Dies*. In a crucial, oft-quoted passage where questions of birth, death, and the invalidation of the subject come together, we find the celebrated account of Malone's "birth into death." After asserting that his "feet are clear already, of the great cunt of existence" (283) and hoping for a "favourable presentation" (283), Malone finally claims: "That is the end of me. I shall say I no more" (283). He keeps this promise for about four pages, breaking it with a short interjection, which in Cartesian fashion falls between constative and performative: "I remember" (287).[3] This gesture of the "I"'s refusal to say "I," which entails, of course, the paradoxical assertion of the I which refuses, will be both played through and interrogated to a dizzying degree in *The Unnamable;* yet in its occurence here in *Malone Dies,* already two key issues are raised which should be examined. First of all, we should look at the tense of the sentence: the "I" can only proclaim its own abolition in the projection of a future—"I shall"—as the moment of its utterance invalidates the content of its promise. The promise to no longer say "I" can only be made, as performative, in the expectation of a future which abolishes the very agent of responsibility of this promise. The "I" can only *promise* its disappearance—it cannot later be there to keep its promise, to countersign, as its *not* being there is what the promise consists of. This difficulty goes beyond any question of sincerity and good faith in regard to narrative speech acts, but rather leads to the postulation of "futures" which can never in fact be "nows." *The Unnamable* is perhaps for this reason so prevalently constructed between anticipation and recollection, slipping tenses obsessively from the "will be" to the "was," just as *Malone Dies* moves from the proleptic "I shall say I no more" to the recapitulatory "I remember."

Is the promise "I shall say I no more" kept or broken with the phrase we find on the first page of *The Unnamable,* "I seem to speak, it is not I, about me, it is not about me" (291)? The very fact that the question can be asked shows that "I shall say I no more" can (and must) be taken two ways. On the one hand, it can mean that the first-person pronoun will no longer be allowed to appear (as in the four subsequent pages of *Malone Dies*); on the other, it can mean that when the "I" appears, it not an I that has said it.

This split seems to emphasize two different ways of effacing the subject. On the one hand, we have a simple disappearance of the pronoun, a refusal to make a gesture of appropriation, to demarcate linguistically a point of origin of discourse. Voice continues. What is refused is the implied authority of self-reference or autobiographical interiority. In place of the "I" we might have the "he"—the third-person pronoun Benveniste refers to as the marker of absence in any enunciation.[4] Still, the "I" that says "I shall not say I" will have kept its promise retrospectively, will have in its future asserted itself by the completion of its deferred promise of negation. This seems similar to a certain slant sometimes given to Blanchot's "neutre," in which the subject is ultimately credited for its own disappearance (by this I mean that there implicitly remains a subject which seems to be granted an even greater authenticity by its refusal to say "I," by its accession to "neutrality"). In Beckett, however, if the moment of the appearance of the full presence of the subject is barred, so is the moment of its disappearance, of its absence. Dispossession is neither an event nor a state.[5] The origin effect, and thus the mark of origin, can never be more than provisionally occluded. Likewise, any moment of originary (or teleological) desubjectification will have to be denied. That is, the "I" of the performative temporality which promises its own future vanishing will also have to be invalidated—in this case, with the repetition of the "I" in the phrase "I remember."

Malone Dies attempts to dodge the paradox of the phrase "I am absent" with a temporal maneuver, which would both save the witnessing "I" 's presence and guarantee its eventual dissolution: I *will* be absent, "I shall say I no more." The subsequent "I remember" both prevents the "I" from disappearing in its future and disqualifies any conception of the prior "I" 's existence as contractual subject in a moment of deictic plenitude. *The Unnamable* will shift the terms of the problem and continue it. Rather than focus, as in *Malone Dies,* on the "I" as a subject who may or may not say "I" again (and who may have been writing the name "Macmann" in "I" 's place), it will focus instead on the "I" which is said, without belonging to something we could call a subject: "I seem to speak, it is not I."

We must not miss the complexity of this movement in *Malone Dies:* the dual necessity and impossibility of both the affirmation of the "I" as witness and its negation as subject is seen *not* in the phrase "I shall say I no more," but in the economy of the movement *from* that phrase *to* "I remember" and back again. *The Unnamable* works in similar fashion, though in greater complexity, and its economy of movement, deferral, necessarily proleptic promises, retrospective summations, and both accretive and dedifferentiating repetition goes a long way to accounting for the well-known difficulty of isolating passages in the book for analysis. As Leslie Hill quite rightly remarks, Beckett's later texts "become radically unquotable" (120), and about *The Unnamable*, he asserts "There exists no intentional message that may be extracted from the verbal motions of the text" (120). These "verbal motions" are necessary because it is precisely the *moment* of logical (and subjective) coincidence which the text is at pains to attack. Given this, the attack itself can only proceed by disqualification, invalidation, and fissuring of the temporality of the finished statement, as exemplified by both the deictic moment of enunciation and the phrasal unity of the sentence—thus the interminable, paratactic sentences the book gives us, the early disappearance of the paragraph as unit, and all the other like maneuvers. Unlike Joyce, Beckett does not address the temporality of the word, but *The Unnamable*, like *Finnegans Wake*, does create a structure of constant decontextualization, in which the frame any given "passage" carves for itself is always radically insufficient as a space for discussing that passage's "meaning."

The oscillations, repetitions, prolepses, and disavowals create a textual rhythm which the exquisitely balanced and paced phrases are careful to maintain in terms of breath, tongue, and ear. One name Beckett gives to this rhythm, and the impossibility of regarding in isolation any of its particular rises or falls, is aporia. But aporia, in addition to naming this sort of rhythm, is also seen in *The Unnamable* as being created by it. For Beckett, aporia is never considered as a stable state of unknowing—seen in this light it resembles too closely ataraxy, the stoic acceptance of knowing that one cannot know. Beckettian aporia is much more painful than this—not only can one not know, one cannot know that one cannot know. Aporia, to truly be aporia, can never be accepted as a certainty. Like the subject, it must be continually asserted and effaced, in a rhythm that can never have a moment of resolution. Just as Descartes links subjectivity and certainty, the model of certainty being the subject's recognition of its own existence, in turn proved by its very capacity to doubt this existence, so inversely Beckett links subjectivity with aporia. In *The Unnamable*'s first paragraph, we find the following passage:

> I seem to speak, it is not I, about me, it is not about me. These few general remarks to begin with. What am I to do, what shall I do, what should I do, in my situation, how proceed? By aporia pure and simple? Or by affirmations and negations invalidated as uttered, or sooner or

later? Generally speaking. There must be other shifts. Otherwise it would be quite hopeless. But it is quite hopeless. I should mention before going any further, any further on, that I say aporia without knowing what it means. Can one be ephectic otherwise than unawares? I don't know. (291)

Note that Beckett leaves the very question of the book's aporetics within an aporetic structure. The I (or not-I) only *suggests* that it will proceed by "aporia pure and simple" or "by affirmations and negations invalidated as uttered, or sooner or later": the grammar never confirms whether this will or will not be the method of exposition. There is, then, an aporia concerning the existence of aporia, as the phrases themselves are "invalidated" by their own question marks. Beckett's handling of aporia, like his treatment of subjectivity, is eminently paradoxical. In "true" aporia, we wouldn't even be sure if we were confronted by aporia. Yet, paradoxically, this very uncertainty is itself aporia's certain mark. We are back into the familiar rhythm: for aporia to be valid, one must not only doubt, but alternate between doubting, and doubting that one doubts. Our task is to avoid letting ourselves be fixed on either side of the oscillation. But the very notion of aporia itself imposes a double bind. Either there is not aporia, and there is not aporia, or there *is* aporia, and then there is not aporia concerning the existence of aporia. Aporia can only be thought through an economy which includes a certain forgetting. As the novel puts it, "I should mention before going any further, any further on, that I say aporia without knowing what it means" (291). Thus, one of the conditions of aporia is the possibility of the manifestation or repetition of words or language in the absence of their significatory plenitude (*Molloy* starts on similar grounds: "I've forgotten how to spell too, and half the words" [7]). As we have seen, in order to function, the cogito cannot extend its skepticism so far as to trouble the meaning of the words of which it consists or the capacity to recognize them. "I think, therefore I am" must be immediately comprehensible for the subject to grasp itself as source of its own emissions of uncertainty. But it is exactly this sort of self-recognition that Beckettian aporia disrupts.

In Beckett, then, the importance of the concept of aporia for subjectivity is with regard to the possibility of auto-affective discourse as structured and regulated by a phenomenal "I." In *The Unnamable,* the capital letter "I" will become the centripetal point of a grammatological separation of mark from meaning and of structure from context and reference. The distinctions between use/mention, presentation/citation, constative/performative, original/repetition, source/reflection are brought to an aporetic crisis around the "I" through the emptying and filling of names and pronouns, and the concomitant alternate definings and troublings of temporal and enunciative sequences. Thus, *The Unnamable* becomes a massive parody of Cartesian auto-affectivity, in that when "speaking" the "narrational effect" constantly "hears" itself as so radically other and incomprehensible that both the terms "auto" and "affect" are thrown into question. The ramifications of this process exceed Beckett's running skirmish with Descartes. Derrida has claimed that auto-affection is not "a modality of experience that characterizes a being that would already be itself" (*Speech and Phenomena,* 82) but that rather auto-affection "produces sameness as self-relation within self-difference; it produces sameness as the non-identical" (82) [produit le même comme rapport à soi dans la différence d'avec soi, le même comme le non-identique (*Voix,* 92)]. This moment of continuity and recognition, the creation of a "same" which allows the "itself" to be articulated, is in crisis in *The Unnamable*, which so systematically hammers the "différence d'avec soi" that the concept of "le même," even considered as "non-identique," is denied. It is this denial which I think precludes any consideration of a "subjectivity" in *The Unnamable* which could be discussed even in the already parodic and absurd terms invited by *Molloy* and *Malone Dies*. I use "denial" here advisedly, however—the denial operates through a rhythm that includes the space of subjective affirmation. These affirmations will be called (and given) names, the names Mahood and Worm, for example, and later pronouns, and the mechanisms of their affirmations will lead us back to the questions of voice, hearing, repetition, and surrogation which we began to discuss in the previous chapter. At this point, however, the relationship between the names and the pronouns by which they come to be replaced must be examined.

The first pages of the book called *The Unnamable* are, paradoxically, filled with names—not only "Malone" and "Molloy," which belong, of course, to the trilogy's first two volumes, but Murphy and Mercier and Camier also make their appearance (even though *Mercier et Camier* was not published until 1970—long after *The Unnamable* had been published in both English and French). These references, not only to the trilogy but to other books signed "Samuel Beckett," naturally create the temptation to authorize the voice making them, to link this "I" of *The Unnamable* to a literal, if not empirical, authorial subject which would be less enmeshed in an economics of fictionalization, trope, and representation than the "mannikins" of Beckett's other fictions. But even assuming for the moment that this "I" represents a unitary, single narrator—a proposition the text will render increasingly questionable—we must still acknowledge that it in no way literally represents "Samuel Beckett" even to the extent, for example, that the "I" in the *Pisan Cantos* represents Ezra Pound. The narration of *The Unnamable* exceeds all bounds of realism, on the one hand, and repudiates any and all signature effect, on the other (something which Molloy, Moran, and Malone are at pains, albeit in ironized ways, to assert). Once this figural aspect of the nameless narration in *The Unnamable* is acknowledged, we have to ask ourselves if there is, in fact, any reason to grant it more authority, to treat it more "literally," than those other figures which are the names Molloy, Moran, Malone, Macmann, Murphy. This is crucial, as it is through these names, along with those of Worm and Mahood, that "unnamability" will be articulated in the book as something other than a name or a pronoun. The narration, or narrator, or "I," seems to move from being an unnamable figure to a figure of unnamability. As such, we need to examine the relations established and, of course, disestablished, between the names and this other in order to understand what might be at stake in their renunciation. These relationships will revolve around questions of representation and the specular, and thus, repetition, but also around questions of communication, listening, and speaking, and thus, another repetition. The "voice" will speak of the proper names in terms of surrogation and exteriority, but the terms of these terms are themselves doubled (temporally and metacritically) and demand the closest scrutiny. Indeed, it is through the mechanics of the positing of the voice as source of the "delegates" that the entire concept of subjective source will be exploded.

To begin with, however, let us acknowledge that the voice certainly does make statements that could lead the reader to take the proper names as its "characters," doubles, or figures. It says, "I have been here, ever since I began to be, my appearances elsewhere having been put in by other parties" (293), and a few pages later, the voice asks, "Why did I have myself represented in the midst of men, the light of day?" (297). The terrain here seems clear: the names are "characters," "representations," "figures," "signs," and with the advent of the voice of *The Unnamable,* we move from character to author, from the fictional to the real, from the image to the object, from the figural to the literal, from the sign to the referent. Yet immediately following the last sentence quoted comes a passage which immensely complicates this formulation:

It seems to me it was none of my doing. We won't go into that now. I can see them still, my delegates. The things they have told me! About men, the light of day. I refused to believe them. But some of it has stuck. But when, through what channels, did I communicate with these gentlemen? (297)

Here, the voice talks of its "delegates" not as characters of its own creation, but almost as the opposite. Rather than that which represents the voice, that *through which* the voice speaks, here the "delegates" are that which speaks *to* the voice, that which gives the voice what it has to speak. If in the first formulation the "delegates" are secondary representations, presumably repetitions of an originary "unnamable" voice, in the second passage it is precisely the "voice" which would be secondary, repeating the voices of its "own" representations. Together, these passages seem to offer a double articulation of the sign, or expressivity as exteriority. Staying within the most classical semiotics, we could say that, on the one hand, we have the relationship between the sign and what it represents, as the "delegates" could be said to have "represented" the voice. On the other hand, the voice tells us it *received information* from these delegates. This gives the relationship between signs and the subject or addressee who reads or interprets them. But how could the "same" sign both represent the "voice" as object to another or others, being thus invested *by* the voice with its ideal meaning, *and* exist as mediating conduit of information to and for the voice it represents? It would seem that the "representations" of the "voice" function semiotically as "representations" in all their exteriority for the voice itself also. In other words, the voice "itself" has no preexpressive knowledge of itself, nor meaning in itself, but passes through the exteriority of the sign in its own auto-representations, on the one hand, and in the hearing of its "own" sentences, on the other (which means inevitably in the *speaking* of them also). If the "mannikins" are no doubt the voice's creations, the voice is *their* creation also. The "voice" cannot be read as presenting an essence in its pure, interiorized form, as it only exists in the space of its own exteriority.[6] Thomas Trezise has brilliantly shown the relevance of Derrida's critique of Husserlian phenomenology for Beckett's work,[7] and we can see the immediate application to the above discussion of his assertion that "subjectivity ('solitary mental life') is always already intersubjective" (24). "Interiority" is always presented in *The Unnamable* as alterity, an exteriority which can only reproduce and double itself.

Trezise rightly cites some of Derrida's comments on consciousness and the "for-itself" (23) to which I, too, would like to refer:

> Ce que nous voudrions finalement donner à penser, c'est que le pour-soi de la présence à soi (für-sich), traditionnellement déterminé dans sa dimension dative, comme auto-donation phénoménologique, réflexive ou pré-réflexive, surgit dans le mouvement de la supplémentarité comme substitution originaire, dans la forme du <<à la place de>> (für etwas) c'est-à-dire, nous l'avons vu, dans l'opération même de la signification en général. Le *pour soi* serait un *à-la-place-de-soi:* mis *pour soi,* au lieu de soi. (Derrida, *Voix,* 99)

> [What we would ultimately like to draw attention to is that the for-itself of self-presence (*für-sich*)—traditionally determined in its dative dimension as phenomenological self-giving, whether reflexive or pre-reflexive—arises in the role of supplement as primordial substitution, in the form "in the place of" (*für etwas*), that is, as we have seen, in the very operation of significance in general. The *for-itself* would be an *in-the-place-of-itself:* put for *itself,* instead of itself. (Derrida, *Speech and Phenomena,* 89)]

This reasoning disqualifies any rigorous opposition of literality to figurality, as any act of naming, any subjective assertion, is always already a placing or positioning of the self for itself. A differential or supplemental conception implies that every name must be a figure for itself, enmeshed in substitutive chains which deny ultimate or originary propriety or self-coincidence. Beckett's overdetermined chain of serially substituted surrogates forces us to think identity in terms of replacement and supplementarity, that is, the nonself-identical. The "mannikins," then, cannot be read in classical high-modernist fashion as masks or personae which represent a discreet, discrete author—*The Unnamable* is not "The Circus Animals' Desertion." In the very complex network of representations in the trilogy, Beckett does not privilege the figure of the author, trapped in his struggle to find the proper objective correlative to exteriorize his solitary interior life. Beckett's comments in "Three Dialogues" on failure and the traditional conceptualization of the "occasion" (*Disjecta,* 142–45) should already put us on our guard against any discourse of mimesis or adequation. But it is sufficient to read *The Unnamable* to avoid this discourse. After continuing to list the information brought to it by the "delegates," the "voice" of *The Unnamable* makes an offhand but crucial comment regarding its relationship to them. Discussing the seemingly endless flow of words these vague "gentlemen" put forth, the "voice" asks:

> When did all this nonsense stop? And has it stopped? A few last questions. Is it merely a lull? There were four or five of them at me, they called that presenting their report. (298)

The "four or five" would seem to refer to the "characters" of the trilogy (Molloy, Moran, Malone, Macmann, and possibly Sapo, considered as separate from Macmann, or perhaps Mahood), but the key phrase here is "presenting their report." For "report" is the exact word Moran uses to designate the narrative Youdi demands of him, paralleling Molloy's claim that he is writing his story at the behest of "others." Thus, even if we do provisionally accommodate ourselves to the idea that the *M* characters were all representations of our "new" narrator, apparently revealed to us this time in his essence, we find ourselves now confronted with a passage that suggests that the "real" delegate of the voice in *Molloy* was neither Molloy nor Moran but Youdi—the addressee of the "report." In terms of the "for itself," *The Unnamable*'s voice identifies as much with that which receives, which demands that this self be given as with the "representation" or construction which is proffered. This is already implied by the constant focus on *hearing* in the trilogy, but the identification here with the "Youdi-position" quite clearly means that the voice that proffers cannot be considered as either the source or essence of the subject, nor as the intention or the referent of the fictional statement, as the "subject" includes that which demands this expression. Youdi is no longer a figure of law or authority, demanding in Kafkaesque fashion that the subject account for itself. On the contrary, the Youdi-position has become as great a part of the subject's accounting as that figured by Moran. The "voice" of *The Unnamable* is both the "characters" who are obliged to express, with nothing to express, *and* the other who demands this expression. Yet again, we see that the "voice" cannot be identified with the existential situation of the writer, confronted with the problem of finding adequate vehicles of "self-expression," as the "voice" is also the voice that demands that that expression take place, in addition to being the voice that supplies (like the delegates) the "content" that is expressed. *The Unnamable* is perhaps the most rigorous attempt we have to include the alterity from which any voice must make the gesture of differentiating itself in every expression. But this does not imply a greater completeness or fidelity in its representation of expression—rather, it implies a rethinking of the kind of completeness or totality that expression or representation could claim, as seen in the book's figuring of expression as always simultaneously excess and lack. "Moran" and "Youdi," then, do not represent subjective positions with which the voice may or may not identify, but parts of an intrasubjective economy, within which the voice finds itself. "Finds itself" should be read literally, in that this economy implies that the voice is *not* automatically available to itself. In fact, it implies that the voice is not "itself."

Various models are available for addressing this kind of structure. An obviously pertinent one is Benveniste's exposition of the dialogic structure of discourse, discussed in the introduction, in which the monologic event is seen as necessarily implying the second-person position, as it is only through difference with this position that the "I" can be articulated. This does not mean that subjectivity can always become an object for its own scrutiny, though this is, of course, implied, but more than that, it means that first-person "monologue" can only exist within the space of the hypothesis of an addressee, which is necessarily exterior to its expression. In other words, it is not sufficient to claim that first-person discourse implies a posterior "you" who would receive it, and thus doubles the subject. This is certainly true, but we must go on to state that the first-person utterance is *already* predicated on its division from the "you" to which it responds. In this sense, the "I" is itself posterior to the implied "you" which makes its possible. Seen in this light, the "I" will never be originary, producing through discourse a specular double, but rather always already in the position of responding, answering, or following. We approach here Beckett's famous "obligation to express"—expression must be an obligation when its possibility is predicated on the existence of that to which it answers. In Beckett, the "I" is not a representative of full subjectivity, but one marker within a subjective economy which necessarily comprises the second-person position, with its implicit demand. In *The Unnamable*, with its emphasis on repetition, citation, the overheard and the oversaid, the "I" is always already spoken and articulates itself by way of the second-person demand, which itself is made possible only by this (belated) "first-person" expression.[8]

In these ways, the trilogy's rendering of "monologue" seems, in many aspects, to explicitly work through certain questions that Jacques Derrida explores through a reading of a "monologue" of obvious centrality for Beckett: that of Molly Bloom in *Ulysses*. Writing of the "yeses" that bracket the Penelope chapter, Derrida embarks on a long and complex argument concerning the relation of the "yes" to the interiority that the traditional notion of monologue claims. Derrida's meditation on the "yes" in *Ulysse gramophone*[9] seems, in many ways, a critical rethinking of Benveniste's article "L'appareil formel de l'énonciation," which considers "oui" and "non" to be among the most important markers of the enunciative position.[10] I cannot go into all the ramifications of Derrida's argument here, but for the purposes of this study, I would like to emphasize two points Derrida makes in various ways: first, that "yes" is a necessary pre-space for any performative or signature effect, for negation as well as affirmation (in the sense that I negate by saying, "Yes, I negate"), and second, that "yes" as phatic affirmation is also a response or address which implies and invokes an other. Derrida writes: "*Yes* indicates that there is address to the other" (*Acts of Literature*, 299). This conception of the other which is interior to monologue Derrida shares with Benveniste, but Derrida will subtly break with the Benvenisten conception of dialogic structure in a manner of great relevance to Beckett. Derrida will deny that address necessarily implies dialogue, as Benveniste claims, asserting instead that address supposes neither voice nor symmetry, "but beforehand the over hastiness of a response which has already become a question" (my translation) [mais d'avance la précipitation d'une réponse qui déjà demande (*Ulysse gramophone*, 127)]. He goes on to explain:

> Car s'il y a de l'autre, s'il y a du *oui,* donc, l'autre ne se laisse plus produire par le même ou par le moi. *Oui,* condition de toute signature et de tout performatif, s'adresse à de l'autre qu'il ne constitue pas et auquel il ne peut que commencer par *demander,* en réponse à une demande toujours antérieure, *de lui demander* de dire *oui.* (*Ulysse gramophone,* 127, Derrida's emphasis)

> [For if there is some other, if there is some *yes,* then the other no longer lets itself be produced by the same or by the ego. *Yes,* the condition of any signature and of any performative, addresses itself to some other which it does not constitute, and it can only begin by *asking* the other, in response to a request that has always already been made, *to ask* it to say *yes.* (*Acts of Literature,* 299)]

For Derrida, subjective affirmation does not simply "implante l'autre en face," as Benveniste would have it (*Problèmes II,* 82). Rather, the "yes" of subjective affirmation is an appeal to be asked to say yes. The "yes," then, is always both too early and too late—a response to that which has not yet asked and an invocation of that which precedes its voice. As Derrida puts it, "time only appears after this singular anachrony" (*Acts of Literature,* 299, translation modified). The originary moment of speaking consciousness, then, is not a moment at all, but an anachrony in which question and response, locutor and addressee each presuppose an anterior other, which, in turn, must be seen to have presupposed it. Neither the yes that asks to be asked, nor the "other" that is asked to ask the yes into affirmation can be considered originary.

In *The Unnamable,* Beckett voices both the "yes" and its unspeakable demand in typically aporetic fashion. All of the narration of the trilogy seems to center around the kind of "oui" which Derrida highlights, with its emphasis on telling one's story in one's name, of signing and counter-signing it, of saying, "Yes, I am speaking, and about myself." But in contrast to "Penelope," the trilogy's narrators always explicitly emphasize that their discourses *are* a response, either asked for or extorted. *The Unnamable* presents a significant shift for the trilogy precisely because it abandons this yes — but not for a no — because the "yes" it relinquishes is the yes that comes *before* the alternative negation/affirmation, the yes that makes that choice possible. In addition, the book's temporal dislocations and oscillations, its rhythm and rhythms, seem to provide an exceptionally powerful staging of Derrida's "anachrony." *The Unnamable* is obsessive in its looping of expression into citation, its self-justifications whose ultimate justification finally is that they justified somebody else's self, its disappropriative statements which inevitably, impossibly, include their own declaration in their disavowal. One of the most insistently repeated and disturbing moments in the book is that at which the "I"'s voice, having heard the demand and responding to it, saying "yes" to it, uncannily finds that in its answering, it has become the articulation of that "other" call, demanding a "yes" which it then starts to hear. Among numerous possible examples, I will cite two long passages, the first of which seems to enact this sort of process, the second to comment on it:

> . . . what am I saying, after my fashion, that I seek, what do I seek now, what it is, it must be that, it can only be that, what it is, what it can be, what what can be, what I seek, no, what I hear, now it comes back to me, all back to me, they say I seek what it is I hear, I hear them, now it comes back to me, what it can possibly be, and where it can possibly come from, since all is silent here, and the walls thick, and how I manage, without feeling an ear on me, or a head, or a body, or a soul, how I

manage, to do what, how I manage, it's not clear, dear dear, you say it's not clear, something is wanting to make it clear, I'll seek, what is wanting, to make everything clear, I'm always seeking something, it's tiring in the end, and it's only the beginning, how I manage, under such conditions, to do what I'm doing, what am I doing, I must find out what I'm doing, tell me what you're doing and I'll ask you how it's possible, I hear, you say I hear, and that I seek, it's a lie, I seek nothing, nothing any more, no matter, let's leave it, no harking, and that I seek, listen to them now, jogging my memory. . . . (387)

My voice. The voice. I hardly hear it any more. I'm going silent. Hearing this voice no more, that's what I call going silent. That is to say I'll hear it still, if I listen hard. I'll listen hard. Listening hard, that['s] what I call going silent. I'll hear it still, broken, faint, unintelligible, if I listen hard. Hearing it still, without hearing what it says, that's what I call going silent. Then it will flare up, like a kindling fire, a dying fire. Mahood explained that to me, and I'll emerge from silence. Hearing too little to be able to speak, that's my silence. That is to say I never stop speaking, but sometimes too low, too far away, too far within, to hear, no, I hear, to understand, not that I ever understand. It fades, it goes in, behind the door, I'm going silent, there's going to be silence, I'll listen, it's worse than speaking, no, no worse, no better. (393).

Hearing, or more precisely, the overheard, is perhaps the dominant figure for this otherness that asks that one speak but is accidentally, impossibly spoken, in all its otherness, itself. The unnamable voice is simultaneously the answer and the demand, in search of a prior origin which would then allow it to end. Derrida's "anachrony" is at work in *The Unnamable* in its constant interrogation of both temporal structures and originary moments—moments which are ironized precisely by being figured as repetitions, just as cogitolike statements are presented as cited. Thus, it is through an examination of the role of hearing that we can approach another modality of the question raised by the relationship of the "voice" to its surrogates—that of the origin of utterance and meaning. For it is the motif of hearing and the overheard in *The Unnamable* which links the anachrony of the demand/response structure and its necessity of belatedness and incompletion with the concept of the temporal origin and causal source.

We have already discussed the way Beckett plays on the cogito by linking consciousness with hearing, but a hearing which separates what is heard from any sure relation to a source. In the passages in *The Unnamable* which first begin to discuss the origin of both the "voice" and its abode, we have an account of what would seem to be the originary apperception of sound. Given the treatment of hearing in the trilogy, this passage is obviously among other things a parodic allegory of the birth of consciousness, and the way Beckett works through hearing, speaking, and repeating here deserves close scrutiny:

> That I am not stone deaf is shown by the sounds that reach me. For though the silence here is almost unbroken, it is not completely so. I remember the first sound heard in this place, I have often heard it since. For I am obliged to assign a beginning to my residence here, if only for the sake of clarity. Hell itself, although eternal, dates from the revolt of Lucifer. . . . So after a long period of immaculate silence a feeble cry was heard, by me. I do not know if Malone heard it too. I was surprised, the word is not too strong. After so long a silence a little cry, stifled outright. What kind of creature uttered it and, if it is the same, still does, from time to time? Impossible to say. . . . Is Malone the culprit? Am I? Is it not perhaps a simple little fart, they can be rending? (295–96)

In terms of its figuring of apperception, this passage breaks down two very crucial distinctions: first, that between self and other, inside and outside, in asking who the culprit is, and second, that between language and noise, or perhaps semiotic systematicity and indexicality, in the hypothesis of the fart. For Descartes' s cogito to work, it is essential to be able to recognize a) oneself as source of the language one is "hearing," and b) the language one is hearing as language with a fixed, univocal meaning. The above passage remains wholly aporetic regarding these two assumptions. If one can't know if the cry one hears has come from oneself, it stands to reason that when one hears speaking one might not know if that speech is coming from oneself or another. The "yes" of subjective assertion may always be overheard and cited, "mentioned" rather than used. But each time the "I" testifies to this, it is within the possibility that it is stating at that moment a testimony not its own—yet "I am not saying this" is an impossible statement.

The further collapsing of the cry into the fart extends this Cartesian demolition, for even if the cry is, in a way, indexical, as in the cry of pain, and thus significantly different from a linguistic proposition, it still maintains a privileged link with language and expression through its association with the mouth and breath and therefore with concepts of spirit, soul, and inspiration.[11] The scatological move in this passage of replacing orality with anality, inspiration with a literal exhalation, the soul and spirit with the fundament ("My work is a matter of fundamental sounds"—*Disjecta*, 109; in addition to the play on "fundamental," note the one on "matter"), speech with shit ("But let me complete my views, before I shit on them"—*The Unnamable*, 338), not only calls into question a certain exalted conception of the muse and the interiority of meaning, but also in relation to the biblical resonances of the passage effects an alternative genesis: In the beginning was the fart. The originary moment, then, although involving the expulsion of air in the production of sound, is anything but the moment of perfect coincidence of sign, meaning, intention, and referent. Later, even the internal animal origin of the noise will be questioned: "Perhaps it is something breaking, some two things colliding. There are sounds here, from time to time, let that suffice" (296).

The question of the origin of this noise, these noises, and their relation to what the "voice" says, and thus to what we read, is not one designed to vanish. But let us note that in any and all cases the origin is still figured as noise, as the *heard*. One aporia *The Unnamable* is at pains to sustain is that surrounding the question of whether what is heard is the demand, the call to which the voice must respond, or whether what is heard is the sound of the voice's "own" response, heard when uttered by the voice as if from the exterior. In *The Unnamable*'s anachrony, the "voice" is never either the response or the demand, Moran or Youdi, but always already both, and not yet either. But it is precisely the "voice" or a "voice" which, at least in the book's early sections, verbally stages the scenes of its own not speaking. A few pages after the last passage quoted, we have a crucial statement of our problem. Speaking of the voice, the "voice" (if after this passage the term still applies) says:

> It is not mine, I have none, I have no voice and must speak, that is all I know, it's round that I must revolve, of that I must speak, with this voice that is not mine, but can only be mine, since there is no one but me, or if there are others, to whom it might belong, they have never come near me. . . . So it is I who speak, all alone, since I can't do otherwise. No, I am speechless. (307)

This passage leaves us in the most perfect aporia concerning the origin of this voice, but again we do seem to proceed from the assumption that there is speech. Once more, we are talking about listening. When I know that I am speaking simply because as I am alone, what I hear must be myself, and *not* because I am aware of having an intention, a thought, or an impulse driving the language, we have abandoned all discourse of origin and moved to one of appropriation, and thus, of pronouns. That is to say, the utterance is proffered in the first person—the implied speaker of the phrase and its subject are meant to coincide. But it is exactly this coincidence that the above passage, along with countless others, denies. If the "I" of the utterance does not refer to me, but "I" am saying it, then I am in effect citing or repeating this "I," "mentioning" it rather than "using" it. But the prose of *The Unnamable* refuses to deliver the contextual boundaries necessary for keeping the use/mention distinction in place. At this point, the relationship of hearing and the heard to consciousness and narration needs to be brought into line with the questions concerning the relationship between the speaking "voice" and the mannikins. Both schemas promise a priority or origin which finds itself in a constant state of deferral, and Beckett links the two, along with the opposition of the proper name to the pronoun, in order to dissolve the authority of any origin effect. The relationships between these three tropes begins to emerge clearly in the following passages.

Speaking of its need "not to peter out" (307), the voice posits the possible necessity of inventing "another fairy tale, yet another, with heads, trunks, arms, legs, and all that follows, let loose in the changeless round of imperfect shadow and dubious light. But I hope and trust not. But I always can if necessary" (307–8). Once again, the suggestion is made that the voice here is the "author" of the previous tales of the trilogy. But let us be on our guard. The "voice" continues immediately after: "For while unfolding my facetiae, the last time that happened to me, or to the other who passes for me, I was not inattentive" (308). The key here is not only the presence of "the other who passes for me," but also of the "or," of the inability to distinguish between the self and this "other." The issue is not one of deciding if it is in fact "me" or the "other" that is in question, or of determining that this other may be Malone writing of Macmann, Molloy writing in his mother's room, or any of the other possible solutions. On the contrary, the aporia opened by the "or" shows that this decision *doesn't matter*, that if the "me" exists in the possibility of its confusion with the "other," then to the extent that the "me" can be shown to "exist," it will exist in the space of its "own" otherness, its lack of self-identity or self-presence, and thus can never serve the role of ultimate source *or* of ultimate referent of the "surrogates."[12] It has merely become one surrogate, one delegate, among many. Its difference from the surrogates we are in the habit of referring to, however, is in its namelessness, in its insistence on the pronominal system as means of reference, and in this we see some of the biggest stakes raised by the concept of "unnamability."

Pronouns, of course, can be assumed by anyone—the guarantee that two or more "I's," in fact, refer to the same "person" can only be made through the establishment of secure deictic contextualizations. But deixis, the here and now of a moment of utterance, is one of the many things the prose of *The Unnamable* refuses—we see this in the celebrated opening, "Where now? Who now? When now?" (291), which addresses the three central deictic coordinates. Not only is there no guarantee that the pronominal surrogates share the same referent, there is the constant suggestion in the book that they do not. At this point, the term "voice" is clearly insufficient, as the existence of a single voice—the deictic guarantee of continuity of reference in *spoken* utterance—is precisely what the book is at pains to deny, along with a similar guarantee, the proper name.[13] Once the pronominal surrogates have been untethered to name, voice, and reference, and offered in their irreducible iterability as a replaceable series, it seems no longer acceptable to refer to what we are given to read or hear in *The Unnamable* as proffered by its "voice." To move to a plural term, "voices," although an improvement, still implies a serial finitude this movement seems to work against. One could speak generally of the narration of *The Unnamable,* but this term also seems to imply a deictic moment (or series of moments) and perspective (or series) from which narration would occur. The pronominal seriality and the continued rejection of enunciative closure, however, argue less for a sequentiality of self-substituting deictics, than for the impossibility of *any* single, full deictic construction. Given the impropriety of these terms and the emphasis *The Unnamable* puts not only on hearing, but on the alterity and accidental indexicality of what is heard, one could make a gesture of the kind *The Unnamable* refuses and henceforward name the "narration-effect" of the book quite simply as "noise." That this noise often presents a source or origin-*effect* that is male, Irish, et cetera, cannot be denied, but as has been amply demonstrated already, the constant and obsessive repudiations of these stable identifications comprise much of the book's burden. We cannot avoid using and working through these effects (or the others named Molloy, Moran, and Malone, for example), but let us respect the text's economy which should prohibit us from hypostatizing them.

In fact, the book seems to refer to its own production as noise and characteristically speaks of this noisesome production in terms of hearing.

In reference to the last time the "I" or "other who passes for me" worked on a fairy tale, we are told:

> And it seemed to me then that I heard a murmur telling of another and less unpleasant method of ending my troubles and that I even succeeded in catching, without ceasing for an instant to emit my he said, and he said to himself, and he asked, and he answered, a certain number of highly promising formulae. (308)

These "highly promising formulae," one might think, are those we are exposed to in the text of *The Unnamable*. But apparently this is not the case, for we are told of what was heard, "I only barely heard it, because of the noise I was engaged in making elsewhere," and later "all is forgotten and I have done nothing, unless what I am doing now is something, and nothing could give me greater satisfaction" (308). This noise which impedes what one wants to hear by being what one says, causes the ear to strain, but strain toward what? Perhaps, we are led to believe, toward the noise which one says: "I strained my ear towards what must have been my voice still" (309). "Noise" is not allowed to stand as a figure of an inauthentic, inadequate vocal expression, which blocks the perception of the true interior murmur, as this noise is made to name the voice which is precisely what one tries to hear. If this is the case, then that "murmur" which went ill heard was itself *already* the noise which impeded hearing. Yet even this rather complex formulation will be further troubled. The noise-voice aporia will be doubled, as it systematically is, by an aporia concerning self and other, inside and outside, effected by speculations concerning the origin of what was termed "my voice." A little bit further on in the discussion, in reference to Mahood, we read: "It is his voice which has often, always, mingled with mine, and sometimes drowned it completely" (309), followed by ensuing aporias as to whether Mahood is still "mingling."[14] The burden of *The Unnamable*, and one of its greatest achievements, is the continual thwarting of the anchoring of the "must have been my voice" to any kind of origin. The Cartesian moment of the simultaneity of utterance with its perception and understanding is always denied. The hearing comes too late, and the noise is repeated in its absence through the form of inscriptions, which both testify to and prevent its silence. On the other hand, the voice always comes too soon in its attempts at extrapolation of the cogito, becoming paradoxically the given noise from which the cogito can be extrapolated. To put it another way, the cogito depends on an indexical perception of consciousness which is universalized in the linguistic form, "I think," as it is only in this *non-indexical* form that the moment of self-apperception can *itself* be doubled and recognized, and thus function as evidence for "I am." Beckett *never* recognizes the logically prior moment of self-apperception—the language is radically uncertain in its reference. The two linguistic movements of the cogito—first, "I think," second, "therefore I am"—do not maintain their temporal seriality (upon which, paradoxically, the proof's logical simultaneity depends). If there is one Beckettian cogito, "I hear, therefore I am," which involves an inversion of Cartesian originary causality, there is also another that inverts the cogito's logical temporality, as many of *The Unnamable*'s enunciations could be glossed as, "Therefore I am, I think."

In fact, thinking and hearing are again explicitly linked in another meditation concerning the "promising formulae," ill heard behind the "noise," and probably forgotten:

> For if I could hear such a music at such a time, I mean while floundering through a ponderous chronicle of moribunds in their courses, moving, clashing, writhing or fallen in short-lived swoons, with how much more reason should I not hear it now, when supposedly I am burdened with myself alone. But this is thinking again. (308)

The references to music, listening, "moribunds," and thinking take us back to Molloy and his "distant music." If Molloy's "distant music" was also that of Gabriel Conroy, let us not forget that in these pages the Biblical-Cartesian originary moment of the first sound which breaks the silence is figured as a fart—itself more distant music for readers of Joyce, as at the end of the explicitly fugal "Sirens" chapter of *Ulysses,* provoked by burgundy and between citations of Emmet's last words, Bloom sounds the last note:

> *Let my epitaph be.* Kraaaaaa. *Written. I have.*
> Pprrpffrrppffff.
> *Done.*
>
> (239)

Bloom's fundamental ex-pression at the moment of the inscription of the epitaph, when an orphaned writing must fill the place opened by the expiration of the subject, may be seen as emblematic of *The Unnamable*'s take on prosopopoeia generally. If the preterition of the written is indeed played off against the aural phenomenality and temporality of the phonetic in the trilogy, there is never a claim to the authority of inspiration, saturation of ideal meaning, and manifest presence of a full subjectivity that an emphasis on the aural realization of the written mark so often implies.[15] The quantity of passages that disclaim the relationship between the "I" that speaks and what is spoken in *The Unnamable,* between the stories recounted and the subject who recounts, between originality and repetition, between pronoun and proper name is staggering. No exhaustive account, with pretensions of handling the problem in its totality, could be undertaken. The book defers and displaces totalistic teleology in a manner that exhausts the exhaustive desire. But if on the one hand, any and all accretive finality is denied by the repetitive processes of self-invalidation of *The Unnamable* (and it is in this sense that critics like myself may be taken to task for a somewhat lax lassoing of *Molloy, Malone Dies,* and *The Unnamable* into a whole called "the trilogy"), symmetrically, the archeological gestures of origin are equally troubled, belated, and displaced. The moment of origin in *The Unnamable* is a moment of debt, but also of nonself-identity and appropriation. One hears oneself as if another, straining toward one's own voice, *and* one hears another (Mahood, the other "mannikins") as if oneself. And if the reader of Beckett is constantly tempted to hear intertextual allusions in the prose yet is never certain of their status, it is precisely because it is the inability to differentiate between the interior and exterior, original and repetition, which all the passages we have been reading stage. Now this differentiation is essential to the cogito's success, even if the cogito's ultimate consequences are the exclusion of virtually everything as external to the space it needs. In the following chapter, I will argue the centrality of the name of Joyce for Beckett's questioning of Cartesian subjectivity and examine how techniques like that which we have examined above rejoin certain strategies of the *Wake,* but for the moment we should turn our attention to a remarkable passage in *The Unnamable,* which like many others, rewrites the cogito.

In the latter sections of the head-in-the-jar story, Beckett frames certain movements through playful allusion to the Latin version of the cogito. Early on the voice asks, "What about trying to *cogitate*" (341) and introduces its conclusion to its considerations with the phrase, "I shall now *sum* up" (344, my emphasis). This summation, however, does not occur before the voice asks if it has an "*ego* all my own" (345, my emphasis). The shift from ergo to ego is emblematic of how Beckett will push the Cartesian discussion into Freudian ground in this amazing sequence which also overwrites the establishment of the Cartesian subject onto the passion of Christ.[16] This series of allusions can be seen as framing a consideration of three different paradigms for thinking subjectivity: philosophical (Cartesian), psychoanalytic (Freudian), and religious (Christian), although Beckett presents these models not in the interest of choosing one as satisfactory, but rather to juxtapose different ways of narrativizing the "story" of the subject. The emphasis on "cogitation" might also point again to the genesis of so much of Descartes in Augustine, which Beckett also notes in "Whoroscope." As H. Porter Abbott has recently pointed out, Augustine prized the Latin word "cogitare" because it seemed to define thinking precisely as an *act* of gathering or collecting one's thoughts. For Augustine, to "think" means to gather or assemble oneself. This is resonant with much of Beckett, for as Abbott persuasively argues, Beckett and Augustine share an idea of self-writing or "cogitating" in the larger sense as performative act rather than constative representation.[17] Indeed, this sort of mental "assembling" is humorously mirrored in the passage under consideration by the physical dispersion and reduction of the head-in-the-jar. That the Cartesian/Augustinian terms are invoked to signal an investigation of the mechanics of the establishment of an "I" is made clear by lines like the following, found farther on in the novel:

> . . . let me now sum up, after this digression, there is I, yes, I feel it, I confess, I give in, there is I . . . I sum up, now that I'm there it's I will do the summing up, it's I will say what is to be said and then say what it was, that will be jolly, I sum up, I and this noise. (388)

The seeming certainty of these lines will also be invalidated, as we shall see later on, but for the moment let us continue our investigation of the passage at hand.

The passage as a whole poses and inconclusively works through the kind of questions that dominate *The Unnamable* throughout. The "narrator" tells a story in the first person which he nevertheless identifies as Mahood's. As the story progresses, however, the narrator's ability to distinguish his voice, experience, and memories from Mahood's gradually decreases, until we must ask ourselves if the assertion that the story is Mahood's is not, in fact, the only part of the story for which Mahood is responsible. The voice flip-flops between a failed attempt to disassociate itself from its story and a failed attempt to identify with it. Certainly, the passage seems to finish on a rather unequivocal (and often quoted) note: "The stories of Mahood are ended. He has realized they could not be about me, he has abandoned, it is I who win, who tried so hard to lose, in order to please him, and be left in peace" (345). However, only a few sentences later, this assertion and others of its ilk will be thrown into doubt: "Do they believe I believe it is I who am speaking? That's theirs too. . . . Do they believe I believe it is I who am asking these questions? That's theirs too, a little distorted perhaps" (345–46).

Given this familiar sort of sequence, I find it hard to qualify this tale, as many do, as "Mahood's story"—this critical act of nomination and attribution, although provisionally made by the narrating voice, closes down the questions the book pries open throughout. And in this passage, these questions are linked to certain Cartesian maneuvers. Thus, after asking, "What about trying to cogitate, while waiting for something intelligible to take place?" (341), the noisy "voice-effect" arrives at a question which will occupy it for some time: "How is it the people do not notice me? I seem to exist for none but Madeleine" (341). The joke here is that "cogitation" leads not to the conclusion "I am," but rather to doubts as to whether one exists, doubts which are founded on the lack of recognition from all but the caretaker and restaurant proprietor, Madeleine. The linkage of existence to a condition of being witnessed adds Bishop Berkeley to the philosophical equation, but before embarking on a consideration of Beckett's use here of one of his favorite motifs, *esse est percipi,* we must turn our eyes to the figure of the witness in this passage—a witness whose names sound another series of resonances. The "Madeleine" of these lines had earlier been referred to as "Marguerite" (340) and will be so named again (344) before the story is over. This offhand conflation and confusion of two names which seem to represent the two central and necessarily distinct female roles in the story of the Passion, reminiscent of the "Mag" passage in *Molloy,*[18] links witnessing to both Berkeley and the Christ story. Certainly, this section of the book poses an ironic martyr—a Christ minus the limbs to be nailed to a cross—but in addition, we should note how the figure of Christ, as the word made flesh, the union of the real and the ideal, the ineffable and the named, theologically represents a transcendence of the problems of semiosis and absence that obsess *The Unnamable.* In other words, Christ represents a state of being and finality of meaning capable of transcending the need for witnessing, or reading, inherent in a perusal of the Old Testament or God's signs as written in "Nature." The Christ-identification could then serve to preclude the need of a witnessing other or ministering mother and open the way to successful solipsism. If the slippage between Madeleine/Marguerite can be seen as a lifting of the bar of the Oedipal repression which would divide the figure of sexual desire from the figure of the mother, and if we keep in mind the Proustian resonances of the maternal and the oral in the name "Madeleine," we might gloss this movement as "Let he who is without sin suck the first stone."

However, the question of witnessing also needs to be looked at in terms of its "Cartesian" consequences. For in articulating its need of a witness, the "voice," in anti-Cartesian fashion, throws the question of its existence outside of its perception of its own consciousness and onto the necessity of someone else's perception of it, and the subsequent perception of that act of perception. This violates two related central Cartesian tenets: that the invisible soul can be known with more certainty than the physical body and the world, and that the workings of reason, the "intelligible," are more reliable than sense-perceptions, the "sensible." But we already know that the "voice" has been "waiting for something intelligible to take place" (341). The utter insufficiency of self-consciousness as mode of knowledge is made manifest by the voice's unflinching inability to determine if it has a consciousness, and if so, what or whose it might be, and if not, what or who is asking the question. The strategy proposed in this passage for circumventing this aporia is a projection of the role of witness onto *another*, who could then be witnessed in turn—a difficult task, when the border between self and other has been so radically destabilized (in fact, it is this destabilization which makes the "projection" necessary to begin with). The "voice" finds itself disturbed by the fact that it is only recognized by one witness, Marguerite/Madeleine, fearing that if no others acknowledge its presence, it will have to conclude that its caretaker is simply hallucinating. Again, the irony consists in the absolute refusal of the "voice" to credit its "own" sense of existence, history, memory, or consciousness as helpful in determining its existence, while being paradoxically forced to rely on its *senses* to witness the hopefully confirming testimony of its existence as given by others.

The issue of the caretaker and her witnessing will subtly slide from Berkeleyan and Cartesian speculations into a Freudian discourse concerning desire, taboo, and ritual, as the depiction of the head-in-the-jar becomes increasingly totemic and the critical discourse increasingly symptomatological. Weighing the evidence of the recent increase in Madeleine's attentions to him, the "voice" interprets them as an argument against its existence, finding them to be symptoms of her impending loss of faith: "No, there is no getting away from it, this woman is losing faith in me. And she is trying to put off the moment when she must finally confess her error by coming every few minutes to see if I am still more or less imaginable in situ" (343). He immediately follows with an even more explicitly Freudian focus on compromise-formations, compensation, and ambivalence: "Similarly the belief in God, in all modesty be it said, is sometimes lost following a period of intensified zeal and observance, it appears" (343). Finally, Beckett spikes a following sentence with particularly resonant Freudian terms, introducing the term *denial,* which has probably been the key concept of the analysis of the caretaker effected up to this point: "That the jar is really standing where they say, all right, *I wouldn't dream of denying it. . . .*" (343, my emphasis).[19] The ruminations concerning Madeleine/Marguerite continue, to culminate with the lines:

> I shall now sum up. The moment is at hand when my only believer must deny me. Nothing has happened. The lanterns have not been lit. Is it the same evening? Perhaps dinner is over. Perhaps Marguerite has come and gone, come again and gone again, without my having noticed her. (344)

The scene of the jar on top of the menu in front of the restaurant fades, never to appear again. The narrative will drift into the hypothesis of Worm, during a transition in which the "voice" remarks:

> It must not be forgotten, sometimes I forget, that all is a question of voices. I say what I am told to say, in the hope that some day they will weary of talking at me. The trouble is I say it wrong, having no ear, no head, no memory. Now I seem to hear them say it is Worm's voice beginning, I pass on the news, for what it is worth. Do they believe I believe it is I who am speaking? That's theirs too. To make me believe I have an ego all my own, and can speak of it, as they of theirs. Another trap to snap me up among the living. (345)

Note that after the "sum" of "sum up," rather than have certainty, we are given denial of belief, in the form of Marguerite who, rather than any apostle, denies the unnamable messiah. "I sum" leads to its speaker's inexistence. We have already looked at a later passage where the word "sum" is used in an attempt to affirm an I: "[T]here is I . . . I sum up, now that I'm there it's I will do the summing up" (388). But not surprisingly, this affirmation, too, will be erased a few pages later: "[C]an it be of me I'm speaking, is it possible, of course not, that's another thing I know, I'll speak of me when I speak no more" (392), and no possible Cartesian "optimism" can survive the repetitions of "It's not I" of the book's dense final pages. In the passage quoted above, then, "I sum up" *does* lead to subjective assertion, to the "there is I," yet its virtual mechanical repetition seems already to lay the ground for the subsequent invalidation of the "I." We saw in the previous chapter how the temporality of the cogito necessitates its continual repetition, and here the "I sum up" seems hardly able to provide the breathing space necessary for the elaboration of its claims. Moreover, we should remember that "sum" here functions as an *English* verb. "I sum up," read against the Latin "sum," seems to change "being" from a prior ontological state, expressed in constative terms, into a subjective action, effected by a performative linguistic statement. In this sense, the gesture of enacting the cogito (cogitating?) could perhaps be described neologistically as "summing," or in English, "amming," rather than being. The "sum" of the cogito, rather than being a constative statement, is something I *do*, I "sum up," again and again. *The Unnamable*'s utterances never have the ontology or temporality of "I am," but rather that of "I am amming." The latter formulation, however, implies a deictic moment at which the performative "amming" could take (its) place. But this ideal subjective space is refused just as forcefully as are the realist spaces of description, story, history, and geography. The "Where now? Who now? When now?" refer just as much to the possibility of predication and logical temporality as to the epistemological problem of knowing with certainty certain particular wheres, whos and whens. We will never stop waiting for "something intelligible to take place." What we do while waiting, "cogitating," is unable to function either in a constative or performative mode. The trilogy does not attack the conventions of realism or the concept of transparent reference to replace them with an interiorized ideal. The ideal subject is invalidated to the same extent as the empirical, social, and contractual ones find themselves to be.

The stakes of cogitating, "amming," "speech acting" are clear, as *The Unnamable* considers successful "speaking" to be the most adequate proof of subjectivity and consciousness: "Do they believe I believe it is I who am speaking? That's theirs too. To make me believe I have an ego all my own, and can speak of it, as they of theirs" (345). Thus, a successful act of speech and self-reference would be tantamount to proof of the I's subjectivity and consciousness. To "witness" its own impossibility, then, each "voice" must disavow its own speech and voicehood. That this disavowal needs a disavowing agent which must be subsequently disavowed ad infinitum, is by now a variation on a theme. This necessary invocation of an other that is no more able to separate itself than is the ego able to appropriate itself, brings us back to the question of the boundaries between inside/outside, self/other. Working through reference to the cogito,

Beckett attacks these divisions through the figures of hearing, listening, speaking, and repeating. There are countless passages devoted to attempts to demarcate a difference between an "I" and a "they," or a "he." In the famous tympanum passage, the narration posits itself neither as outside nor inside but as the space of their difference:

> . . . perhaps that's what I feel, an outside and an inside and me in the middle, perhaps that's what I am, the thing that divides the world in two, on the one side the outside, on the other the inside, that can be as thin as foil, I'm neither one side nor the other, I'm in the middle, I'm the partition, I've two surfaces and no thickness, perhaps that's what I feel, myself vibrating, I'm the tympanum. (383)

It is not fortuitous that the figure for this difference is the eardrum, as hearing has been the central figure throughout for the interrogation of the problem of exteriority and identity, on every level. Yet if we go back to what seems to be Beckett's explicitly Freudian invocation of the "ego all my own," we should remember that Freud himself defines the ego precisely as a "mental projection of the surface of the body" (*Ego and the Id*, 26). As such, we see the strict parallelism between Malone's progressive loss of his body and the loss of the first-person pronoun in *The Unnamable*. Beckett writes the Cartesian "mind/body" problem over the Freudian oppositions of projection and introjection, in both cases troubling the dividing margin between inside and outside on which both thinkers depend.[20] It is worth noting, however, that in Freud, the ego, the agency charged with establishing and preserving the difference between self and other (largely through utilization of the space of the unconscious) is itself predicated on a misrecognition of this division, on an interiorization of a representation of the body. The fictive status of the psychic tympanum is on this level recognized. In addition to the Freudian turn given to the mind/body difference, Beckett also writes the cogito over Freudian conceptions of parapraxis, of language as both symptom and structure of subjective articulations. As we have seen, as early as "Whoroscope," Beckett saw Descartes as a neurotic and interpreted his writings through a symptomatic lens, and in *Watt* and the trilogy, the linkage of Cartesian system building and hyperrationality to paranoia and obsessional thoughts is clear. In addition to Beckett's wide reading in psychoanalytic literature, we should note his analysis with W. R. Bion, which seems at least as crucial for his intellectual orientation as for his psychoemotional one. And of course, Beckett directly participated in the monumental collision of the questions of language, consciousness, subjectivity, and symptom represented by *Finnegans Wake*. Indeed, one aspect of his involvement in the project can only be qualified as "Beckettian": when working as Joyce's amanuensis, he copied and read aloud great portions of the Joycean text. And if Beckett's writings cannot be considered post-Wakeian or post-Joycean in that they in no way extend or manipulate Joyce's techniques, strategies, or stylistic maneuvers, I still feel the utter dislocation and dispossession of subjectivity and consciousness found in Beckett's prose stems from a profound understanding of the real stakes of *Finnegans Wake,* in terms of the relationships it creates between language and subjectivity. We have already looked at Beckett's thematization of *response,* of response as being in some ways prior to, and an invocation of, that to which it responds. In the following chapter, I would like to consider the possibility that the thematization of response and echo itself is, in its way, Beckett's impossible response to Joyce.

5. Narcissistic Echoes

Joyce's Wake and the *Texts for Nothing*

The tradition of emphasizing the admittedly significant differences between Beckett and Joyce in terms of style, technique, and mood has been one of the most deeply entrenched in Beckett criticism and needs no recapitulation here. Indeed, it has become commonplace to view Beckett's divergences from Joyce as representing at the very least a distinct ideological break and sometimes even a repudiation. To this effect is usually evoked the oft-quoted distinction Beckett himself seems to have made between Joyce's omnipotence ("The more Joyce knew the more he could") and his own interest in "impotence."[1] More recent criticism, however, is starting to reexamine this relationship. In addition to an increasing awareness of the extent and plenitude of Joycean references and allusions in Beckett—and we have seen our share already in this study—there also seems to be an increasing sense that in very different ways the two authors often raise similar problems and questions. H. Porter Abbott has recently called into question the familiar oedipal schema of potent Joyce the "supreme artist" and impotent Beckett the "rebellious ephebe (arch botcher)" by emphasizing their shared stress on incompletion and interminability, pointing out that in *Finnegans Wake* Joyce had written "in such a way that readers would continue experiencing forever what he had experienced for the last fourteen years of his life. He had succeeded in creating an art without end. Work forever in progress, it was work that, to use Beckett's continual refrain, 'must go on.'"[2] Another book which opens a path for linking the writers, though this is not its explicit concern, is Jean-Michel Rabaté's *Joyce Upon the Void: The Genesis of Doubt.* As the book's title and introduction make clear, Rabaté reads Joyce through the lens of the issue of "doubt," in its religious, philosophical, and psychoanalytic resonances. Rabaté remarks that he chooses the word "doubt" rather than terms like "indeterminacy" or "uncertainty" precisely to allow this conceptual overwriting to occur,[3] but the fact that he chooses and is able to focus on a specifically Joycean *aporetics* already shows a clear proximity to the Beckettian project that is not normally acknowledged. In fact, in a recent collection of essays dedicated to the Joyce/Beckett relationship, *Re: Joyce 'n Beckett,* Ed Jewinski makes this point explicitly. After discussing the well known problems the *Wake* presents to literary critical conceptions of closure, fixed meaning, and stable reference, Jewinski briefly refers to the question of aporia in Derrida. He then goes on to write:

> Beckett, too, relies on the word "aporia," especially in the opening section of *The Unnamable,* a text that concentrates on the narrator's inability to clarify, explain, or "name" his experiences. . . . The end result of Beckett's fiction—its constant habit of placing its readers into the same state of "aporia" as the narrators—*resembles in effect, although not in style or technique, Joyce's accomplishment in Finnegans Wake.* (Carey and Jewinski, 169–70, my emphasis)[4]

In the context of this recent trend, I would like to suggest that in certain fundamental ways Beckett's postwar texts present us with one of the first and most incisive responses that we have to Joyce—and particularly the Joyce of the *Wake.* Indeed, I think the very Beckettian concern with belatedness and secondarity, already implicit in anything defined as "response," is itself an outgrowth of and reflection on the Joycean project and its "interminable" nature as Abbott and, as we shall see, Jacques Derrida characterize it.

The question of response, as we have already seen in the previous chapter, involves a temporal structure in many ways more complex than the simple chronology of statement and counterstatement or question and answer, which it seems, at first, blush to imply. We shall return to the temporal issues raised by the concept of the "response," but for the moment let us turn to another issue raised by it which has considerable bearing on the Beckettian project: namely, the dialectic of subjective positioning implied by "response structure." Obviously, any utterance, gesture, or significatory practice qualified as a response automatically implies a reversal—in relation to the problematically "previous" statement—of the positions of sender and addressee. A response is what happens at the moment an addressee of a particular message becomes, in turn, a sender whose message is then destined for the site whence the "first" message came. In this sense, a "response" consists of an addressee, in turn, addressing the origin of its own designation as addressee. So if responses respond to a sender who now becomes an addressee, they always also necessarily respond to one's *having been* an addressee, to one's capacity to be spoken *to,* to hear. Responses are always in part self-addressed apostrophes to the ear. The belatedness and repetition which are part of the structure of the response, along with the element of auto-address it implies, perhaps allow us to think the response in terms of a narcissistic echo, a noninaugural reproduction of the subject.

However, in the trilogy, as we have seen, the two enunciatory positions on which the "response" depends—"sender" and "receiver," "speaker and listener"—are destabilized beyond recognition: the ear that hears, hears one's self, the voice that speaks, speaks another. At this point, the terms "self" and "other," "subject" and "object," though remaining in a necessary circulation, lose their capacity to ground the structures of diegesis, introspection, and auto-inscription the trilogy works through, along with that of "response," already implicit in the assumption of the first-person pronoun. In the next few pages I would like to consider the possibility that this inability to respond, and therefore, this inability ever *not* to respond, that is, to inaugurate, is itself a kind of response to Joyce, a response which being programmed by Joyce's text gives itself by failing to respond, echoing and doubling instead. From this perspective, to respond to Joyce would not be to distance oneself, to answer from one's own perspective and position, as should the typical "strong" writer, but rather to speak from within Joyce, to become Joyce's symptom. This likewise means to have "Joyce"—his name and his letters—speak and write within oneself.

The issues implicitly raised by this problematic can be considered in a broader context. The question of responding, and thus of belatedness and secondarity, is not only highlighted in Beckett's work, but also seems symptomatic of current intellectual attempts to define our contemporaneity. In recent years, the insistence of terms like "poststructuralist" or "postmodernist," whatever their actual utility, belies a need of defining terms which present themselves as articulations of responses, or repositionings with regard to some sort of anteriority—one which, in fact, is often mythical. That this issue is not only implicit in Beckett's relationship to earlier writers and writing practices, but explicit in the economies of his texts, seems worthy of notice—Beckett might be the exemplary "postmodern" author because of his interrogation of posteriority. What remains to be seen is how Beckettian posteriority positions itself as after Joyce, and to this effect we should remember, in turn, the extent to which Joyce's own project depends on the secondary and the belated in its relation to language. As I shall go on to argue, if Beckett and Joyce share an obsession with narcissism in the content of their narratives, in their writing practices each invokes a complementary notion of the echo. For both, the narcissistic object is always constantly in construction through a graphematic movement of inscription which cannot help but reveal the nonoriginary character of this apparently "primal" object of desire. That is, the allegedly "primal" narcissistic object is not immediately available but is itself the product of a syntax and thus of differencings. Yet the "subject" of this desire, defined only in relation to that at which it gazes, can in the end have no more originary a status than the "object" it attempts to take itself for. Both writers present the subject constantly trying to "respond" to itself, and for both, though in differently modulated inflections, language is the measure and the instrument of the alterity of the subject's desire even when—especially when—that desire seeks to obviate alterity through a closed solipsistic system of narcissism.

In Joyce's work up to and including *Ulysses,* a privileged emblem of the rupture of narcissistic solipsism is the cliché, as seen in Stephen Dedalus's myriad poetic clichés which serve to deflate his ascendance to the sublime, or in the more complex structural embedding of the cliché in *Ulysses* which counterbalances the thrust toward what could be called the solipsistic novel, a self-sufficient textual "world" wholly contained within itself. This undecidable dialectic between the perfectly coherent, ideal, auto-referential novelistic world and the raw historical contingency of the clichéd tag is a result of the interrogation of the subjective position of the narrator which Joyce's project implies. Concerning this issue, Joyce is clearly the follower of Flaubert, who also realized that the creation of the perfectly self-contained novel, about "nothing," dependent on nothing external and held together by style alone, would inevitably entail the evacuation of the conventional novelistic subjective positioning of the narrator, the structural element traditionally the most responsible for providing the sort of "content" Flaubert wished to avoid. The Flaubertian valorization of "style" leads ineluctably to subjective withdrawal on the level of narration, in order to better let the "language" speak. However, the abstraction of "language" as such upon which a notion of "style" must depend if it is no longer to be thought of as a mere vehicle of "content" creates certain problems of its own: if a book is "about nothing," then language is no longer a vehicle simply and transparently expressing an idea or subject. In such a situation, how does one recognize the "mot juste"? On what grounds can a word be "right"? Such a conception of "style" clearly divorces the idea of felicity from expressive adequation to a subjective or objective referent that must be represented. Now, this focus on language as an object of investigation in its own right rather than as expressive medium can take many directions. But if one rejects symbolist idealism, language "as such" inevitably becomes language as it is used—the empirical praxis of usage and thus context. Citation replaces inspiration, irony becomes a mode of the sublime, and for an entire strain of modernism we reach the defining moment at which the "mot juste" vertiginously melts into the cliché or found tag.[5] Yet as soon as the qualitative opposition between the "right word" and the "cliché" is deconstructed, the subject as authentic, inaugural agent disappears, becoming only a vehicle of language and not the contrary. Once "language" speaks, the "subject" in its conventional acceptation grows uncannily silent, and the novels of Joyce and Beckett "speak" from within this echoing silence. To see how this comes about, we must briefly trace the evolution of the question of the cliché in the three writers in question.

Ezra Pound was the first to fully comprehend the importance of Flaubert for Joyce and of *Bouvard et Pécuchet* for *Ulysses*. Pound entirely realized the sense in which *Ulysses* was a vast collection of *idées reçues*, clichés, and contemporary nonsense—not only that which is "expressed" by the characters, but that practiced by novelists, as the many parodies and pastiches show.[6] In this, *Ulysses* is also a descendent of *Madame Bovary*, which explicitly repeats the subject matter and structure of the kind of novel Flaubert was attacking most savagely. Yet, if *Ulysses* revels in a certain kind of exhaustion of language and creates its wounded transcendences, it might be argued, only through an ecstatic sidestep into a sort of found poetics of the abject, *Finnegans Wake*, on the other hand, might seem to practice a *renewal* of language, in which debased clichés are abandoned for the freshness of a newly minted idiolect. Joyce, however, seems not to have fallen for the lure of an originary language capable of maintaining an inviolate singularity. For *Finnegans Wake* itself is almost entirely constructed of sentences which point to the secondariness, the familiarity, the ring of recognition of so many of those in *Ulysses,* but which never quite arrive at their destination. Indeed, it is only through their difference from recognizable commonplaces that the book's mechanics of distortion, difference, and delay can be engaged. Yet it is precisely by not arriving at their destination that they elaborate and extend one of the functions of the cliché in *Ulysses.*

The cliché, the proverbial phrase, the customary response give a rather obvious and perhaps banal example of how the function, structure, and history of language determine the subject at least as much as the subject creates itself through language. A cliché demonstrates the otherness speaking through us, speaking us like a language, not to the extent that it is inadequate, incorrect, inappropriate, insincere, or simply wrong, but to the extent that it is an *automatic* response. Clichés are metonymy in action—their mechanism is that a sign, or an event read semiotically, provokes in response another sign, whose articulation is produced only by a habit of contiguity with the initial sign. In "Le Dictionnaire des idées reçues," Flaubert often insists that a cliché consists precisely of always associating one word with another or certain others. For example, under "cachet," he writes, "toujours suivi de 'tout particulier'" (*Bouvard,* 495), while "chaleur" is "toujours 'insupportable'" (497), and "histrion" must be "toujours précédé de 'vil'" (527), to give just a small portion of his list. Again, the point is not that heat is not unbearable nor that histrionics cannot be vile. Rather, Flaubert is fascinated and appalled by language's capacity to create our responses for us. And as Ruth Amossy and Elisheva Rosen point out, this fascination arises not only from horror at conventional "wisdom" in contrast to enlightened understanding but even more from a sense that clichés are no more than a privileged window on the automatism which is constitutive of all language. Rather than an anomalous *exception* to adequate usage, the cliché becomes the hyperbolic *example* of the working of language generally.[7] And as the writer's job is to lay bare language in its essence, the "right word" and the "cliché" begin to converge toward the same vanishing point.[8] Thus, Pound's comprehension of Flaubert falls short when he goes no further than to consider him a clinician collecting a symptomatology of idiocy. If Flaubert could so famously identify himself with Madame Bovary, it is because his analysis precluded his exclusion of himself from the affected and infected.

The implications and indeed some of the history of this view of language and subjectivity can be quite economically gauged by considering another curious echo, this time resonating between two of the century's most prominent French thinkers on language and literature.

Jean-Paul Sartre, writing on Flaubert, characterized his relationship to language in these terms:

> A ce niveau, Flaubert ne croit pas qu'*on parle: on est parlé;* le langage, en tant qu'ensemble pratico-inerte et structuré, a son organisation propre de matérialité scellée: ainsi, résonnant tout seul en nous, selon ses lois . . . il nous infecte d'une pensée à l'envers (produite par les mots au lieu qu'elle les gouverne) qui n'est que la conséquence du travail sémantique ou, si l'on veut, sa contre-finalité. Le langage pour Flaubert, n'est autre que la Bêtise, en tant que, laissée à elle-même, la matérialité verbale s'organise en semi-extériorité et produit une *pensée-matière.*[9] (*Idiot de la famille,* 622)
>
> [On this level, Flaubert does not believe that *people speak—people are spoken.* Language, as a practico-inert and structured whole, has its own organization of sealed materiality; thus, echoing within us by itself and according to its own laws . . . it infects us with a thinking turned inside out (produced by words rather than governing them) which is only the consequence of semantic labor, or, if you like, its counterfinality. Language for Flaubert is nothing but stupidity, since verbal materiality left to itself is organized semi-externally and produces a kind of *thought-matter.* (*Family Idiot,* 602–3, translation modified)]

Meanwhile Jacques Lacan, early on in his seminar on Joyce, delivered the following typically central Lacanian "digression":

> Ce sont les hasards qui nous poussent à droite et à gauche, et dont nous faisons—car c'est nous qui le tressons comme tel—notre destin. Nous en faisons notre destin, parce que nous parlons. Nous croyons que nous disons ce que nous voulons, mais c'est ce qu'ont voulu les autres, plus particulièrement notre famille, qui nous parle. Entendez-là ce *nous* comme un complément direct. Nous sommes parlés, et à cause de ça, nous faisons, des hasards qui nous poussent, quelque chose de tramé. (Lacan, *Joyce avec Lacan,* 22–23)
>
> [It is chance which throws us hither and thither and out of which we make—for we are the ones who weave it together as such—our destiny. We make our destiny from it because we speak. We think we say what we mean and want, but it is what others meant and wanted, especially

our family, which speaks us. Take this *us* as a direct object. We are spoken and because of this we weave together the chance occurrences that buffet us into a fabric. (my translation)]

It is this shared concept less of the "speaking subject" than of the "spoken subject" which is of interest here. "We are spoken," both writers agree, yet an entire paradigm shift can be discerned between Sartre's condemnation of an inauthentic, alien "infection" and Lacan's mode of simple constatation. The natural order that Sartre's argument implies, in which the primacy of the idea or "thought" would govern a language viewed as a wholly exterior implement, is not even present as a nostalgia in Lacan, who here has clearly broken with that brand of existentialism. Yet for our purposes, it is striking that in an ostensible commentary on Joyce, Lacan evokes none other than the most typical Beckettian enunciative situation, found in especially pronounced form in *The Unnamable* and the *Texts for Nothing,* in which the "narrators" are *literally* presented as "spoken" as much as "speaking," "citing" rather than "expressing" as can be seen in these two passages from the *Texts:* "Leave, I was going to say leave all that. What matter who's speaking, someone said what matter who's speaking" (*Stories and Texts for Nothing,* 85); and "He has me say things saying it's not me, there's profundity for you, he has me who say[s] nothing say it's not me. . . . That's how he speaks, this evening, how he has me speak, how he speaks to himself, how I speak, there is only me" (*Stories and Texts for Nothing,* 92). The dominant figure for consciousness in Beckett, "being spoken," has then a definite history which runs through Joyce but also, as Sartre points out, back to their major precursor, Flaubert. A certain path can be traced from Flaubert to the Joyce of *Ulysses,* from *Ulysses* to *Finnegans Wake,* and finally from the "Work in Progress" to the Beckettian subject.

Although Beckett's seemingly shorn, crystalline style does not engage the cliché as directly and insistently as Joyce's writing, around the question of linguistic automatism, a rapprochement between the two authors must be made. One need only evoke Lucky's speech or *Watt*'s systematic permutations to be reminded of the pressure of language as subjective drive or motor, along with the weight of past erudition, usage, and verbal detritus. The question is indeed that of a certain writing's relation to the stock: of available words, but also of available set phrases, combined strings, syntactic and narrative chains, cultural character types and mythemes, et cetera. Wyndham Lewis, for example, famously criticized Joyce as being entirely devoid of "worldview" (88) or virtually any other sort of intellectual originality, to such an extent did he find *Ulysses* to be built through stock characters and conventions. Now in terms of *Finnegans Wake* what needs to be examined is not any sort of clean "break" from belatedness and automatism, from citation, but the uncanny distancing of the familiar which the text relies on as its dominant stylistic support. The troubling, even annoying "translatability" of the text is dependent throughout on its constant proximity to words, names, citations, and phrases that, while not being actualized, lend the book the insistent, echoing distortion which is its most distinctive trait. The only way the text can make its interpreters strain toward what is not quite there is by appealing to a common reservoir of reference. The *Wake* makes constant appeal to the carved-out, prepared, always already available spaces the language has in reserve; not unlike *Watt,* whose dominant stylistic strategy is to present the language's syntagmatic structures as the ultimate motor of meaning, to be almost randomly fueled by ultimately inconsequential paradigmatic filler. The standard opposition between Joyce's last two novels needs to be rethought: the *Wake* mobilizes automatism as much as *Ulysses* on the one hand, while on the other, through irony and transposition *Ulysses plays* on the mobilized automatisms just as much as the *Wake.*

However, the *Wake* does differ from *Ulysses* in how it positions itself in relation to the ubiquity of the laws of English or to English as law. For if *Ulysses* points constantly to the domination of the language's law over the entire enunciative scene, the *Wake* foregrounds this law precisely by transgressing it, by constructing signifying scenes which take on their larger meaning only through their status as violation of these laws. Just as on the narrative level, Earwicker's voyeuristic observation of the girls in Phoenix Park gradually seems less a cause for fear of punishment than a pretext to enact a self-objectifying encounter with the law he transgressed, so on the stylistic level, the book's constant differencing of itself from the laws of English is only legible as such to the extent that it appeals to the articulations of the law it upbraids. Indeed, the complexity of Earwicker's desire is revealed in the comical abundance of slips in which he compulsively exposes that which he ostensibly is most concerned to hide, just as the language of the *Wake* often presents itself as a misquotation, a *linguistic* slip away from a familiar word or phrase. Thus, we move from the dominant figure of the cliché in *Ulysses* to *lapsus* in the *Wake.*

It is hardly surprising that this would be the case in Joyce's book of the night, for as Jean-Michel Rabaté points out, Joyce was well aware that the English "sleep" derives etymologically from the Old English "slæpan" and thus the Latin "labi," which means "to slip": "Sleep is a gigantic *lapsus. . . . a lapsus linguae and a lapsus calami*." [10] *Ulysses* and the *Wake* present a sort of Scylla and Charybdis in that while the cliché serves to disqualify an originary point of interior departure for conscious intention, the *lapsus* represents the failure of speech acts to arrive at the destination that is consciously intended for them. The two figures are symmetrical in Joyce, whose *Wake* often gives us the spectacle of automatized clichés failing to articulate themselves. The question to bear in mind here is that of the stakes of this displacing of the automatic. As early as the midthirties, Beckett was already asking similar questions in his "German diaries." There, in the context of what might be mistaken for a discussion of the purely sonorous qualities of language, Beckett qualifies the "Work in Progress" as the only possible development from *Ulysses* and criticizes the latter on these grounds: "*Ulysses* falsifies the unconscious, or the 'monologue intérieur,' in so far as it is obliged to express it as a teleology." This appears to be due to literature's structural need to work in terms of what Beckett calls "chronologies" rather than "simultaneities," which distorts the unconscious as such: "I provoke loud amusement by description of a man at such a degree of culture that he cannot have a simple or even predominating idea." [11] Beckett seems to be groping his way toward a rejection of a "teleological" view of the unconscious which would consider it as a hidden but still structurally self-identical form of intention or consciousness, capable of thus being "revealed" in mimetic sentences. His emphasis on simultaneity, and elsewhere, "dissonance," implies a more sophisticated view of the entire scene of consciousness as structured itself through interminable differencings and noncoincidences within its own articulations, but without a single self-identical "content" which could be arrived at. This is what the "Work in Progress" comes closer to achieving by refusing to actualize and articulate a single determinate content, either "conscious" or "unconscious." The *Wake*'s constant evocation of familiar phrases which are nevertheless left occluded creates a crisis of "teleological" meaning. The oscillation between the phrase that is there and the phrase that is not first makes the literally absent phrase appear, and second, robs the printed phrase of its "full" (if dispersed and deferred) meaning. Neither phrase is allowed to take place, each appearing in the space of the other's difference, each legible only in its alterity from its own articulation. This is Beckett's "simultaneity" and "dissonance," a constant movement of meaning in which meaning can only exist in its own slipping away from itself.

And Beckett, following on from Joyce and the question of parapraxis, will also slip away from the sort of "teleological" unconscious which, for example, his early story "A Case in a Thousand" might seem to point to.

Certainly, parapraxis is one of the dominant modes of signifying performance in a book like *Molloy*, in which both the narrators tell the tale of a series of misfires and mistakes, and in the case of Moran especially, consistently mistake their own motives. Indeed, if Molloy seems more foregone than Moran, he also seems more reasonable as he harbors far fewer illusions concerning the place of his consciousness with regard to the entire scene of his mental life. But if the trilogy starts with the *lapsus* and *acte manqué*, by the time we reach *The Unnamable*, their prominence has been greatly reduced, for in the final book of the trilogy the predicative structure of egoic assertion against which a *lapsus* might erupt is itself most often refused. As we have seen, the book destroys the appropriative and identificatory solidity of an "I" capable of clearly delimiting an inside and an outside to consciousness and intention and consequently banishing the "unconscious" to the absent third-person position of the "id," the "it." Without an "ego all my own," the standard analytic reading of the *lapsus* as an incursion of the unconscious is hard to maintain. In a book like *The Unnamable*, what ego structure is left to be broached? Yet it is in this methodical staging of the dissolution of the transcendental ego as origin and arbiter of language and meaning that Beckett distinguishes himself as distinctively post-Joycean, and all protestations of "impotence" aside, Beckett is no less methodical and rigorous than Joyce. Beckett pushes onward from the literally destructuring and displacing interrogation of language, desire, and *lapsus* in the "Work in Progress," but also inward: for if Joyce's final work stages magnificently the performative workings of language and the unconscious—language as unconscious—to such an extent that the subject as such disappears, Joyce's work does not address the phantasmatic place of the subject *within* this larger problematic. Joyce does not present the subject's witnessing of and testimony to its own nonself-identity—perhaps the central scene of Beckett's prose. The *Wake*'s radicality largely lies in its elimination of a stable narrative subjective position. For example, the *Wake* is wholly immune to a rhetorical reading focused on irony, as it simply refuses to construct the sort of allegedly static subjective positions and assertions which are irony's target. If the hermetic *Wake* is an "open" text, it is only inasmuch as it strives to resist the economy of closure and exclusion necessitated by the temporality of the performative speech acts of the speaking subject. The question which returns in Beckett's work is that of the necessarily noninaugural subject as performative nodal point of the sort of identifications, exclusions, and repetitions which echo throughout Joyce. This means that Beckett enacts a return to a question Joyce seems to have left suspended after the *Portrait:* the narcissistic articulation of the shattered scene of enunciation, the subject's deferred apperception of "itself" as echo, remainder, alterity. Such a moment is largely deferred by Joyce beyond the very borders of the *Wake*'s covers, but his procedure implies it and at times hints darkly at it. The grammar of appropriation which fails to arrive in Beckett, the deictic slip displacing origin, are really variations on the Joycean problematic, as the very pronoun "I" becomes a sort of cliché one can never do other than cite. Likewise, the question of the status of the cogito if "I" repeat it without knowing with certainty what it means is reminiscent of the Flaubert of *Bouvard et Pécuchet*. Much of Beckett can be read as a monumental heave of the *Wake* and its implications into the gears of the traditional narrative apparatus of auto-analysis and introspection. Beckett returns with no illusions to a task which Joyce and Flaubert had done much to throw into ridicule: investigating how the subject might take itself as its own object, how it might think and even speak the implications of its own thinking and speaking.

Indeed, by raising these questions it seems that Beckett is also posing the question of the subjective position of the *reader* of the *Wake*. When I wrote above of the "literally destructuring and displacing" powers of the book, my argument slid onto a necessarily shaky empirical ground; yet a certain sense of the dislocation of one's own subjectivity is a common symptom among the book's readers. Jean-Michel Rabaté has even suggested that the *Wake* is a kind of parapraxis machine, creating its effects in us. Writing about the interplay of phonetic and graphematic punning, and about the reader's implication in the construction of meaning in the book, Rabaté states: "The hearing glance implied by this paradoxical notion of reading-as-writing and of writing-as-reading functions as a kind of parapraxis, a *lapsus* which yet fulfills the programme of the machine: the *lapsus* arrives too early or too late to a meaning which it mistakenly imagines to be there, begging thus the question of sense" (112).[12] It only requires a slight extension of Rabaté's point to argue that the *Wake*'s dislocations of language *create* parapraxis in us, make us (necessarily) parapractitioners. Commenting on Beckett's famous assessment of Joyce's *Work in Progress*, "His writing is not *about* something; *it is that something itself*" (*Disjecta*, 27), Rabaté writes: "Beckett's words make it possible to begin to understand how *Finnegans Wake* does not describe the dream [of Earwicker], does not inform about it, but generates it, is this dream in gesture *and* in gestation" (*Joyce upon the Void,* 123). This dream can only be "generated" in "us"—we don't read, and perhaps, analyze, someone else's dream. On the contrary, we *dream* the dream of *Finnegans Wake,* and it, in its dreaming, analyzes us. The above framework suggests an economy of transsubjective parapraxis, in which it is precisely the *reader* of the book who is "spoken," or perhaps "read."

Such a framework would coincide at least in part with the opinion of Jacques Derrida. In his essay on *Finnegans Wake,* "Deux mots pour Joyce,"[13] Derrida, perhaps elaborating on the well-known conception of *Finnegans Wake* as a machine, or "word machine," defines the *Ulysses-Finnegans Wake* system more precisely as a supercomputer (*Ulysse gramophone,* 22–23; Attridge and Ferrer, 147). By this conceit, he is referring not only to the encyclopedic massiveness of the works, but also to their enormous "coordinational" capacities, the way they metonymically and self-referentially rewrite and overwrite themselves and history, assembling and dispersing vast amounts of reference, wildly intricate traces and chains of signification, into the smallest and most unstable "places"—places which in all propriety can be neither simply phonetic or graphic. Derrida asserts that Joyce's work forces the reader "to be in his [Joyce's] memory," and then goes on to elaborate in this fashion:

> Être en mémoire de lui: non pas nécessairement vous souvenir de lui, non, être en sa mémoire, habiter une mémoire désormais plus grande que votre souvenir et ce qu'il peut rassembler, en un seul instant ou en un seul vocable, de cultures, langues, mythologies, religions, philosophies, sciences, histoires de l'esprit ou des littératures. (*Ulysse gramophone,* 21–22)

> [Being *in memory of him:* not necessarily to remember him, no, but to be in his memory, to inhabit his memory, which is henceforth greater than all your finite memory can, in a single instant or a single vocable, gather up of cultures, languages, mythologies, religions, philosophies, sciences, history of mind and of literatures. (Attridge and Ferrer, 147, emphasis in translation only)]

Thus, Derrida focuses on the uncanny way in which a reader of the *Wake* feels himself or herself to be already written into the book, rather than a reader of it. It follows from this that the Joyce "computer" is not there for the reader to program but on the contrary programs the reader who tries to approach it. Derrida calls it a "hypermnesiac machine" that exists "to compute you, control you, forbid you the slightest inaugural syllable because you can say nothing that is not programmed on this 1000th generation computer— *Ulysses, Finnegans Wake*" (Attridge and Ferrer, 147). To read Joyce, then, is to read within the knowledge that one's own response to the reading has already been written by Joyce: "I don't know if you can love that, without resentment and jealousy. Can one forgive this hypermnesia which *a priori* indebts you, and in advance and forever inscribes you in the book you are reading" (Attridge and Ferrer, 147, translation slightly modified). We can only forgive this, Derrida argues, by remembering also that Joyce, in his relationship to language generally, suffered the same effects we submit to in "reading" his work:

> On ne peut le pardonner, cet acte de guerre babelien, que s'il se produit toujours, de tout temps, à chaque événement d'écriture, suspendant ainsi la responsabilité de chacun. On ne peut le pardonner que si on se rappelle que Joyce lui-même a dû subir cette situation. On se le rappelle parce qu'il a voulu d'abord nous le rappeler. De cette situation, il fut le patient, c'est son thème, je préfère dire son schème. (*Ulysse gramophone*, 22)

> [We can forgive this Babelian act of war only if it has always happened, with each event of writing, thus suspending the responsibility of each of us. We can forgive it only if we remember that Joyce himself had to endure this situation. We remember this because he wanted first of all to remind us of it. Of this situation he was the patient, that is his theme, or as I prefer, his scheme. (Attridge and Ferrer, 147)] [14]

Derrida's suggestion that Joyce's texts in some way make off with the capacity to *answer* them, with "responsabilité" in its literal sense, can be seen extended in Beckett's work, so often predicated on the *demand* for a response (from Youdi, from the "others" who collect Molloy's writings, from *The Unnamable*'s unnamed hordes, to give a few obvious examples) and the inability to give it, or at least to give it oneself, as oneself. When we read Joyce, we are always already spoken by Joyce, and it is this "spoken" subject which makes its entirely deconstructed reappearance in *The Unnamable* and the *Texts for Nothing*. If the *Wake* is indeed an analyzing machine, it is largely because of its structural break from the introspective tradition with which it shares many concerns, that is, its refusal to postulate its text as emanating from an analytic subject. The absence of an arbiter of self-knowledge in the *Wake* prevents us, the readers, from isolating and subsequently identifying with an analytic position. There is no point of stability from which the meaning of meanings can be evaluated. Thus as readers, rather than define meaning we become it. Indeed, on a narrative level Joyce consistently shunned the auto-analytic structure in which the analytic role is internalized to correspond to the narrator's "I." The *Portrait*, for example, is not an allegory of autobiography but an ironic novel about a person engaged in an autobiographical project. Beckett is post-Joycean in his effort to return to an interrogation of subjective positing while registering Joyce's complications of the narrative and linguistic assumptions on which it is based. Yet Beckett's "introspection" is no more teleological than the *Wake*, because there "is" nothing inside to be found. Beckett's "simultaneity" comes from the necessary doubling of an "I" whose constitution is possible only *within* the economy of its own echoing and not on either end of it. His dissonance is found in the multitude of figures which refuse to allow this redoubled "I" a moment of self-identity. Beckett's uncanny subject returns from the other side of *Bouvard et Pécuchet* and the "Work in Progress," itself now in progress and like both those works, interminable, but reintroducing the question of auto-affect through its engagement with the appropriative problematics of first-person narration. Thus in the trilogy and the *Texts,* we find less the speaking subject than the spoken subject, insisting that it echoes and repeats, and telling its own story precisely by recounting how it is told by someone else—by its lack of coincidence with its own desires, by its experience of its "self" as no less alien than "others," by its unnamability. In this, Beckett shows himself to be a reader of, that is, read by, Joyce.

The *Texts for Nothing* occupy an interesting place in Beckett's canon. Although they are certainly as condensed and complex as anything Beckett ever wrote, they receive comparatively little critical attention. Written in French after *L'Innomable,* the *Textes pour rien* are usually—and rightly—seen as covering much of the same ground as the previous novel, without really extending or significantly rearticulating its concerns. It is an understandable commonplace of Beckettian criticism that the intensity of the linguistic and literary dispossession of *L'innomable* left Beckett in some sort of an "impasse" as to how to go on writing. Indeed, a 1951 letter from Beckett to his publisher Jérôme Lindon indicates that Beckett himself felt this to be the case:

Je suis très content que vous ayez envie d'arriver rapidement à *L'inno-mable*. Comme je vous l'ai dit, c'est à ce dernier travail que je tiens le plus, quoiqu'il m'ait mis dans de sales draps. J'essaie de m'en sortir. Mais je ne m'en sors pas. Je ne sais pas si ça pourra faire un livre. Ce sera peut-être un temps pour rien. (*Disjecta*, 104)

[I am very happy that you wish to arrive rapidly at *The Unnamable*. As I have told you, this is the work I care about the most, although it has left me in a fine mess. I'm trying to get out of it. But I'm not getting out of it. I don't know if it will turn out to be a book. Maybe it's just a rest-note. (my translation)]

The text in question is, in fact, the *Textes pour rien,* and the most common critical view is that, given their similarities to *L'innomable,* they do *not* help Beckett arise from his "sales draps," which, depending on the critic, get washed either through Beckett's genre shift into drama and theater, or by the stylistic departure represented by *Comment c'est.* I do not want to challenge this kind of reading—it is clear that Beckett *had* pushed one sort of thing as far as it could go, or at least as far as he could push it, and *did* need to find a way of shifting gears and moods in order to continue. However, apart from the consideration demanded by the stunning brilliance of the *Texts,* it seems ironic that in the corpus of the prophet of failure, of incapacity and inability, of not going on, these works are passed over *because* they fail and are unable to move Beckett "onward."[15] If it is indeed the case that the *Texts* neither articulate the problem, as does the trilogy, nor seem to move out of it, as do "Fin de partie" and *Comment c'est,* the very fact that they *repeat* the impasse, hopelessly and overtly restating it, their very *impassiveness,* should earn them special consideration. In fact, if Beckett's trilogy is one of the first and most dazzling "post-Joycean" works, the *Texts* are perhaps the first "post-Beckettian" texts ever written, questioning what can come after *The Unnamable,* as Beckett's letter indicates. As such, and in their answer, which is in many ways, "more of the same," in their refusal to go forward or onward (progressivist concepts Beckett will interrogate right through *Worstward Ho*), the *Texts,* in their (relative) dismissal, are read *symptomatically,* as *symptoms* of having written, or read, the trilogy. But the symptom itself, no less than failure, is a key concept in Beckett's works, which never fail to investigate symptomological production and signification. Bearing in mind that the *Texts* largely do simply (!) repeat the problems of *The Unnamable,* and that much of the work done up to now, in this study and others, on *The Un-*

namable can simply (!) be applied and extended to the *Texts,* I would like to focus on the element of repetition, that sense of superfluity, the *excess* that the *Texts* have come to represent in Beckettian criticism.[16]

The very first text starts off in terrain extremely familiar to any reader of the trilogy: "Suddenly, no, at last, long last, I couldn't any more, I couldn't go on. Someone said, You can't stay here. I couldn't stay there and I couldn't go on" (75). The inability to either "stay" or "go on" recalls, of course, the final pages of *The Unnamable,* while the "Someone said, You can't stay here" is reminiscent of Molloy's various encounters with figures of authority and the final words of *Molloy,* part 1, "Molloy could stay, where he happened to be" (91). The self-canceling, oxymoronic style is common to both works and will be omnipresent throughout the *Texts.* The *Texts,* then, which are so often *qualified* as an impasse, immediately state as their *explicit subject matter* the question of impasse, the impossibility of "going on." But already, they give us "impasse" in a singularly Beckettian shape. Normally, an impasse is considered to be that which impedes progress, that which stops one from going on. But in the first *Text,* there is not only the impossibility of going on, there is also the impossibility of staying where one is. It should be noted that if Beckett constantly describes barriers and impediments to movements, movement itself is never figured as a self-evidently positive, desirable goal. The "barriers" in and of themselves only present problems because one is not allowed not to move; one cannot stay where one happens to be. This means that the impasse in Beckett is less a block, a barrier, than a double bind. Stasis and movement are equally denied. It also means that in relation to Beckett's "historical" writerly impasse, the "temps pour rien" or rest-note represented by the *Texts,* to the extent that they are a repetition of the trilogy, is itself an experiment precisely in staying where one is, in not going on. Perhaps the key question then is not what prevents progress, what stops one from going on, but rather what impels and forces one even to try.[17] The answer in the first *Text* is that externalized voice which commands: "You can't stay here"—the voice that establishes the status of addressee that Beckettian narration is always at pains to uncannily maintain, even in midutterance.

To "go on," then, physically, is to *respond* to the voice's imperative, through a "speech" made by the body, in its act of acquiescing by "moving." No wonder to "go on" in Beckett is almost always both to go on moving, walking, cycling, crawling, et cetera, and to go on thinking, talking, discoursing, writing.[18] The parallel between these two forms of "going on" allows Beckett a large space for humor by conflating the absurd structures of his "narratives" with the ridiculous modes of locomotion of their mannikins. But it also introduces another level of irony concerning Beckett's structuring of inter- and intrasubjective relations (this distinction never being firm in his work). As many critics have noted, the impossible Beckettian stasis is quite clearly associated with death: both Molloy and Malone, for example, ask nothing better than to be left alone to die, yet find themselves forced, Molloy by his keepers, Malone by that space called time, to respond. This desire for stasis, joined with the obsessional repetitions and attempts to recapture past states of being, often seen in Beckett, can all be and have been linked to the Freudian conception of the death drive.[19] However, this "death drive" in Beckett is in no way a sadistic, other voice, aimed at the annihilation of the ego. On the contrary, the forms of static suffering bring only a *jouissance* (which admittedly can only be maintained by their own occasional interruption)—the sadistic voice is rather the paternalized, overdetermined, superego-like voice which says: "Move! Talk! Write! Live!" The Beckettian "subject," like Kafka's, is often subordinated to this voice as law, but the agony for the Beckettian "subject" is the knowledge that it will *never* obtain from this voice the death sentence which it seeks. To continue in Freudian terms, one might suggest that Beckett shows a cheerful acceptance by the ego of itself as object of death drives, resisted by a "superego" agency whose sadism consists of its rejection of the masochistic wish. Through this mechanism, everyone is (dis)satisfied. Or to put it another way, satisfaction and its other are not easily distinguishable.

The subject's existence, however, is always conceptualized not only in relation to but also *within* this voice—Beckett never sustains the possibility of the "ego" achieving independence from it, nor the rigorous conceptualization of the voice's "externality." This "externality," when it appears, should rather be considered as a moment of articulation, within which utterance finds and loses itself. Following the previous chapter's investigation of the Beckettian merging of the call and the response, here we should note that the "externalized" imperative in Beckett is always itself also the voice of response, itself an answer to the "I couldn't go on" so often heard. In the *Texts for Nothing,* perhaps even more than in *The Unnamable,* we are presented with the spectacle of the subject's alterity in the form of a constant exchange of nonoriginary, interposable "I" 's and "you" 's. Indeed, if the Freudian schema divides the "self" into an "I," an "it," and an "over-I," in some ways assimilable to a "him," Beckett can be seen as attempting to add to this grammar a "you," [20] which in itself would observe no more

strictly demarcated limits than the interarticulating Freudian functions.[21]
In fact, the relationship of the grammatical categories of person and number to subjectivity is explicitly raised in the *Texts*. In the twelfth *Text,* a
voice, speaking on the by-now familiar "other," utters the following:

> And this other now, obviously, what's to be said of this latest other, with
> his babble of homeless mes and untenanted hims, this other without
> number or person whose abandoned being we haunt, nothing. There's
> a pretty three in one, and what a one, what a no one. (134)

Noteworthy in this passage is the parallelism and opposition of the
"me"'s and the "him"'s—the "him"'s, untenanted, are figured as empty
containers, whereas the "me's" are figured as errant units, without stable
lodging or place. The opposition here seems clear: "him" is a stable "place,"
but an empty one, substanceless, while "me" is an actual "thing," but one
which cannot be fixed, located, nailed down. Does this suggest a solution
in which "me" would take up "residence" in "him"? This could perhaps
be assimilated to what might be Malone's projective story, writing himself
(if indeed this is the case) through the figure of Macmann. But if him and
me are clearly offered here as complementary opposites, we still need to
examine the particularity of this opposition. "Untenanted him" suggests
a word, "him," that is *empty,* that *holds nothing.* The implication seems
obvious: the pronoun "him," the third person, when stated, refers to no
one. There is no *actual* person referred to—there is no him, only "him."
In this sense, one might be tempted to argue that "him" is untenanted
because it is only a *figure* for the "me." In other words, the "him" could
be read as a *figure* or mannikin created by a discoursing "I"—this would
tie in well, for example, with the "fabler" of *Company* who finds himself
in the end "alone." Following this reading, "him" is "untenanted" because
there is no other person—I am (is) alone.

But let us turn our attention now to the expression "homeless mes."
If an "untenanted him" is an *empty* "him," a "him" not filled out by a
referent, what is a "homeless me"? It is a "me" which apparently has no
fixed *place,* no site to anchor it, to house it. This could mean that the
"me" is the subject, without a pronoun in which to lodge itself. However, as "me" is a deictic pronoun, a homeless "me" is not a "me" at all.
The "me" cannot be thought in terms of homelessness, of enunciatory
exile. Its meaning comes entirely and only from its lodging in an actual
or hypothetical voice. A "homeless me" is not simply a referent without
a sign, but rather unsignifiable, not merely anonymous, but unnamable.

The situations of the "him" and the "me," *seemingly* opposed, are actually analogous, both indicating deictic markers untethered to referents. What is different is the figuration of this relationship. For the "him," the missing referent is the missing resident, whereas for the "me," the missing referent is the missing abode. This juxtaposition refuses to figure language as a logically prior structure, "inhabited" by speakers, while also refusing to privilege the primacy of an empirical, physical, prelinguistic "reality," to which language would attach itself. Even more, both figures link subjectivity to the temporality of the deictic moment, and both articulate an expressive-referential disjunction which Beckett finds constitutive of both "language" and its unnamable other. "Untenanted him" figures the mark *itself* as locus, which, in principle, can either be empty or filled, while "homeless me" figures the mark as some sort of discrete element, which seeks to lodge itself in the subject. As noted, the *juxtaposition* of these two contradictory figures refuses to grant primacy to empiricized or idealized conceptions of either "language" or the "real"—the logic of the two figures is articulated through their collision. But if we separate them for the moment, we will hear other resonances.

The "untenanted hims," which present language as a fillable structure or space, and the "homeless mes," with their vision of language as swarming elements trying to fill the subject, correspond well to two of the modalities of Beckettian narration: that of the voice bloated with words forcing themselves out in its utterance, and that of the voice trying to fill up and exist in the words that it, unbelieving, utters. What must be noted is the homology between the phantasm of being reamed with words and that of the inability to fill them, assume them. The hinge separating and linking the two is the reversal of the sense of space and substance, or more precisely, the articulation of "outside" and "inside." But if a missed encounter between language and subjectivity is sketched in both these figures, subjectivity—as a discrete "substance" capable of existing outside of language and deixis—is also rejected. We have no metaphysical attempt to recover the subject's "truth" beyond the spoken and the speaking tongues.

This is seen quite clearly in the equation of the "other without number or person" with "nothing" (134). This grammarless, "antithetical" other does not achieve by its extradition from language either the revelation of its being, or the revelation of its lack of being. The "pretty three in one," as Beckett's parody of the trinity would have it, is both "nothing" *and* "what a one"—in other words, neither wholly a "one" nor a "no one." This logic of the neither/nor is perhaps what links this passage with the question of the trinity, itself invoked to respond to the no less paradoxical nature of Christ's divinity/manhood. After the rhetoric of lodging concerning the pronouns, we are apparently told that all of them, including the abode-like "hims," are themselves inside the emptiness of the abandoned being of the other. The "trinity" seems to consist of the "other" without number or person, its or their "abandoned being,"[22] and the "we" which inhabits the abandoned being. This would *seem* to cast the articulating pronouns in the role of the animating holy ghost, and this ties in with Beckett's anal parodies of spirit and inspiration seen in *The Unnamable*. Important for the moment, however, is to note that by putting the "untenanted hims" *inside* the "abandoned being," Beckett once again dislodges any final assumptions one could make concerning language as ultimate lodging place.

The other without number or person, whose abandoned being swarms with pronouns, is far from an entirely new conception when it arises, but some of the early passages of the fourth *Text* seem to relate to it especially explicitly. The *Text* begins:

> Where would I go, if I could go, who would I be, if I could be, what would I say, if I had a voice, who says this, saying it's me? Answer simply, someone answer simply. It's the same old stranger as ever, for whom alone accusative I exist, in the pit of my inexistence, of his, of ours, there's a simple answer. (91)

Alain Badiou has recently found in this passage what he takes to be the three central Beckettian questions, and writes interestingly: "Au fameux <<Que puis-je connaître? Que dois-je faire? Que puis-je espérer?>> de Kant, répond, dans les *Textes pour rien,* le triplet: Où irais-je si je pouvais aller? Que serais-je si je pouvais être? Que dirais-je si j'avais une voix?" (*l'increvable,* 12).[23] Badiou's isolation of the textual vortices represented by these categories in Beckett is fruitful, but one should note that, as we saw in the introduction, unlike Kant's questions, Beckett's are all posed in the *conditional*—the answers given are necessarily hypothetical, as the litany of "ifs" already tells us that, in fact, I *can't* go, I *can't* be, and I have *no* voice. For Beckett, unlike Kant, outside the realm of the hypothetical, these questions have already been answered. In very logical fashion, the text asks the naive but reasonable question that follows the assertions that I have no voice and that I don't exist: "who says this, saying it's me?" In this typical Beckettian move, the "I" denies its "own" speech by attributing it to a third ("who says this?"), while, of course, this very move also simultaneously undermines the attribution itself of speech to another. This sort of system, probably the prevalent trope of *The Unnamable,* was clearly of obsessive interest to Beckett. For our purposes, we must note the way in which it depends on and creates a third, a "him" or "they" or "it" no less problematic than the "I" which invokes this third in a move that must logically invalidate the invocation it presents. The fourth *Text* is particularly explicit in its discussion of the third and the first person: speaking of the "old stranger" (who of course in principle is the one who speaks when we read "I"), the "I" continues, "If at least he would dignify me with the third person, like his other figments, not he, he'll be satisfied with nothing less than me, for his me" (92). Again, this grammar posits a "him" who would like to take on a "me" as tenant; however, the enunciative situation posits that the "I" talking of the "him" is, *in fact,* the him impersonating the I—which would give us an "I" *whose speaking* takes a "him" for its "him" (in other words, if it is "he" who says "I," my "me" is his "him." Of course, no "I" can ever say this. We know this amply by now).

In the passage quoted above, an interesting addition to the subjective grammar of number and person is that of case—"The same old stranger as ever, for whom alone *accusative* I exist" (my emphasis). This mention of case is absent in the French text, which reads, "C'est le même inconnu que toujours, le seul pour qui j'existe" (*Nouvelles and Textes pour rien,* 139), and the disjunction explains on one level the mention of the accusative: the French text is grammatically unambiguous, but the English text could be read both as "I exist for that stranger—not for anyone else" *and* "I exist for that stranger—no one else does." "Accusative," then, tells us that "alone" modifies the object, not the subject, of the phrase. This is all good and well, but it hardly exhausts the function of "accusative" in this passage— after all, Beckett could easily have written "The same old stranger as ever, the only one for whom I exist," if he had wanted to avoid the awkward, metalinguistic interpolation, as he had in the original French. The addition of "accusative," however, seems to highlight the entire structure of the relationship between the different grammatical persons, in which the specular noncoincidence of the "I" as subject and object (or nominative and accusative cases) is figured as, and is a figure for, difference in person in terms of pronoun and verb conjugation. The failure of the "I" and "me" to coincide indicates a rupture between the accusative and nominative cases of subjective auto-designation. Indeed, Beckett has given us the most extended meditation on the Lacanian dictum: "Il ne s'agit pas de savoir si je parle de moi de façon conforme à ce que je suis, mais si, quand j'en parle, je suis le même que celui dont je parle" (*Ecrits I,* 276) [It is not a question of knowing whether I speak of myself in a way that conforms to what I am, but rather of knowing, when I speak, whether I am the same as that of which I speak (*Ecrits: A Selection*, 165, translation slightly modified)]. The Beckettian answer is an emphatic "no," but that answer in and of itself does not sum up Beckett's questioning of the positioning of objects, or the self as object, in other words, "accusative existence."[24]

The relationship that the passage establishes between the grammatical persons can, perhaps, in certain ways be subsumed under the term "accusative," inasmuch as the "I" only exists at all as object for the he—that is, in the *accusative*. In this sense, in the sentence, "It's the same old stranger as ever, for whom alone accusative I exist" (91), "alone" and "accusative" must also be read as modifying "I"—that is to say, "I" exist(s) only *as object* for the "stranger." This assertion must be understood on two levels. First, in terms of the narrative, the "I" which "speaks" this text has no existence "outside" the existence/inexistence of the "stranger." This is reminiscent of the head-in-the-jar story, in which the voice seeks to have its being ascertained by a witnessing. Second, this phrase is also illustrative of the manifold instances in which the "I" is not allowed a nominative authority, is distanced from the source of utterance it is meant to designate, and is nudged into the position not of logical cause or origin of speech as the nominative case implies but rather of object or effect—in other words, the accusative. The "accusative I" or "accusative voice" is one of the most significant of Beckett's stylistic inventions, occupying a middle space between the nominative "I" and the standard accusative "me." The "accusative I" is the particularly Beckettian articulation of the subject as posited, and posited by itself, but without an agent that could possibly have a moment or place. But this sort of displacing of moment and place—crucial to Beckett's representation of subjectivity—occurs on another level in the English version of this passage, as the words "for whom alone accusative" are almost a direct quotation of a line from Beckett's early poem "Sanies I."

"Sanies I," one of Beckett's more interesting early poems, for the most part describes a narrator's long journey astride a bicycle, at the end of which he finally espies a woman identified as object, or onetime object, of desires. After an extremely long string of adjectival and prepositional clauses, we are given these lines at the beginning of the final stanza:

I see main verb at last
her whom alone in the accusative
I have dismounted to love

gliding towards me dauntless nautch-girl on the face of the waters
dauntless daughter of desires in the old black and flamingo
get along with you now take the six the seven the eight or the little
    single-decker
take a bus for all I care walk cadge a lift. . . .

                                      (*Collected Poems*, 18)

If the insertion of the metalinguistic "accusative" is somewhat out of
the ordinary in the *Texts,* here it forms part of the consistent pattern of
self-reflexive stylistic commentary of Beckett's early work, seen also in the
comment "main verb at last." Of course, the poem's Apollinairean lack
of punctuation leaves the phrase "main verb at last" itself in a kind of
aporia—given the poem's self-reflexivity, we could read the phrase not as
a parenthetical description of the verb "see," but rather as its *object:* the
narrator-poet could be insisting that at this point he "sees" (at last) his
main verb. The fact that there is no other "main verb" leads us to read
the phrase parenthetically, but still, within the space of the line, its diacritical status is somewhat challenged. The designation "accusative" will
wobble in an analogous way. Paring out the "commentary," we could write
the first three lines of the stanza like this: "I see/her whom alone/I have
dismounted to love"—this would refer to dismounting the bicycle and
exchanging the erotically charged ride (described in line 7 as "heaven in
the sphincter") for the sexual encounter. "In the accusative," modifying
"alone," becomes then a somewhat sophomoric sexual quibble concerning the beloved's sexual activities, to wit, "I have dismounted to love no
one but her" and *not* "No one but I has dismounted to love her." The
note concerning the "accusative" economically implies that the narrator
has but one lover, while the "dauntless daughter of desires" has many.
The irony of Beckett's self-reflexive insertions is that rather than clarify
linguistic relations and eliminate ambiguity, both their supersensitivity
to innuendo and the structural ambiguity of their grammatical placement tend to encourage and emphasize readings focused on the *lapsus*
and double-meaning. It is only the *addition* "in the accusative" which,
by highlighting the placement of "alone," serves to imply the beloved's
promiscuity through implicit contrast—an inference we would not have
made without the "clarifying" comment. "In the accusative," then, raises
and intensifies the entire question of object, of the articulation of grammatical relationships or perhaps of a grammar of object relations, which
the avowedly paratactic poem had been at pains to defer. We see in germ

here the anxiety concerning origin, destination, and reference of utterance which will become such a major theme in the later writings.

To a large extent, the poem is constructed around the tension between its grammatical indeterminacy (absence of punctuation; use of paratactic constructions) and its attempt to semantically and diacritically supplement this willful lack. But to whatever extent the diacritical comments counter the grammatical uncertainty, to an equal extent the grammatical indeterminacy prevents any definitive, unproblematic application of the diacritical directives. For example, the three lines, "I see main verb at last/her whom alone in the accusative/I have dismounted to love" could also be read as indicating that "her" should be taken as the direct object not only of "see" but also of "dismounted." That is, if these lines of the poem turn on the obscene equivalence of mounting the bicycle and mounting the daughter of desires (both, let us remember, erotically invested objects), the stanza, with its desire to distance the girl, to put her on a trolley or bus, and its celebration of the pleasures of the pedal [25] and saddle, could, in fact, be suggesting that the narrator, in order to love, must dismount not the bicycle but the girl. This places us squarely within the thematics of solipsism, narcissism, voyeurism, and onanism so prevalent in the early Beckett. This tangent of the poem's undecidable structure seems somewhat similar to Murphy's drive to replace Celia as object with a narcissistic focus on himself—played out through the punning oscillation between Celia the woman and the celestial star chart on which Murphy's destiny is inscribed.

The manner in which the poem (incompletely) enacts a rejection of woman in favor of bicycle (the explicit theme of the story "Fingal" from *More Pricks than Kicks*) cannot be excluded from the network of possible relations of object the poem constructs. In the context of our discussion of the *Texts for Nothing*, we need to emphasize the way Beckett writes the question of the specular division of the subject's self-positing—often presented as a linguistic or philosophical issue, and especially in the *Texts*—onto an erotics of narcissism and self-objectification. The grammatical contortions around person, subject, and auto-designation are linked to a general economy of narcissism and object choice. In emphasizing this link, the nod in the fourth *Text* to "Sanies I" forms a part of Beckett's meticulous investigation of the relationships between drive, desire, and language. Throughout Beckett, the privileged figure of both the mirage of subjective coherence and of the registration of structures of desire is the body. And the body parallels "subjective consciousness" in Beckett in arriving belatedly, as effect of those drives of which it should normally be the source.

Beckett's bodies speak, just as Beckett's voices are spoken. This entails a careful consideration of the question of the relationship between "body," "mind," and "language" in Beckett, in terms of sexuality and drive. For if the body and its exigencies is a more than frequent theme in Beckett, the problem of the relationship between body, drive, and language exceeds any conception of the body as referent (or source) of desire, and thus of the body's *representability* in language, or language's ability or lack thereof to express desire.[26] Rather, it is through language that objectification, and thus the body as object, is articulated. If the body is a crucial problem in Beckett, it is because it, like the speaking subjects Beckett presents, is constantly *being created* through language, and *not* because it in some way exceeds language, or marks a site of which language falls short.[27] Writing of the discovery by Austin and Lacan of "acts as language effects," Shoshana Felman remarks that the conception of the "act" as a production of the "speaking body" will explode "the metaphysical dichotomy between the domain of the 'mental' and the domain of the 'physical,' [and] break down the opposition between body and spirit, between matter and language" (*Literary Speech Act*, 94). Felman goes on to quote Lacan to the effect that: "A body . . . is speech arising as such" (94).[28] In Beckett, the process of subjective and linguistic articulation is never only a response to, but also a construction of, something which could be called the body, just as the body's actions, movements, and motions are always in Beckett a form of speech or speaking, a locomotive (Molloy) and somatic (Malone) language.[29]

Lacan, in discussing the drives, has called them "l'écho dans le corps du fait qu'il y a un dire" [the echo in the body of the fact that there is saying (notes; my translation)], and this beautiful phrase could itself be applied to *Finnegans Wake,* in which the echo of language, both as system and as the impossibility of a particular system's closure, is made to resound in the body of language "itself," as the portmanteau words are given as only the echoes of "originals" whose full divination is prohibited to the reader. Yet, if full semantic articulation is denied in the *Wake,* it is paradoxically denied through the assertion of the phonic and graphic materiality of the echoing litters of the ruptured signs. Indeed, the language of the *Wake* is perhaps also the "Echo's Bones" which name the collection of poetry in which "Sanies I" was first published. Certainly, it is around the echo — the other sound of the *Wake's* words, the repetitive mouthing of Beckett's "voices" — that Beckett and Joyce meet. But in each case, it is echo without "origin," echo which cannot be traced, echo as trace of constitutive

otherness. The "words" of the *Wake* and the grammar of Beckettian so-
liloquies both imply a "without" which cannot be exteriorized, which
remains steadfastly within that which is defined as separation from it. This
sense of otherness which could not exist in the mode of presence, which is
not a modified tense of the present, nor space of the present, is what links
the Beckettian and Joycean projects to that of Derrida. It is in the terms
mentioned above that Derrida writes of the Freudian unconscious in "La
Différance," and he seems to rejoin Beckett's suspicion of the unconscious
as "teleology" when he describes it as an "alterity" which is not a "hidden, virtual, or potential self-presence" (*Margins,* 20). In arguing that the
unconscious is not a "thing" or a "virtual or masked consciousness" (21),
Derrida claims that the unconscious "differs from, and defers itself; which
doubtless means that it is woven of differences, and also that it sends out
delegates, representatives, proxies; but without any chance that the giver
of proxies might 'exist,' might be present, be 'itself' somewhere" (20–21).[30]
A nonexistent sender of "delegates, representatives, proxies," with no presence of its own, describes with frightening precision the situation Beckett
"called" *The Unnamable.*

But the parallelism and interplay of Beckett's treatment of "mind" and
"body," linguistic subjectivity and sensory physicality, also needs to be emphasized. The "body" with its "drives" is no less than the unconscious an
echoing membrane of differing and deferring delegates in Beckett's work.
No more than the unconscious, or the "proper meaning" of the *Wake*'s
words, could the body present itself as such, and *not* because of any fissure
of language, or language's inability to be the "things" which it represents.
The relationship between language and the body, a favorite subject in
Beckettian criticism, must not be looked at in terms of representation and
adequation, but rather in terms of extension, continuation, displacement,
mood, and voicing. If the mouth is often viewed in psychoanalysis as the
privileged meeting place of the body and the word, drive and expression,
physicality and symbolization, Beckett, like Joyce, is more concerned with
the "other precipitates," with the other orifice where letter and litter—that
is, language and body as *exteriority,* disjecta, sanies, or trash heaps—fall
together.[31] If Beckett and Joyce both tend to privilege the anus, it is *properly* no more a part of the body than of the page. The body as language,
language as body—to give respectively the primary Beckettian and Joycean
inflections of the problem—allow the exterior and interior to remain
places, but displaced, nonsymmetrical places. The question of litter in the

sense of remainder, of what perhaps outlasts the speech-timed "moment" of Cartesian self-apperception, is the explicit concern of the final *Text for Nothing,* in which the question of voice is extended into that of trace:

> Whose voice, no one's, there is no one, there's a voice without a mouth, and somewhere a kind of hearing, something compelled to hear, and somewhere a hand, it calls that a hand, it wants to make a hand, or if not a hand something somewhere that can leave a trace, of what is made, of what is said, you can't do with less, no, that's romancing, more romancing, there is nothing but a voice murmuring a trace. A trace, it wants to leave a trace, yes, like air leaves among the leaves, among the grass, among the sand, it's with that it would make a life, but soon it will be the end, it won't be long now, there won't be any life, there won't have been any life, there will be silence, the air quite still that trembled once an instant, the tiny flurry of dust quite settled. (137)

The written trace is abandoned as soon as it is invoked in favor of the wind metaphors, which give us something quite different. For the leaves and the grass only register the wind while it is passing through them; they leave no after-mark of the wind having passed—no monument, no wake. In terms of temporality, they are like the speech of the voice, yet even as contemporaneous traces, they still serve to make the invisible wind apperceptible. In this way, the words of the voice are likewise traces of the voice's passing, neither representations nor expressions but indices of its moments—moments which, of course, will not have been. I have already referred to Rabaté's paradoxical conception of the "hearing glance" in *Finnegans Wake.* Parallel to this, the Beckettian Narcissus could be said to gaze at his own echoes, to witness that trace-of-self which precisely by being trace defeats the "narcissism" it is invoked to satisfy. The figure of Narcissus is one of the most prominent sites of classical allusion in Beckett's early work.[32] Beckett's reading of Narcissus places no emphasis on self-love or successful egotism; rather, Narcissus is the figure of the refusal to take an object, the refusal to accept the location of erotic satisfaction or even investment outside of oneself.[33] And as in Ovid's telling of the myth, the hills and mountains that now render the echoes of our voices to us are the metamorphosis of the bones of Echo after she died of grief from Narcissus's rejection of her love, the title "Echo's Bones and other precipitates" might imply that the poems therein represent that which returns the poet's voice to his ears—to wit, the space left by the absence of the other as object. This sort of "narcissism," then, would consist of the appropriation of the echo of the other as oneself, as one's voice, which, in turn, could only make itself heard through its own disappropriation. That the poems posit themselves as the trace of body of the abandoned, grief-stricken dead woman could also be linked to Beckett's mourning and guilt concerning the death of his cousin, Peggy Sinclair, in May 1933.[34] The early *Dream of Fair to Middling Women,* however, shows a scene in which the protagonist, Belacqua, finally finds himself smitten with love and exchanges his rampant narcissism for an infatuation with the crepuscular "Alba":

> Then lo! she is at the window, she is taking stock of her cage. Now under the threat of night the evening is albescent, its hues have blanched, it is dim white and palpable, it pillows and mutes her head. So that as from transparent polished glass or, if you prefer, from tranquil shining waters, the details of his face return so feeble that a pearl on a white brow comes not less promptly to his pupils, so now he sees her vigilant face and in him is reversed the error that lit love between the man (if you can call such a spineless creature a man) and the pool. For she had closed the eyes. (174–75)

What this very difficult paragraph seems to describe is Belacqua's increasing difficulty in seeing the reflection of his own image in the Alba's eyes, due to the falling night, followed by the impossibility of so doing upon her closing of her eyes, which leaves him no choice but to see the woman herself. At this point, the "error that lit love between the man . . . and the pool" is reversed. That is not to say the error of narcissism is corrected; rather, Belacqua exchanges the error of self-love for what the narrator portrays as the *equal error* of love for another. This complex passage of exchanges between self and other, alterity and interiority, image, object, and reflection, is also a kind of echo, being little more than a direct translation of canto 3 of Dante's *Paradiso,* where we find:

> Quali per vetri trasparenti e tersi,
> o ver per acque nitide e tranquille,
> non sì profonde che i fondi sien persi,
> tornan d'i nostri visi le postille
> debili sì, che perla in bianca fronte
> non vien men forte a le nostre pupille;
> tali vid'io più facce a parlar pronte;

per ch'io dentro a l'error contrario corsi
a quel ch'accese amor tra l'omo e'l fonte.
(lines 10–18)[35]

Beckett's plays on this passage are evident. For example, when Dante mentions the "contrary error," he means that of taking real beings (the angels) to be images, as opposed to Narcissus, who took his image for reality. As we have seen, Beckett's text implies something quite different. Note that Dante takes the image of the face reflected in a pool as a metaphor to describe the apparition of these faces of Paradise; this metaphor is first qualified itself by a kind of metametaphor—the image of the pearl on the white brow—and then used to foreshadow the reference to Narcissus. Beckett, however, replaces the "*our* eyes" of generic optic experience with "*his* pupils"—a reference only to the body of the object of description. This in turn suspends the "so that" between an expression of causality creating metaphorical equivalence and an expression of temporality, implying something like "now he sees his face" et cetera. In Beckett, the metaphorical clause concerning the pool and the pearl cannot be read as modifying only the appearance of the Alba's face to his vision, because this passage, devoted to the beauty of the Alba's eyes, stipulates that the narcissistic error is "reversed" only when the Alba *closes* her eyes, denying Belacqua his vision of himself as beautified by the limpid pools of her "dark eyes of the beautiful" (174). These figures of Belacqua's embellished visions of himself, as read through Narcissus, give us yet another possible play on the name "Bel/Acqua." This entire scene should be read against Murphy's gaze into the eyes of Mr. Endon, which renders, rather than the recognition of another, nothing but Murphy's own image in reflection.

But if narcissism is usually figured as visual or specular, from Ovid through Lacan, the narcissistic "moment" or Beckettian mirror-stage would seem to be not only specular, but also comprised of a vocal temporality, in which Dante's echo is allowed to be heard, and which acknowledges the echoing possibility of repetition, duplication, and parasitism inherent in any lovable "image," whether specular or aural. This vocal temporality means that the "moment" is no longer a moment at all. Beckett's narcissistic structure is in fact unthinkable without the component of the echo—that is, subjectivity as a temporality of belated returns and retrievals, which both enable and disable the apparently static structure of specular self-contemplation. It is in this context that Beckett's investigations of the linguistic temporality of Descartes's cogito need to be examined. This sort of "echoing narcissism" defies any easy opposition between visual/aural, image/language, body/mind, or imaginary/symbolic. It also raises the question of the relation between repetition and response—if Narcissus refuses the other represented by Echo, let us not forget that Echo can only offer herself as a doubling or extension of that voice by which Narcissus proclaims his love for himself. In this way, Echo would be not even a space of narcissistic projection—a narcissistic object—but rather an echo of the narcissistic *desire,* of the voice of auto-eroticism.

To respond to Joyce, then, to take up the responsibility of Joyce's texts, can be neither to answer in one's "own" voice, nor to echo Joyce's, but rather to register the echo in all acts of voicing and tracing, and paradoxically, to *see* the echo of the other in one's own self-tracings. This leads to a reexamination of certain conceptions of fidelity, filiality, and mastery in terms of the relationship between the two writers, especially, as I argued at the outset, the focus on Beckettian "impotence." Whatever Beckett may thematize, his texts show a multilingual erudition, stylistic range, and linguistic virtuosity every bit as intimidating as Joyce's. If *Ulysses* enacted the "death of style," Beckett, without returning to naive mimetologist or expressivist positions, becomes style's Lazarus.[36] And if Beckett on occasion works through somewhat minimalist procedures, in contrast to other avant-garde authors, he never divests himself of his almost unrivaled writerly powers. If there is a contrast to be drawn between Beckett and Joyce, it is in terms of their relationships to the linguistic and textual effects they each masterfully allow to be produced. Here Derrida's somewhat "transferential" model of reading *Finnegans Wake* might once again be useful. Derrida seems to suggest that behind the Joycean text implicitly lurks, to use Lacan's phrase, the "sujet supposé savoir," or rather, the text itself becomes an object of transference, before which the reader is divested of mastery. I have been arguing that Beckett *stages* this divestment, stages the sense of having already had one's story told (or lived). But as Derrida points out, *Finnegans Wake* is already itself divided, and through its "hypermnesic" economy, it is forced also to live its own failure to "master" the differential structure it opens. The distinction exists then in the subjective spacings the two writers employ. The seemingly subjectless *Finnegans Wake* structurally forces the reader to (fail to) occupy the space of the subject of enunciation, while the trilogy and the *Texts* obsessively (fail to) provide these pseudo-subjects themselves. Parallel to this, the sensualization and physicalization of language in *Finnegans Wake,* with its emphasis on the aural and optic qualities of its words and letters, is mirrored in Beckett by what Joyce's procedure already implies: a semioticization or symptomatic construction of the body. The concept of the symptom implies the body as trope, its needs being that which answers as much as that which must be answered. Likewise, any notion of a "symptomatic language" must acknowledge language's capacity to embody drives, needs, and desires rather than simply "represent" them. The "symptom" and the "response," in fact, share a structure of secondarity, of the "post." Each is meant to refer to something in some way logically prior—in one case, the "repressed drive" or "desire," in the other, the address or statement. But as Freud considers at length in "Inhibitions, Symptoms and Anxiety," a symptom can never simply be reduced to the libidinal directive it replaces—the substitutive process itself allows it to be bound into new psychic formations by the ego, which, in turn, will reshape and re-form that which it "originally" represented. In this sense, the symptom could be said to create the desire or drive just as much as the desire or drive could be said to give birth to the symptom.[37] The symptom, then, can never achieve semiotic transparency or finality.

Likewise, just as answer can never be originary—the entire concept of "response" presupposing a prior "question"—the answer can never achieve finality either (as "Ithaca" in *Ulysses* makes clear). As answer, it is always *offered,* given, and must await a subsequent recognition, confirmation, or countersignature—acts which themselves can only necessitate further responses. The *Texts for Nothing* are the last Beckettian work to focus primarily on the unanswerable answer, the unreceivable response. As such, they form the last Beckettian text to be structurally interminable. In the next chapter, we will look at the late texts from the eighties which return to some of the earliest Beckettian issues—those of movement, stasis, and change.

6. "For Nothing to Be Changed"

Fabling Arrival in the Late Prose

Toward the end of the first section of *Molloy* is one of the most commonly cited passages in all of Beckett. Speaking of his representations of his own speech and consciousness, Molloy informs us:

> And when I say I said, etc., all I mean is that I knew confusedly things were so, without knowing exactly what it was all about. And every time I say, I said this, or I said that, or speak of a voice saying, far away inside me, Molloy, and then a fine phrase more or less clear and simple, or find myself compelled to attribute to others intelligible words, or hear my own voice uttering to others more or less articulate sounds, I am merely complying with the convention that demands you either lie or hold your peace. For what really happened was quite different. And I did not say, Yet a little while, at the rate things are going, etc., but that resembled perhaps what I would have said, if I had been able. In reality I said nothing at all, but I heard a murmur, something gone wrong with the silence, and I pricked up my ears, like an animal I imagine, which gives a start and pretends to be dead. (88)

This passage is, of course, extremely important in its disavowal of speech, expression, and the literality of the story which Molloy has been recounting up to this point. Critics have made much of Molloy's distress at the troubling of the "silence," along with the notion of language and diegesis as a sort of originary translation. But this sequence is not only about language's lying unreliability or literal inadequacy—on another level, it is about language's efficacy and necessity. I would like to continue this passage, extending its citation slightly further than the norm:

> And then sometimes there arose within me, confusedly, a kind of consciousness, which I express by saying, I said, etc., or, Don't do it Molloy, or, Is that your mother's name? said the sergeant, I quote from memory. Or which I express without sinking to the level of oratio recta, but by means of other figures quite as deceitful, as for example, It seemed to me that, etc., or, I had the impression that, etc., for it seemed to me nothing at all, and I had no impression of any kind, but simply somewhere something had changed, so that I too had to change, or the world too had to change, in order for nothing to be changed. And it was these little adjustments, as between Galileo's vessels, that I can only express by saying, I feared that, or, I hoped that, or, Is that your mother's name? said the sergeant, for example, and that I might doubtless have expressed otherwise and better, if I had gone to the trouble. (88)

The point to which I want to call attention here is the sense of language, and even consciousness, as response and maneuver, or as Beckett calls it, "adjustment"—adjustment mobilized in the interest of stasis and preservation. The goal of these adjustments, "as between Galileo's vessels," paradoxically, is to restore the state of things prevailing before their necessity, to ensure that nothing be changed. What this means is that if language is problematic, it is not only or even primarily because it is false, distant from truth or from the truth of Molloy's experience, but also because it exists only in order to obviate itself, to retract or redress. Discourse exists to re-create the conditions in which it was not yet necessary—inscription aims at its own erasure. Indeed, the expression we read as Molloy's tale, no less than the events recounted therein, seems to exist not in the interest of "expression," but rather in the hope of bringing about or maintaining desired conditions—conditions which would seem to include the tale's own termination. "Change," then, is only a detour on the greater road to stasis, a delicate balancing of the relationship obtaining between the without and the within, which can be affected from either side of the border.

The focus on the tactical retreat or the Penelope-like dialectic of interminable weaving and unweaving is not original with Beckett. More striking is it that *language* is the name given to this sort of adjustment, be it internal or external. This implies, of course, a need to maintain a perspective on language as performative, on speaking not as a means of expression but as an act which produces effects on people and results in the "world." For example, one says certain words to gain peace from a sergeant. But the passage tells us that not only the world but also Molloy could be changed to accomplish the preservation of balance—Molloy includes in his list of "adjustments" the phrases, "I feared that" and "I hoped that." This gives us in all its radicality a conception of consciousness and interior monologue as performative. The passage is explicit: "I feared" and "I hoped" are not expressions of Molloy's anxiety at his realization that adjustment is necessary—*they are the adjustments themselves.* The passage doesn't really seem to claim that Molloy's consciousness is ineffable, beyond language, when it states that in "reality" Molloy said nothing at all, but on the contrary asserts that that which we might wish to express as "Molloy's consciousness" is itself *already* expressive and nonoriginary.[1] We have here a formulation of consciousness not as the "expressed" but rather as expression, and "expression" not as mimesis but as performative.[2]

These considerations have several implications, concerning not only language, but also the ends and goals of all the kinds of movements and initiatives seen in *Molloy.* First of all, one might conclude that all of Molloy's wanderings are undertaken in the interest of going nowhere, just as all of Molloy's utterances are proffered in the interest of saying nothing, or perhaps of not having said.[3] This does not imply, for example, that Molloy does not wish to see his mother, but rather that the act of seeing his mother itself represents a certain return or restoration. Note that Molloy never does see her—given this structure, this is perhaps exactly his way of arriving at her. Second, one must examine the consideration of consciousness and concomitantly language as defensive and protective, geared not toward representation, expression, or even formulation of attitudes, ideas, or mental conditions, but rather toward production and constitution of these conditions. The concept of the auto-performative is yet another (and one of the most striking) in the long list of Beckettian figures of the subject's alterity, which we have been examining throughout. In addition, however, it calls our attention to everything invested in and accomplished by the act of discoursing over and above the expression of "content." In the context of the passage above, we are reminded that the continuation of the interminable Beckettian monologue, the "on" that survives the opposition of can't and can, is not simply an "expression" of the situation of the Beckettian "narrator," but is itself one of the "little adjustments" made "in order for nothing to be changed." In such circumstances, we must ask in relation both to linguistic discourse and physical motion exactly what a concept such as "on" might mean.

That is to say, if movement, change, and discourse are adjustments acted out to bring about stasis and constancy, they can no longer be symmetrically opposed to "contraries" such as immobility, stability, or silence. These seemingly opposed pairs must be read not as opposites, but rather as different movements and moves within a restricted economy of stasis. "Going on" is no longer the *opposite* of "standing still" but rather a *form* of standing still, a variation on standing still. Earlier on in *Molloy,* Beckett hints at this pseudo-equivalence when Molloy reflects: "For in me there have always been two fools, among others, one asking nothing better than to stay where he is and the other imagining that life might be slightly less horrible a little further on" (48). Indeed, the early Beckett seems concerned with a collapsing of the oppositions of coming and going, entering and exiting, progressing and regressing into a generalized movement—named by an anonymous narrator "gress" or "gression" (*More Pricks,* 38). This generalized movement is contrasted to generalized motionlessness. Later, the emphasis shifts to the collapsing of the opposition movement/stasis itself, seen vividly in the oxymoronic title of Beckett's last prose work, "Stirrings Still" (which also plays on "still" as temporal adverb). If in Beckett there is in fact a move from rendering coming and going equivalent, to rendering moving and staying equivalent, the implications for many Beckettian texts are considerable. In *The Unnamable,* for example, the final "I can't go on, I'll go on" alternative would have to be reread as a pseudo-alternative, giving us less the double bind than a form of nonchoice, of variations on the same. Yet, if any essential opposition is denied to the pair movement/stasis, their definition and delineation as differing modalities never ceases to obsess Beckett as a crucial task and decision. One might well ask how in Beckett "going on" can really be differentiated from "standing still," but let us not forget the pains Beckett takes to ask that question. If the difference between the two is far from certain, the question for Beckett is equally far from moot. Much of Beckett, and especially the later Beckett, can be read as an investigation into the possible meaning of "on" and "onwards," progress and regression, profit and loss, and finally better and worse, within an economy of dedifferentiation, repetition, and death.

Company is a text which raises many of the questions we have been considering so far concerning the status of "on" in Beckett, and the parallelisms Beckett draws between discoursing, walking, thinking, and surviving.

Among its series of strikingly luminous scenes, episodes of walking and trekking are prominent (they will be even more so in the following *Ill Seen Ill Said, Worstward Ho,* and "Stirrings Still"). The long walks of the hearer, his father, and his father's shade prepare the way for the crawling and eventually supine "fabler" with whom the story ends. As the "fabler" is figured as the "producer" (albeit nonoriginary) of the "fable" we read as *Company,* the constellation of tropes turning on movement, distance, return, and physical positionality is progressively linked to questions of discoursing, recounting, speaking and hearing—in short, of *narrative* positionality.

Company tells the story of four major "walks," in many ways similar, and their positionings with regard to the surrounding passages, along with the sense of seriality that emerges from their repetitiousness, make them one of the key elements in the sense of stasis, return, and incompletion which pervades the book. The first walk recounted occurs on the day of the hearer's birth and is undertaken by the hearer's father, who leaves for a daylong "tramp in the mountains" motivated by "his aversion to the pains and general unpleasantness of labour and delivery" (13). When he arrives back home ten hours later, he learns to his dismay that labour "was still in swing" (14), and he prepares to set off once more when the maid rushes to tell him, "it was over at last. Over!" (14). This passage gives a relatively rare Beckettian "realist" portrait of a cold and distant husband, unwilling or unable either to offer comfort to his wife or to tolerate his impotence in the face of her suffering, and not significantly moved by the imminence of the arrival of his offspring. It also puts into play in very subdued fashion certain ironies and queries more familiar in the Beckettian corpus. Immediately evident among them is the fact that the passage which describes our hero's birth terminates not on an inaugural note but with the word "Over!", complete with exclamation point. This is a familiar Beckettian take on life's promise and possibilities—the relationship to the inevitable closure of death, with which Beckett becomes increasingly concerned in the late texts, becomes the defining mark of entry into life. The passage also moves through the history of birth, delivery, and conception in a highly provocative way, which will lead into questions concerning artistic and intellectual conception and engendering. On the most literal level, it stages the absence of the father from the parental relationship in the starkest of terms. The moment of birth, which both links and separates the mother and child, in no way requires the presence of the father—in fact, the father cannot help but be excluded from the umbilical moment. The obvious absence of the father from gestation and birth leads to consideration of the venerable issue of the relationship of the father to the child he engenders, and that of "engendering" itself, which, in turn, is mirrored in *Company* by questions concerning the genesis and origin of the stories it tells, and the relationship between the recounting creator and recounted creature. The question of the link between father and son, begetter and begotten, and of its figuration in terms of a rhetoric of source and reflection, origin and copy, artist and artefact, goes back at least to Plato and unrelentingly onwards. As Stephen Dedalus says in Joyce's *Ulysses:*

> Fatherhood, in the sense of conscious begetting, is unknown to man. It is a mystical estate, an apostolic succession, from only begetter to only begotten. On that mystery and not on the madonna which the cunning Italian intellect flung to the mob of Europe the church is founded and founded irremovably because founded, like the world, macro and microcosm, upon the void. Upon incertitude, upon unlikelihood. *Amor matris,* subjective and objective genitive, may be the only true thing in life. Paternity may be a legal fiction. (170)

A close look at this passage from *Ulysses* would no doubt take us too far afield. However, Stephen's reflections on begetting, consciousness, incertitude, and "paternity as a legal fiction" are all neatly evoked by the opening sentence of the passage from *Company:* "You first saw the light in the room you most likely were conceived in" (12). The logistical collapsing of conception and birth, along with the father's deliberate absence by tramping, creates a complex tropological network of entrances, exits, lodgings, evictions, beginnings, and, as we saw, endings.[4] The passage, moving from conception to childbirth, from the sexual act to the father's wandering, stages the replacement of the father by the son in the conjugal bed and the mother's body, and depicts the father's response to this replacement—in terms quite reminiscent of *Ulysses*—as a kind of exile. However, if the passage echoes Dedalus's conception of paternity as an ideological effect of patriarchy—arbitrary, legalistic, and proprietary—*Company* differs on the question of *amor matris.* The very first of the recounted stories in the book details what is presented as an incomprehensible distance and lack of comprehension on the part of the mother toward the child when he asks her if the blue sky "is not in reality much more distant than it appears" (11). Receiving no answer, the child mentally reframes his question to ask if the sky "does not appear much less distant than in reality it is." The passage concludes: "For some reason you could never fathom this question must have angered her exceedingly. For she shook off your little hand and made you a cutting retort you have never forgotten" (11). The repetition of the same question in inverted form, and the pseudo-dialogue revolving around the establishment of distance and proximity in relation to the mother, seem archetypical of Beckett's concerns. In this anecdote concerned precisely with the very question of distance and proximity (that of the sky to the earth), the child no less than his father becomes the exile, and indeed, the figure of the exile, the expelled, the banished in Beckett's work does not seem to have been sufficiently explored. The relationship of "exile" to literary creation in Joyce is well known, but turning back to the passage from *Ulysses,* we should note that in his discussion of Shakespeare, Stephen explicitly links the question of paternity to that of artistic "begetting" and creation. In *Company,* the issue of the fabler, or creator as he is sometimes called, is foregrounded along with the entire question of literary or perhaps psychotic creation, and the relation that pertains between creator and creature. The casually dropped tag "darkness visible" (19) serves to call up the great *locus classicus* of this topic, *Paradise Lost,* which similarly treats it in strikingly oedipal terms.[5] Beckett also will deal with the question of engendering in literary and artistic terms in *Company,* along with literature's possible relationship to some sort of auto-engendering, which would effectively complete the replacement of the father inaugurated at conception.

This will be staged in the book's second great "tramp," which follows immediately on the heels of the first. The passage begins, "You are an old man plodding along a narrow country road. You have been out since break of day and now it is evening" (14), which recalls the ten-hour excursion of the hearer's father. The rather brief episode goes on to recount the hearer's pause to calculate the number of miles he has probably walked in his lifetime and ends as follows:

> Halted too at your elbow during these computations your father's shade. In his old tramping rags. Finally on side by side from nought anew. (15)

The episode, in relation to the previous, marks two important shifts: the hearer goes from newborn to old man, the father from quick to shade. Along with these shifts, we have the hearer depicted in a fashion which makes him greatly resemble his father as recounted in the first tramp. One imagines the hearer fleeing not the scene of a child's birth but that of his own, as he staggers toward his death. But rather than simply replace the father, the hearer also doubles and is doubled by his father. On the one hand, the image of the two relics walking side by side erases the generational difference, reinscribing the paternal relationship in a fraternal mode. The sense of shared exile, already hinted at, is reinforced; however, here we have not the classical Freudian scheme of brothers exiled by the autocratic father, but rather that of men exiled from the female body. In this respect, the juxtaposition of the issue of distance with that of the mother takes on its full resonance, along with Beckett's careful extension of the rhetoric of distance in the passage: "For some reason you could never *fathom*" (11, my emphasis). That the hearer walks, as we know his father did, and with his father's shade besides, in the *shadow* of his father, certainly heightens the sense of the hearer's repetition of his father, his assumption of his father's position. But note that he doesn't actually walk with his father, but with his father's *shade*—what the hearer has for company is not his father but his father's *death,* which follows him endlessly on his aimless tramping and accompanies his obsessive, useless calculations. The overtones of Hamlet are obvious and perhaps echo Stephen Dedalus once more. The hearer, then, is in no way unequivocally posited as the absent engenderer, or even the substitute for the engenderer in his absence. Still, this positioning will be suggested in a variety of ways in the text, most notably through its metadiscursive commentaries. The question of authorship is slyly introduced into this constellation by the phrase "nought anew," which seems to be an auto-citation by Beckett of *Murphy,* the first line of which reads, "The sun shone, having no alternative, on the nothing new" (1). Note that the passage in *Company* ends precisely with an absence of finality, with the Beckettian siglum of entropy and deferral, "on":[6] "Finally on side by side from the nought anew." The passage is both a consideration of the relationship with the father as a means of going on, in the senses of continuing and repeating, and a consideration of paternity as that which goes on, that which defeats finality and conclusion.

A few pages later, we are given another tramp by the hearer and his father's shade—one which seems a direct continuation of the previous. The episode begins "Nowhere in particular on the way from A to Z" (23) and briefly establishes a scene of wandering. I will quote slightly more than the last half of the episode in full:

> Nowhere in particular on the way from A to Z. Or say for verisimilitude the Ballyogan Road. . . . Father's shade to right and a little to the rear. So many times already round the earth. Topcoat once green stiff with age and grime from chin to insteps. Battered once buff block hat and quarter boots still a match. No other garments if any to be seen. Out

since break of day and night now falling. Reckoning ended on together from nought anew. As if bound for Stepaside. When suddenly you cut through the hedge and vanish hobbling east across the gallops. (23–24)

"Reckoning ended on together from nought anew" takes us back to the earlier tramp's "Finally on side by side from nought anew" (15). But what to make of this tramp's concluding interruption, of the apparent rupture of the measured, countable gait, and the stepping aside from Stepaside? Is this entire passage to be read as a side step, a di-gression or *parekbasis,* a moment where the "on"ward movement doubles back, or re-turns? John Freccero, in the context of Dante's journeying, has pointed out the "analogy between a literal journey and interpretation," and notes: "In the ancient world, this descent in search of understanding was known as a *katabasis*" (107). "Parabasis," then, is not only the irony of the "self-conscious narrator," or the "author's intrusion that disrupts the fictional illusion," as Paul de Man puts it (*Blindness and Insight,* 218–19). More pre-cisely, it is the irony that consists in the disruption of textual teleology and directionality, which turns away from the promised end or final mo-ment capable of the retroactive bestowal of meaning and significance on (for example) what otherwise might very well be a random collection of fragments or chance-ridden history.[7] This sort of stepping aside is always a part of the Beckettian "on" which affirms its impossibility of terminating, of reaching a suitable conclusion. "On" is always away and aside. Dante's wanderings represent both a digression from the right path and a journey inside himself. In exemplary Christian fashion, Dante recuperates his loss into greater gain at the end of the road. Beckett's irony is poignant in that he shares Dante's notion of the digressive interior journey, but figures it as interminable. Thus the logic behind Beckett's embracing of Dante's Belac-qua: in the *Commedia,* Purgatory is the only realm which allows change and transformation, and accordingly, a notion of movement and progress. The dominant figures of spacing and space in Purgatory are neither the pits, plains, and ice wastes of Hell nor the thrones and glowing rose petals of Heaven, but rather roads, paths, and passes. Belacqua, who chooses to sit rather than walk, is the figure who strives for stasis in the realm of change—a striving which, in the long view, is doomed. Every soul in Pur-gatory makes it to Paradise in "the end." Belacqua, then, could be seen as an antiteleological figure within the *Commedia,* as an allegorical figure of parabasis. Likewise, the Beckettian Ulysses is Dante's, who doesn't in the end stay returned to his proper place, except in the Hell which Beckettian protagonists lack and regret. Typically, Beckett throws his trope into convolutions—the hearer doesn't step aside; he steps aside from Stepaside, which perhaps means that he fails to digress. The irony is apparent and instructive: when we are forced to acknowledge that stepping aside from Stepaside might represent a failure to digress, we are no longer able to clearly define the difference between digression and progress, and thus, the allied differences between means and end, substance and ornament, or even literal and figural. The above suggestions may seem somewhat far-fetched, but immediately following the tramp discussed above comes a metadiscursive discussion dealing with just this sort of problem. The word "digression" imposes itself; if anything in the history of literature qualifies as "an author's intrusion which disrupts the fictional illusion," these bits from *Company* certainly do. I quote the passage in full:

> For why or? Why in another dark or in the same? And whose voice asking this? Who asks, Whose voice asking this? And answers, His so-ever who devises it all. In the same dark as his creature or in another. For company. Who asks in the end, Who asks? And in the end answers as above? And adds long after to himself, Unless another still. Nowhere to be found. Nowhere to be sought. The unthinkable last of all. Un-namable. Last person. I. Quick leave him. (24)

The baffling syntax of the beginning of this passage raises even more questions than those it expressly articulates. "For why or" may certainly refer to the "or" of "in another dark or in the same," which immediately follows and which has prior to this point already been used several times to describe the situation of the enigmatic "creator" or "devisor" (cf. *Company*, 8, 22). But this certainly does not explain the extremely unidiomatic "For why," whose very strangeness calls attention to the role of the word "or" generally in *Company*. Indeed, one of the book's principal stylistic traits could be called its "orness"—often two conflicting constatations of a given situation or condition will be placed on either side of an "or," with neither being assigned definitive validity. The "or," then, is one of the text's major devices for troubling ontological stability and grounding.[8] An obvious in-stance of such a troubling question is that of the location of the "creator," who is said to be "in another dark or in the same," but whenever this sort of "or" comes into play, regardless of the specific issue at hand, the cre-ator's role and position is foregrounded. We are constantly reminded that we are reading "somebody's" story and not, even with disbelief willingly suspended, a set of fictively true "facts." However, we are equally denied any sort of representation of the "process" of artistic creation, in which the author's "real choices" would be displayed—the "voice" that says "or" is as fictive, as "or-ridden," as his fictions, as the above passage, among others, makes clear. To escape from a naively mimetic reading of *Company*, it is necessary to look at the emphasis on the "or" as an emphasis more on the status of the subject of enunciation, rather than a focus on any particular fictive enunciator. This brings us back to the problems of fixing ultimate intentional finality to particular utterances that we examined in our readings of the trilogy. It also remains quite in line with de Man's reading of ironic authorial intrusion, the effect of which "is not a heightened realism, an affirmation of the priority of a historical over a fictional act. . . . The problem is familiar to students of point of view in a fictional narrative, in the distinction they have learned to make between the persona of the author and the persona of the fictional narrator. The moment when this difference is asserted is precisely the moment when the author does not return to the world" (*Blindness and Insight,* 219). Not only the inability either to return to or to leave the world, but indeed the drawing of boundaries that makes such a conceptualization possible, is one of the major questions of *Company*.

The "or," then, is a stylistic modality of the gyre of questions asking who asks, and who asks who asks—questions begging the rhetorical need to interminably step aside in favor of another enunciator. The passage, with its "ors" and its "whos," elucidates all the problems involved in asserting that one is not sidestepping, that meaning is anchored in origin and destination. If it is the "or" generally which is in question here, one particular instance of it of special interest to us is found in the previous tramp passage: "Nowhere in particular on the way from A to Z. Or say for verisimilitude the Ballyogan Road" (23). Here one may very well ask "For why or?" Why the shift to "verisimilitude"—hardly the dominant mood of the ghostly tramp passages. Why the shift from mythic generality to the specificity of the proper name, and the cultural, geographical, and linguistic baggage it carries? The Ballyogan Road seems to replace (although the "or" refuses to acknowledge this replacement as definitive) a generic "way from A to Z." This vaguely archetypal path, however, is strewn with a fair amount of baggage itself. First of all, "A to Z" implies teleology and completion—a path with a definite and identifiable beginning and end. Likewise, A to Z scan the trajectory of the alphabet. Once again, discoursing and wandering, linguistic acts and physical acts, seem to be placed in parallel. All of this is refused, or at least supplemented by the historical and linguistic particular, which in its play on "Stepaside" opens out again into the mythic-allegorical mode of wandering as writing/talking, and arriving as completion/meaning.

But as the "Who asks?" passage makes clear, arrival, completion, and meaning cannot be thought apart from departure, inauguration, and expression. The insistence of the passage on the interminable need of an other in narrative structure, which is to say linguistic structure, and the inability of any other to achieve finality, is familiar to any reader of *The Unnamable,* and indeed this book is alluded to by name, if such a paradoxical statement is permissible. The characterization of "I" not as first person but as *last* person is a perfectly clear articulation of the idea that as the "I" grounds enunciation it is as much a figure of finality as of origin, or more precisely, is the figuring of origin *as* finality, and vice versa. Unnamability is at least as much concerned with this imputed lastness as with any sort of primariness. The text's multitude of "ors" must then be considered not as tokens of verisimilitude, grounding the "last" first voice of the "author at work," but rather as supplements to lastness, as what comes "after" the "unthinkable" last voice.[9] This entire problematic is allegorized in the gradual collapsing of the "devisor" and the "devised" as the text progresses. In fact, the strategy of juxtaposing tramping, movement, directionality, and arrival with passages concerned with narrative directionality and stability will give way to a virtual collapsing of movement into discourse at the book's end.

The fourth tramp in *Company* marks a crucial point on this trajectory and establishes one of the most important divisions in the text. It comes almost exactly at the book's midpoint, and in terms of the "memories" that the voice recounts, it creates a break between those of childhood and those of maturity, signaled by the first words of the episode immediately following the tramp's conclusion, "Bloom of adulthood. Imagine a whiff of that" (38).[10] The text of this tramp and the "Bloom of adulthood" passage are also by far the two longest episodes of the book. The lingering question of lastness or finality is immediately raised by this passage: "The last time you went out the snow lay on the ground" (35). The passage goes on to recount a final traversing of a long familiar route, one which the hearer could at this point cover with eyes closed. It picks up several motifs and tags from the earlier tramps, informing us that the hearer no longer counts his steps, "For the simple reason they number each day the same. Average day in day out the same. The way being always the same. You keep count of the days and every tenth day multiply. And add" (36–37).

The hearer is also told, "Your father's shade is not with you any more. It fell out long ago" (37), and we learn that the hearer is plodding on "from nought anew" (37). The ending of this passage on ending, itself recounting a passage to ending, is of some significance for our purposes:

> The foot falls unbidden in midstep or next for lift cleaves to the ground bringing the body to a stand. Then a speechlessness whereof the gist, Can they go on? Or better, Shall they go on? The barest gist. Stilled when finally as always hitherto they do. You lie in the dark with closed eyes and see the scene. As you could not at the time. The dark cope of sky. The dazzling land. You at a standstill in the midst. The quarter boots sunk to the tops. The skirts of the greatcoat resting on the snow. In the old bowed head in the old block hat speechless misgiving. Halfway across the pasture on your beeline to the gap. The unerring feet fast. You look behind you as you could not then and see their trail. A great swerve. Withershins. Almost as if all at once the heart too heavy. In the end too heavy. (37–38)

Note the immediate concatenation this passage presents of motionlessness and speechlessness, followed by the question of "on": "Can they go on? Or better, Shall they go on?" The shift from "can" to "shall" asks to be read as a rewriting of the final pages of *The Unnamable* and implies an insufficiency of the Cartesian categories of possible and impossible in the consideration of "on." In other words, if the response to the question "Can they go on?" does not necessarily foreclose the question "Shall they go on?" one might presume that "on," in some manner, transcends the category of possibility. Thus, the juxtaposition "I can't go on, I'll go on" could perhaps be read not as an alternative, but rather as an oxymoronic constatation of "on-ness." We shall return to this idea in our examination of *Worstward Ho*. One should also note that once again "speechlessness" is differentiated from any metaphysical "silence"—it too has its "gist."[11]

Immediately striking in this passage, however, is its concern with lastness and finality. The question of lastness is tied here to subjectivity not through consideration of the "first last" person, the "I," but through the familiar Beckettian motif of self-apperception: "You lie in the dark with closed eyes and see the scene. As you could not at the time." If we have left the "unthinkable last of all" and remained with the "you," we have not abandoned the impossible attempt to think lastness, to know one's own lastness. Beckett here stages a crucial move away from *The Unnamable*: rather than try to speak lastness, in an enunciative moment of transcendent simultaneity (as hoped for by Malone and refused in *The Unnamable*), the arena of knowledge in *Company* and *Ill Seen Ill Said* is scopic. *Company,* by its insistence on the second person, begins by abandoning the desire to speak oneself, to speak as oneself: late in the text the voice confirms, "the first personal singular and a fortiori plural pronoun had never any place in your vocabulary" (61). The unthinkable last person will be replaced by a last eye, and indeed the enigmatic "know happiness" which closes *Ill Seen Ill Said* seems to refer more to the gluttonous, insatiable orb than to the old lady, in all probability devised herself for company. For this strange sort of autobiography, with its parade of images and sensations, the term "scopic" is preferable to any conception of "specularity" that one might be tempted to invoke. For *Company* is bereft of the exemplary autobiographical desire to reveal oneself to oneself, to make visible the obscure and give face to the faceless, to engender one's own double. The will to see is linked to an evident pleasure in the opacity of the visible. The text is devoid of all uncanny effects of strangeness and familiarity. Nothing returns. The most uncanny element of *Company* is its failure to be uncanny. To speak seeing, or more precisely, to have seeing spoken, is not so much a question of mimesis and the referential and evocative powers of language, but of repositioning the enunciative position and likewise the space of the subject of knowledge (and ignorance). The impossibility of any ultimate lastness of the deviser ("Yet another then. Of whom nothing. Devising figments to temper his nothingness. . . . Devised deviser devising it all for company" [46]) figured by the refusal of the "I," is echoed by the eye's inability to receive its visions, to invest them with something beyond their own glistening brilliance. Because of this, the shift of object from the apparently autobiographical in *Company* to the clearly fanciful in *Ill Seen Ill Said* is wholly logical—the autobiographical moment in *Company* never is given, not even in the habitual form of disguise, denial, or displacement. The narcissism of self-apperception or displaced identification gives way to a properly spectacular narrative desire to see the end. One of the early passages which set the ground rules for *Company* states the impossibility of the first person in terms which clarify this shift:

> Use of the second person marks the voice. That of the third that cankerous other. Could he speak to and of whom the voice speaks there would be a first. But he cannot. He shall not. You cannot. You shall not. (8)

The impossibility of the first person comes not only from the impossibility of self-reference ("of whom"), but equally from the impossibility of auto-address ("to whom"). The question is not only one of memory and self-knowledge, of speaking "truthfully" and accurately about one's past, but also of the capacity to speak to oneself, to hear oneself, to witness one's own identifications and subjective positionings. In this sense the "to" is prior to any "of," and perhaps this is why Beckett places it first. In any case, it is just this sort of witnessing which is missing from *Company* and which makes a theoretical impossibility of the "addition to company" consisting of: "A voice in the first person singular. Murmuring now and then, Yes I remember" (16). It would be equally impossible to have a voice say, "No, I don't remember."

The narrative movement of *Company,* itself unfurled before the hooded eye of the hearer that it moves, devising the deviser by whom it has been devised, cannot end with a subjective moment of recognition ("Yes I remember") or even its denial, nor with a completed enunciation, as every enunciation begs another enunciator ("And whose voice asking this? Who asks, Whose voice asking this?"). The book has no choice but to tramp "on," and this is exactly what it does, in a final motionless tramp which feigns to merge the identity of the recounted hearer with the deviser who recounts.

As the text moves toward its close, increasing attention is given to the deviser. The deviser's situation is narrated by a third-person voice (thus necessitating a "new" deviser to accomplish this narration), which considers his location, habitation, motivations for "devising," and means of locomotion. Specifically, the deviser crawls, "from nought anew" (49), while attempting to sum up the distances he has covered. As the third-person descriptions of the deviser increasingly come to verbally echo the second-person descriptions of the hearer, it is not surprising to see the "crawling creator" eventually end up in a position highly evocative of that of the hearer. Several episodes recount his crawling and falling, until finally he finishes lying prone alone in the dark (56). The temptation here is to conclude that the deviser has been the hearer all along, pretending not to recognize his own memories and history. However, the hearer lies not prone but supine—the first page of *Company* tells that the hearer lies "on his back" (7), a position explicitly denied to the deviser. At this point, we have the prone deviser and the supine hearer, each in search of company, and if the "hearer" has been "devised," the deviser is devised no less. We are told he is "Devising it all himself included for company" (43), and later, after the deviser abandons the idea of naming the hearer M and himself W, we read, "Even M must go. So W reminds himself of his creature so far created. W? But W too is creature. Figment" (45). It is in this situation that we are given the book's final passage. Written in the second person, it addresses the hearer and takes as its starting point the inability to tramp. This final paragraph, which poses as a myth of the genesis of the text of *Company,* proposes that fabling is, in fact, inaugurated by the end of tramping. It begins as follows:

> Somehow at any price to make an end when you could go out no more you sat huddled in the dark. Having covered in your day some twenty-five thousand leagues or roughly thrice the girdle. And never once overstepped a radius of one from home. Home! . . . The place is windowless. . . . Thus you now on your back in the dark once sat huddled there your body having shown you it could go out no more. . . . With at your elbow for long years your father's shade in his old tramping rags and then for long years alone. Adding step after step to the ever mounting sum of those already accomplished. Halting now and then with bowed head to fix the score. Then on from nought anew. (60–61)

At this point, readers will probably expect the deviser to recount to the hearer how he came to be in the situation in which he was found in the book's first pages. We will not be disappointed, but the trajectory is incompleted with typical Beckettian subtlety. Just as the crawling creator entered into an oscillation between crawling and falling before finally settling prone, here the hearer oscillates between sitting and lying supine before finally lying to rise no more:

> From time to time with unexpected grace you lie. Simultaneously the various parts set out. The arms unclasp the knees. The head lifts. The legs start to straighten. The trunk tilts backward. And together these and countless others continue on their respective ways till they can go no further and together come to rest. Supine now you resume your fable where the act of lying cut it short. And persist till the converse operation cuts it short again. So in the dark now huddled and now supine you toil in vain. And just as from the former position to the latter the shift grows easier in time and more alacrious so from the latter to the former the reverse is true. Till from the occasional relief it was supineness becomes habitual and finally the rule. You now on your back in the dark shall not rise to your arse again to clasp your legs in your arms and bow down your head till it can bow down no further. But with face upturned for good labour in vain at your fable. (61–62)

This passage marks a crux in the story. It is the first time the hearer, rather than the deviser, is referred to as engaged in fabling, and in this way, the tables are effectively turned; the hearer is no longer the mythic creation of a lonely deviser, but rather the creating deviser is the fable of a lonely hearer. The turn needs to be savored: we move from the fable of a deviser devising a creature for company, to a fable of a "figment" devising a creature/creator who would have created him. Here we rejoin the early focus on the father, as the hearer's fable consists in creating his own creator. If a common autobiographical fantasy is to in some way write one's being, and thus engender oneself (Whitman is a good example of this), the fabler oddly writes not his own double but a father/begetter/deviser, who in turn "speaks" him. The deviser no longer devises his double for company—the text refuses the somewhat trite staging of the autobiographical impulse it at times feigns to present. In the final paragraph, the writing-drive, or fabling-drive, is precisely a drive to be fabled, or written. This is how the text concludes:

> Till finally you hear how words are coming to an end. With every inane word a little nearer to the last. And how the fable too. The fable of one with you in the dark. The fable of one fabling of one with you in the dark. And how better in the end labour lost and silence. And you as you always were.
> Alone. (62–63)

The little odyssey of trampings and crawlings, speeches and silences, ends in stasis and repetition: "And you as you always were." The book, with its strategies, calculations, retractions, and reconsiderations could perhaps be seen as one of Molloy's "adjustments" insuring that nothing be changed. Indeed, the text highlights the continuity between going out, going on, and fabling on, devising on. The stasis is presented as the best alternative to an approaching "end" which must remain unknowable. We are promised that the "fable" is petering out: "Till finally you hear how words are coming to an end." However, the fable's ending can only be told within the fable—not only because it must be printed in the text, but because the promise seems to be said by the voice whose very existence constitutes the fable's core. The haunting feel of the end of *Company*, I think, comes less from the somewhat Borgesian reversal, in which the "author" is shown to be in truth a creation of its "character," than from the reversal of investments it enacts. The hearer is no longer the figure of the author's projections of his life into fiction, of the self-representing "characters" he creates, and the deviser is no longer the figure of the author's perverse need to create and populate. Instead, the hearer becomes a projection of the authorial position, and the deviser the projection of the "character." The author, then, to the extent this fable is allowed to hold, is motivated by the fantasy of not being the author—of a voicelessness and unnamability so acute they can only be proclaimed by an other in the realm of the figural. The hearer and deviser seem obvious figures of the scission of the subject into speaker and spoken, recounter and recounted,[12] and the echoes progressively linking the two serve to reinforce this impression. But the text in the end never does assert that the crawling creator came to lie on his back in the dark and fable a voice coming to him—he remains prone. Likewise, when the hearer is identified as source of the fable, it is by the second-person voice which his fabling would logically have had to have created.[13] We have a repetition of the complexities of the relationship between Molloy and Moran—in *Company* not only have we no secure grounds for concluding that the deviser is a figure for the hearer, or vice versa, we can't even be sure in the end that they really refer to the same person. The identification of the hearer as fabler renders the status of the voice that says "And you as you always were. Alone" as wholly undecidable as that of the voice that has been saying "he" throughout—after all we could be listening here to the deviser's fantasy. We don't simply have a representation of language splitting a single subject into two—apparently, within the ontology of the text the deviser and hearer "really are" two, or perhaps none. In the end, we the readers are as we always were: in ignorance concerning the figural grounding of the text, clearly within the allegorical, but unable to differentiate the figures from the referents, the vehicles from the tenors, the destinations from the digressions. Like the hearer and the deviser, we end only with a sense of distance traversed—we can count sentences and images as they count paces. At the end of *Company* it is not clear what, if anything, has happened, but it seems fair to say something has gone *on*—the word itself is inscribed in the text's concluding "Alone."

Worstward Ho begins with the word "On" (7), and the text can be read as an example of sheer directionality. If the title indicates that the goal of this onward movement is the "worst," the worst "itself" can only be a direction and never a place. As Alan Astro puts it, "one can only go 'worst*ward*,' toward the worst, without hope of attaining it. For what is worse: the worst, or what is almost the worst? The almost-the-worst is less perfect, and therefore worse than the worst" (204). Therefore, the goal must be, as the text often words it, "better worse" (8) rather than worst. On the first page, the text states the desire and imperative to "Fail better" (7), and in this way the book is clearly an extension of and meditation on the "Three Dialogues" and the paradox of failure as goal. How does one "fail better"? If the goal is the worst, which is better: "better worse" or "worse worse"? These are not idle questions. If one takes failure as one's end (in all the senses of the word), as Astro makes clear, "worse" is a "better worse" than "worst." But is not a "better worse," by the fact of being better, necessarily a "worse worse"? And if it is, doesn't this worseness then make it better, which would, in turn, worsen it, ad infinitum? If one's goal is the worst, how can the terms "better" or "worse" remain operative? If they are used in the absence of their operations, what is then mobilized? Beckett seems to be sketching a movement toward loss, the arrival at which could resist being rearticulated as gain. The paradox seems identical to the one "B" fails to solve in the "Three Dialogues," when after asserting that "to be an artist is to fail" (*Disjecta*, 145), he refuses to make of "fidelity to failure" (145) a condition of success. "B"'s question could be phrased, How can one simply fail without succeeding at failure? As Leslie Hill elegantly puts it, "What Beckett refuses here is the dialectical sleight-of-hand by which negativity is converted into deferred positivity and the failure of rhetoric into a rhetoric of failure" (122).[14] "Worseness" can only be a movement, a rhythm, which horribly must include moments of its own amelioration. Thus, Beckett must celebrate/lament, "The words too whosesoever. What room for worse! How almost true they sometimes almost ring! How wanting in inanity! Say the night is young alas and take heart" (21). In these respects, *Worstward Ho* is not only an extension of the "Three Dialogues," but also a subtle revision of some of its treatment of this question.[15] In the crucial dialogue on Bram van Velde, "B" states, "There is more than a difference of degree between being short, short of the world, short of self, and being without these esteemed commodities. The one is a predicament, the other not" (143). Although equally concerned with loss and impossibility in the later text, Beckett seems more cagey concerning the dangers of speaking of loss and absence in absolutist terms, and the Hegelianism lurking in the qualitative distinction between being "short of" and "without." In *Worstward Ho,* he writes:

Worse less. By no stretch more. Worse for want of better less. Less best. No. Naught best. Best worse. No. Not best worse. Naught not best worse. Less best worse. No. Least. Least best worse. Least never to be naught. Never to naught be brought. Never by naught be nulled. Unnullable least. Say that best worse. With leastening words say least best worse. For want of worser worst. Unlessenable least best worse. (32)

If "least never to be naught" is here a better worse than the "without" of 1949's "Three Dialogues," the litany of "nos" in this passage should make us aware of another type of directionality in *Worstward Ho*, for just as "ward" puns on "word," "no" is simply "on" read backwards:[16] "Back is on. Somehow on" (37), as the book puts it. But "on" read back and backward is also "no," the note with which the text finishes: "Said nohow on" (47). "On" and "no" are not only mirrors of each other—they are graphic marks whose difference is established through the decision taken concerning the direction from which to approach their letters: this in a text which emphasizes "back" and which hints that going on and back amount to the same.[17] The movement "on" is less an opposition to than a modality of the "no" of the celebrated Beckettian negativity. When Didi and Gogo exclaim that there is "nothing to be done," they are not relieved from doing—they simply do nothing rather than something. "On," by moving "no" backwards, likewise "does" the nothing, attempting to delicately extend in a modality that would escape either affirmation or negation. That this play is staged graphically means *Worstward Ho* is also about the movement through and the reversal of letters and phonemes, progressing toward a word that can only be a "ward"—a direction of the "worst" and a ward of "wardness," of the inconclusiveness of directionality. This is a Wakeian progress, stagings of graphic "ricorsi."[18]

Like *Company* and *Ill Seen Ill Said*, *Worstward Ho* is meticulous in its questionings of the origins of the language and images we are given, and of the mediation of the latter by the former. The very first paragraph supplements "Say on," with "Be said on," before introducing the opposition implicitly maintained throughout between "no" and "on": "Said nohow on" (7). The next paragraph clarifies the situation: "Say for be said. Missaid. From now say for be missaid" (7). We can take this to mean that when we read "say" we should not assume someone "saying" but rather something "being said," and moreover, being missaid. Naturally, this implies the usual inscrutability of the voice's origin and doubts as to its accuracy, but the fact that "say" is allowed to remain even as shorthand suggests Beckett's understanding that the myth of words saying themselves is really the symmetrical inverse of the metaphysical conception of a full subjectivity as origin of meaning. The crux for Beckett, from *Molloy* through the end, is that there has to be a "saying," an enunciation, regardless of the status of the enunciator. In *Worstward Ho,* Beckett addresses the site of the saying in these terms: "On back better worse to fail the head said seat of all. Germ of all. All? If of all of it too" (19). If *Worstward Ho* is being devised by a head for company then the devising head must be a device itself. The "Who asks?" of *Company* must then be asked again:

> Whose words? Ask in vain. Or not in vain if say no knowing. No saying. No words for him whose words. Him? One. No words for one whose words. One? It. No words for it whose words. Better worse so. (20)

Later, we will be told that "it" doesn't "say" but rather "secretes" words impossible to understand, "No knowing what it is the words it secretes say. No saying. No saying what it all is they somehow say" (30). The secreted words come increasingly to be called "ooze," and in reference to the longed-for end, "No ooze for when ooze gone" (41). "Gone," although unsayable, unimaginable, and unoozable, is depicted as the impossible best worse of all:

> Gnawing to be gone. Less no good. Worse no good. Only one good. Gone. Gone for good. Till then gnaw on. All gnaw on. To be gone. (42)

If there is "no ooze for when ooze gone," gone can't be given in the text. "Gone" will have been said, as its only mode of existence is its saying, but it will have been missaid:

> Said is missaid. Whenever said said said missaid. From now said alone. No more from now now said and now missaid. From now said alone. Said for missaid. For be missaid. (37)

This missaying is not opposed to a truth, to a true-saying to be mourned or sought after. "Gone" can't "go" — "can't go on" both does and doesn't continue, neither appears nor disappears. The text began, "On. Say on. Be said on. Somehow on. Till nohow on. Said nohow on" (7), which implies that the text will somehow go on until it can no way go on, or that it will tell of a nearly impossible going on, until it reaches the true impossibility of going on. However, the final words of the book belie this structure:

> Enough. Sudden enough. Sudden all far. No move and sudden all far. All least. Three pins. One pinhole. In dimmost dim. Vasts apart. At

bounds of boundless void. Whence no farther. Best worse no farther. Nohow less. Nohow worse. Nohow naught. Nohow on.

Said nohow on. (47)

The addition of the culminating sentence shows that this passage oozes not that the end has come, but that the end has been said. We haven't moved from going on to not going on, but from having said somehow on to having said nohow on. However, let us remember that "said is missaid"—the text ends not in an oozeless silence, but in the afinality of the missaying of an ending. The movement toward loss and death is a movement through language and within language. *Worstward Ho* proposes "Blanks for when words gone" (41), while acknowledging there is "Nothing save what they [words] say" (29). *Ill Seen Ill Said* can tell of the eye's final closing, but *Worstward Ho* eschews the temptation of oozing the end of oozing—it chooses to ooze of the end oozing. In *Ill Seen Ill Said*, Beckett writes in the last paragraph "Farewell to farewell," which can perhaps be taken as Beckett's leave-taking of the leave-takings which comprise so much of the burden of all three books of the trilogy, "Waiting for Godot," and many other works.[19] I have been arguing that by focusing on saying and missaying, *Worstward Ho* indeed refuses the farewell that Beckett had claimed to have finished with. However, the situation is somewhat complicated by Beckett's final text, "Stirrings Still."

"Stirrings Still" can be seen as something of a coda to the late trilogy. It stages a wandering over a grass field inevitably reminiscent of *Company* and makes several verbal allusions to both *Ill Seen Ill Said* and *Worstward Ho*. Both works seem to be evoked in the sentence, "Then he sought help in the thought of one hastening westward at sundown to obtain a better view of Venus and found it of none" (*As the Story was Told*, 122).[20] However, "Stirrings Still" is undeniably a farewell, giving us from its inception the case of an unnamed man bidding farewell to himself: "One night as he sat at his table head on hands he saw himself rise and go" (113). But the end it gives us is precisely ending without end. As opposed to *Company*, the text focuses on the uncanny and finds the uncanny aspect of the final grass field to reside in its boundlessness, or endlessness: "For he could recall no field of grass from even the very heart of which no limit of any kind was to be discovered but always in some quarter or another some end in sight such as a fence or other manner of bourne from which to return" (123). As his ears and eyes move "from bad to worse" (123–24), he moves "on through the long hoar grass resigned to not knowing where he was or how he got there or where he was going or how to get back to whence he knew not how he came. So on unknowing and no end in sight" (125). His undirected onward tramp, "no end in sight," is only interrupted when he stops to listen:

So on till stayed when to his ears from deep within oh how and here a word he could not catch it were to end where never till then. Rest then before again from not long to so long that perhaps never again and then again faint from deep within oh how and here that missing word again it were to end where never till then. (126)

Having stopped his tramping in order to (fail to) hear, he is faced with a decision:

Was he then now to press on regardless now in one direction and now in another or on the other hand stir no more as the case might be that is as that missing word might be which if to warn such as sad or bad for example then of course in spite of all the one and if the reverse then of course the other that is stir no more. (127–28)

It is in this dilemma that we leave him:

"Such and much more such the hubbub in his mind so-called till nothing left from deep within but only ever fainter oh to end. No matter how no matter where. Time and grief and self so-called. Oh all to end" (128).

The ending of "Stirrings Still" gives us almost all the major motifs of the late trilogy condensed and compacted. The final question of whether it is less worse to stay still or to move on actually echoes Molloy's "two fools," and the directionlessness and interminability of the deathward wandering ("now in one direction now in another") finely tunes the tramps of *Company* and the mock stoicism of *Worstward Ho*. But at the end of the end, Beckett gives us again the old standby of the voice, the ear, and the word. The ending is neither the absolute silence evoked by *The Unnamable* nor the transcendent transcription longed for by Malone. We end with the word, but in its indistinguishability. We end not with silence but with the audibility of the word's missingness—an audibility linked with that strange alternative (already in the title) which is perhaps not one, to either stay still or to stir. To hear that the word is not there, to hear the word that is not there, seems close to hearing or uttering the "missaying" which at the end of *Worstward Ho* "says" "nohow on." "Missaying" and "mishearing," of course, block all conceptions of both perfect expression and perfect comprehension, with an insistent blockage that disallows even the conceptualization of any "true" saying or hearing to which these "errors" could be opposed. The "deep within" will make itself (mis)heard, and silence is only the sound of the word's inaudibility. The movement of language and listening again goes on where the movement of tramping seems to leave off. "Oh all to end," the story ends, in its nonsilence. One thinks of another Beckettian speculation concerning what can come after speech, another positing of a destination which is not silence, this time from the *Texts for Nothing:* "But first stop talking and get on with your weeping" (105). A few sentences later, however, we are told that tears cannot be the right "tone," being too easy, as easy as "mirth." The text ends with a pledge to tell stories, in a phrase where the promise is simultaneous with the discoursing gift and curse: "I give you my word" (105).

Conclusion

Canceling Spaces

"All I say cancels out, I'll have said nothing," (*Stories,* 28) says Beckett's nameless narrator of "The Calmative." And it is difficult indeed to state the sum of the achievements of an author who so consistently strove for erasure, to constantly say in order to have finally said nothing. To claim, as one might be tempted, that he said *the* nothing serves only to bestow the kind of negative solidity which Beckett wished to deny. There is no nothing in Beckett—ultimately, it is only for this reason that it is possible not to say anything. And if Beckett's work is to be seen as a subtraction, it is not a subtraction of the world or the self but only of their own positings. Throughout this study, I have attempted to bring into focus the marks or traces left by this effort of subtraction, and I believe the most effective critical reading of Beckett might perhaps take the form of a charting or mapping, similar to the calculations he so often gives us, especially in the later texts, of the endless tramps which mark terrain without creating a destination. The intertextual overlappings, to say nothing of the intratextual circlings, repetitions, and overweavings, create an abundance of paths and figures which I have not been able even to begin to trace here.

Thus, my emphasis on Beckett's investigations of subjectivity and consciousness in the prose has not been an effort to anchor these potential drifts to a fixed and stable theoretical question, even if for local strategic reasons this may at times seem to be the case. On the contrary, my desire has been to show how scrupulous Beckett is in refusing to allow traditional

philosophical, literary, historical, and psychoanalytic notions of subjectivity, consciousness, or intention to be turned into bulwarks of meaning
to orient, control, and finally recuperate the oscillations of erasure. If the
metaphysical subject remains a crucial issue for Beckett, it is largely because its deconstruction is necessary for the textual movements to be freed
from an ideal tether that would prohibit their flux. But of course, to de-
construct the subject in such a fashion bestows a necessarily "textual" constitution upon it also. It is for these reasons that the issue of the Beckettian
"subject" cannot be separated from that of the Beckettian text.

In the prose, the textual space or staging ground for the "self-canceling"
operations is most often the remnants of the metaphysical subject, while
in the theater the staging ground is of course quite literally the stage.
This implies that for Beckett prose and theater are not simply two different "media" for examining the question of the "subject." Rather, I would
like to suggest that the structuring role often occupied by the "subject" in
the prose is taken by the literal materiality of the scenic space in the theater, that in many respects the "subject" of the prose is replaced not by
the "character" but by the *stage* in the theater. Such an equivalence seems
improbable only until one remembers that in the Cartesian philosophical tradition within which Beckett writes, the "materiality" of subjectivity
can only be experienced linguistically, that the subject *is* language. This
means that novelistic space, being predicated on language, is necessarily
dependent on the enunciating subject as the space of narrative as much as
theater is predicated upon the space of the stage.

One immediate implication of such a framework would be a cau-
tion against establishing an equivalence between the Beckettian narrating
subject-effects as given in the trilogy or the *Texts,* for example, and the
"characters" we might find on his stage. For example, it seems to me a
mistake to assimilate "Mouth" in "Not I" to such a narrating instance, for
"Mouth" is *herself* staged, by the lighting and blocking, of course, but even
more so by the observing, listening "Auditor" that the play also stipulates.
An emphasis on "Mouth" as "character" would lead to the psychologism
that we saw was inadequate to account for the prose "voices"—rather, it is
the economy enacted by the entire circuit Mouth-Auditor-staging which
would perhaps provide an appropriate parallel to the circular disavowals
of the voice-effects in the major prose. The *character* "Mouth" functions
much more like the "mannikins" of the prose, the entire stage scene needing to be examined to judge of possible proximity to the prose subject-
effect.[1] Moreover, a reading stressing the stage personae as "mannikins" is

consonant with Beckett's fabled impatience with his actors' attempts to understand the "psychology" of the roles they were interpreting—these roles are markers within a larger problematic, not "people."

A brief look at *Ohio Impromptu* can also help us begin to see what sort of issues would need to be theorized in a full-scale analysis of the relationship between Beckett's theater and prose. In a brilliant recent reading of the play, H. Porter Abbott has shown that it gives us what he calls a "literary convention" turned "inside out" (*Beckett Writing Beckett*, 165–83). Abbott sees the play as a reversal of a classic topos of the nineteenth-century novel: the night at the theater. There, the real spectacle is of course not the performance of the players but that of the audience of social players—coming to be seen and to be seen being seen. Meanwhile, the gradations of the theater's seats allow the novelist to place the entire economic scope of his or her society in a space "sufficiently compact to be commanded by the eye" (166). The oscillation between the characters' drama and that on the stage accords the novelist an ideal space for bravura effects of narrative orchestration, ironic juxtaposition, and ekphrastic figuration. *Ohio Impromptu,* however, with its "Reader," "Listener," and book, gives us just the opposite, literally *staging* a scene of reading: "Point for point, the situation in *Ohio Impromptu* is an absolute inversion of the nineteenth-century device of *theatrum theatri*. Where the latter was a prose-narrative presentation of the arena of staged performance, the former is a staged presentation of the arena of prose narrative" (169). The novelistic night at the theater takes an eminently public and social spectacle and internalizes it within the covers of a book, offering it to the private, protected, and idealized space of the reader's consciousness—that which is by conventional definition unavailable to another without mediation (of course, in Beckett that space is unavailable to the self meant to live it without mediation, but this is another matter). The point here, as Abbott makes clear, is that the theater scene is not coincidentally public—we are not dealing with a contingent question of generic form—its entire meaning derives from its social role as public event. This in contrast to the "mind" of the subject as traditionally conceived within a ubiquitous nineteenth-century framework, that is, that which is ineluctably private, incommunicable, unspectacular, fundamentally unknowable for another despite any and all wishes for expression or exteriorization. Thus, the traditional romantic pathos of being locked in solitude, which, though evocative of it, is in the end very different from the Beckettian problem of being haunted by company.

Now, one of the earliest explicit linkages of *reading* to this kind of interiority is found in book 6 of Augustine's *Confessions,* where the author observes with some surprise Ambrose reading the bible to himself, silently: "When he read, his eyes scanned the page and his heart explored the meaning, but his voice was silent and his tongue was still" (114). This practice was apparently somewhat unusual, as Augustine ventures various hypotheses as to why Ambrose would choose to read silently, "to himself" only, and not for the hearing of others (114). But within the structure of Augustine's story the event is extremely significant for other reasons, for in this chapter also devoted to the evils of the theater, we learn that Ambrose's chief message was "*The written law inflicts death, whereas the spiritual law brings life*" (116, emphasis in original). Thus, reading to oneself means an internalization of the text, a "spiritualization" in the literal sense of the word, that is, the animation or the giving of life to the letter, and a privileging of interior, ideal meaning over material sign, for Ambrose's great intellectual achievement, as far as Augustine was concerned, was precisely his ability to disclose "the spiritual meaning of texts which, taken literally, appeared to contain the most unlikely doctrines" (116).

Ohio Impromptu casts this entire scene into derision. First of all, by staging the ideally identical pair "Listener" and "Reader," like so much of the prose it figures reading to oneself, like talking to oneself, not as ideal subjective self-presence, but rather subjective doubling and division. And by the very act of placing this figure in the theater, the play takes the incommunicable, necessarily private space of the inner world of reading, in which the "voice" of our consciousness fuses with the text we read, and stages it precisely as perceptible — as spectacle for another. If the novelistic "night at the theater" is in some ways voyeuristic — offering the specularity of the public space to a reader who is removed and protected from it — *Ohio Impromptu* reverses this situation through its structural paranoia, in which the inner voice of the soul is materialized as dead letter (as emphasized by the "Listener"'s demands for repetition) and given to be overheard. The translation of sign into meaning and letter into spirit implied by Ambrose's silent reading is here reversed — the silent soliloquy of the voice of the soul is doubled into the roles of hearer and listener, aurally materialized, and proffered as an object necessitous of interpretation to an audience, as we shall see, comprised of specialists. Thus in *Ohio Impromptu* Beckett does not only stage reading, but also presents reading and the written book as a stage, and indeed Beckett's prose can be seen as the other stage of the theater, its double where the ubiquitous searching "eye" of the drama uncannily returns in the form of its homonymous siglum: the no less searching hearing/speaking "I" of the novels.

Ohio Impromptu was written specially for a conference devoted to Beckett's work, and Abbott subtly elucidates many of the ways in which the play seems specifically to address its initial performance situation, through complex winks at an audience of Beckett experts and through its presentation of a somewhat scholarly scene of reading and interpretation. James Knowlson's biography only confirms Abbott's intuition, as there Knowlson reports that Beckett himself acknowledged the metonymical thrust of certain details that could not leave an audience of Beckett specialists unmoved: the "Latin Quarter" hat and the "Isle of Swans" were references to Joyce.[2] *Ohio Impromptu* was first performed before its specialized audience only three years after the first Beckett biography was published, and also seems, as Abbott has argued about *Company* (18–19), an attempt to respond to and play with a new biographical intertext against which Beckett knew his work would now inevitably be read. By its deliberate appeal to the legibility of this new text through the details mentioned above, the scene of *Ohio Impromptu* takes place before a different other stage where Beckett and Joyce, grown into indistinguishable ancient relics, read out to each other the texts of their own lives, as Beckett so often had in predictable doubling fashion read aloud Joyce's text to Joyce himself years earlier. *Finnegans Wake,* for its part, destroys on the level of the sentence and the word the ideal readerly interiority, or the "spiritualization" of text out of letter and into meaning, as insistently as any piece of "literature" ever conceived.

The cursory readings above are only hints at how to begin investigating the status of narrative, "character," and language in the theater in view of the issues we have explored in the prose; evidently, they leave the crucial question of the theater's ocular, aural, and physical space untouched. A working hypothesis for an investigation of these aspects of Beckett's theater would be to shift from Descartes to Berkeley and examine to what extent "ocular proof" is there challenged in analogous ways to the attacks on the linguistic cogito in the prose. Such an approach seems especially promising with regard to "Film" and the television plays, where the entire scenic space is compressed into an easily voided screen. On the other hand, the radio plays present obvious difficulties to such a tactic and, given the provisos mentioned in the introduction, probably lend themselves primarily to the kinds of analyses conducted on the prose. In addition to redrawing conventional genre boundaries, such a study would also need to continue to investigate the role of language and echo as a kind of supplement to the problematics of vision and reflection in the drama; subsequently, an examination of the question of vision as it doubles speech in the prose would be a necessary extension to what I have undertaken here. In this way the Beckettian stage in the largest sense could begin to be constructed, within the space of all the irreducible local differences.

Yet if different stages offer themselves for Beckett's erasures, these stages are never empty or void; if the goal of the works is for all to be erased, the traces of the acts of erasure are left in exquisite definition. And what these traces leave as legible is precisely their status as trace, their incompletion, their unfinishedness. Thus the celebrated difficulty of "extracting" meaning from the Beckettian text, but also the palimpsestic, overdetermined economy of the prose, always winding elsewhere, resonating, looking forward and back. The result is the paradox facing critic or reader that in spite of an evident "meaninglessness" due to the erasure of all final meanings that could anchor or solve the text, and thus a resistance to interpretation, Beckett's works overflow with local "meanings" derived from an enormous variety of the dominant discourses of Occidental culture, which beg for comment. One feels at once that there is no work to be done, and an enormous amount of work to do. No less than Joyce, Beckett gives us an inventory of the detritus from which we write ourselves, but without proffering the lure of a circling, winding list, ever spiraling back toward itself as it curls away. Beckett instead offers variations of the possible rhythms of these possible inscriptions, as they extend, replace, and preserve themselves and us in their wake: all forms of sanies, disjecta and precipitates, the static record of Echo's bones, the sound of feet as they had fallen, all that fall.

Notes

All page citations for Beckett works are from the Grove Press editions listed in the Bibliography, unless otherwise noted.

Introduction

1. "As a rule, man's attitude is one of refusal. Man reared up against the movement that was carrying him away but in so doing only hurried it along, made its speed dizzying" (Bataille, 69; my translation).

2. See Dickinson, 246.

3. See Trezise for a notable example. The first page of his preface asserts "There may well be no writer of this century who has more radically questioned the foundations of humanism than Samuel Beckett" (ix), and in his conclusion, he stresses the prominence of "compulsion" and "powerlessness" over "freedom" and "power" (168).

4. Beckett, *Disjecta*, 139.

5. The differences effaced between, say, Derrida and Lacan, by including them under a blanket designation such as "poststructuralism," are obvious. When I refer to "poststructuralism," I refer in no way to something I would consider to be a unified or coherent body of thought, but rather to an amalgam of critical and theoretical questionings which in *Anglo-American* criticism have been grouped together. The issue is largely one of institutional reception, and when I mention "poststructuralist" approaches, I am employing a shorthand reference to a certain group of writers and issues, and not a descriptive term.

6. In addition to the two books mentioned above, notable recent works on Beckett relying heavily on literary theory or philosophy include books by Alan Astro, Richard Begam, Stephen Connor, Carla Locatelli, Thomas Trezise, and David Watson. Connor's book was the first to appear, in 1988. In addition, one could mention recent books in French by Bruno Clément and Michel Bernard.

7. Trezise, for example, argues that Beckett's prose "reflects moreover his fundamental affinity with such relatively marginal but important figures as Georges Bataille and Maurice Blanchot and, a generation later, the more publicized philosophers of difference, Gilles Deleuze and Jacques Derrida" (5).

8. See, for example, L. A. C. Dobrez's "Samuel Beckett and the Impossibility of Lit. Crit." Other typical examples would be this passage from Hill, referring to the plethora of critical approaches, "To write on Beckett after all this implies rashness, obstinacy, even naivety. What remains to be said?" (ix) or Astro's admission "A new book on the subject [Samuel Beckett] could hardly be totally original" (xi).

9. See Derrida, *Acts of Literature*, 60–61.

10. Again unambiguously stated by Hill: "This book would not have been written were it not for some frustration or dissatisfaction with much of the commentary and analysis devoted to Beckett's work. For this reader, Beckett's critics— despite exceptions—have often seemed too willing to domesticate the author's texts and too ready to recuperate them within well-worn and reductive norms" (ix–x).

11. A key work in this respect is Marjorie Perloff's "Between Verse and Prose: Beckett and the New Poetry" (in Gontarski, ed., *On Beckett*, 191–206), in which Perloff, through a careful listening to Beckett's syntax, rhythms, and rhymes, convincingly argues the similarities of Beckett's later prose work to certain strains in contemporary poetry, hinting that Beckett belongs as much in discussions and histories of poetry as of prose (193). On new trends in criticism, there is Jean-Michel Rabaté's recent assertion that Beckett is increasingly being seen as a "poète": "ce qui suggère une lisibilité nouvelle de l'ensemble de la production de l'auteur, depuis les premiers poèmes hermétiques jusqu'aux dernières tentatives allant vers un ressassement minimaliste" (which suggests a new legibility for the entirety of the author's production, from the first hermetic poems to the last sketches moving in the direction of minimalist repetition and restatement), in Rabaté, ed., *Samuel Beckett*, 3.

12. One traditional method has been to deny the interiority that one fails to find by arguing for the limpid *literality* of Beckett's work. This insistence on clarity can be recuperated by both absurdist and mystical readings, in addition to historical ones. I, too, shall question interiority, although in another key. However, my treatment of the problem will certainly overlap with the more recent emphasis on intertextuality in Beckett, which I take to be another strategy for disrupting interiority.

13. I have taken a very tentative step in this direction in my "Mirror-Resembling Screens: Yeats, Beckett, and '. . . But the Clouds. . . .'"

14. Yeats's wrestlings with these questions are found principally in two essays, "Symbolism in Painting" and "The Symbolism of Poetry," both included in *Essays and Introductions*. The above quotations come from the former essay (147).

15. A poetics in which these values are invoked and also interrogated to the point of their own dissolution would be Pound's (especially in relation to "Imagism") with its insistence on "Direct treatment of the 'thing' whether subjective or objective" (3), the constatation that "the proper and perfect symbol is the natural object" (9), the linkage of authority and "credit" to the proper name, and the obsession with the proper name itself—both that of the author, and those that one finds on virtually every page of the *Cantos*. A more straightforward expression of this ideology can be found in Emerson's essay "The Poet": "By virtue of this science the poet is the Namer or Language-maker, naming things sometimes after their appearance, sometimes after their essence, and giving to every one its own

name and not another's, thereby rejoicing the intellect, which delights in detachment or boundary" (271).

16. I use "agency of speech" here as I feel that terms like "narrator" or "speaker" or "voice" do not apply to *The Unnamable*, for reasons which shall be explained at length.

17. The term "thetic" is borrowed from Julia Kristeva, who discusses a "coupure thétique" in the process of a child's development of a subjective identity separate from the mother's body and "objects" generally, a development necessitating and enabled by the ability to construct predicative phrases. Kristeva writes, "Nous appellerons *thétique* la séparation du sujet d'avec le continuum perceptif et pulsionnel où le met sa dépendance du corps de la mère; cette séparation altérante et infinitisante est coextensive à la capacité d'asserter, par une émission signifiante, la position d'un objet-référent identifiable" (Kristeva, Milner, and Ruwet, eds., 252) [We shall call *thetic* the subject's separation from the continuum of drive and perception into which it was placed by its dependence on the mother's body; this altering and interminable separation is coextensive with the capacity to assert, through a signifying sound, the position of an identifiable referent-object] (my translation, Kristeva's emphasis). For the full context of Kristeva's long and complex argument, see her article, "La fonction prédicative et le sujet parlant," in Kristeva, Milner, and Ruwet, from which this citation was taken.

18. Although this is not the case, of course, in terms of philosophy.

19. De Man deals with the issues of catachresis and prosopopoeia most explicitly in his essays "Hypogram and Inscription," in *The Resistance to Theory* (27–53), and "Autobiography as De-Facement," in *The Rhetoric of Romanticism* (67–81). An attempt to consolidate de Man's speculations on these figures into the coherent theory of trope and figure he at times proposes proves extremely problematic. Still, de Man's intuition of the crucial role of these two figures seems as perspicacious as ever.

20. "The pure work implies the elocutory disappearance of the poet, who cedes the initiative to the words, set in motion by the collision of their differences" (my translation).

21. In this respect, the issue of deixis seems to be at the heart of de Man's speculations on "prosopopoeia" as the phenomenalization of a present voice.

22. See Benveniste, *Problèmes I*, 251–57, for the original French "La nature des pronoms."

23. "[U]ne notion constante et 'objective,' apte à rester virtuelle ou à s'actualiser dans un objet singulier, et qui demeure toujours identique dans la représentation qu'elle éveille" (Benveniste, *Problèmes I*, 252).

24. See Benveniste, *Problèmes I*, 258–66, for the French "De la subjectivité dans le langage."

25. "La 'subjectivité' dont nous traitons ici est la capacité du locuteur à se poser comme 'sujet.' . . . Est 'ego' qui *dit* 'ego'" (Benveniste, *Problèmes I*, 259–60).

26. Obviously, these concerns are eminently Proustian also. Proust's obsession with distinguishing between dreams and reality, along with his focus on the question of subjective continuity, self-knowledge, and error, make him a quintessentially Cartesian writer to a rather large degree. I find that Beckett, having read Proust and Descartes at about the same period of his life, comes up with an extremely "Cartesian" Proust, and in "Whoroscope," a quite "Proustian" Descartes. For another discussion of the crucial role of deictics in Beckett, see Angela Moorjani's "Beckett's Devious Deictics" in Butler and Davis, eds., 20–30. Moorjani links Beckett's deictic destabilization, or *débrayage,* as she calls it, to a cryptonymic theory of abnormal mourning, derived from the work of Abraham and Torok.

27. "L'acte s'identifie donc avec l'énoncé de l'acte. Le signifié est identique au référent. . . . Un énoncé performatif n'est pas tel en ce qu'il peut modifier la situation d'un individu, mais en tant qu'il est *par lui-même* un acte. L'énoncé *est* l'acte" (Benveniste, *Problèmes I,* 274).

28. Benveniste, *Problèmes II,* 79–88. All subsequent translations of this work are mine.

29. "Mais immédiatement, dès qu'il se déclare locuteur et assume la langue, il implante *l'autre* en face de lui, quel que soit le degré de présence qu'il attribue à cet autre. Toute énonciation est, explicite ou implicite, une allocution, elle postule un allocutaire" (Benveniste, *Problèmes II,* 82).

30. "[D]oit être posé, malgré l'apparence, comme une variété du dialogue, structure fondamentale. Le 'monologue' est un dialogue intériorisé, formulé en 'langage intérieur,' entre un moi locuteur et un moi écouteur" (Benveniste, *Problèmes II,* 85).

31. Blanchot, *Infinite Conversation,* 380.

32. Blanchot, *Space of Literature* (28). The translator has chosen the term "third person" for Blanchot's enigmatic "il": " 'il,' c'est moi-même devenu personne, autrui devenu l'autre, c'est que, là où je suis, je ne puisse plus m'adresser à moi et que celui qui s'adresse à moi, ne dise pas 'Je,' ne soit pas lui-même" (Blanchot, *Espace,* 23).

Chapter I

1. See Bair, 242, who quotes a December 20, 1936, letter to George Reavey.

2. The "German Letter," for all its emphasis on silence, actually enforces this point. Beckett writes, "Is there any reason why that terrible materiality of the word surface should not be capable of being dissolved, like for example the sound surface, torn by enormous pauses, of Beethoven's seventh Symphony, so that through whole pages we can perceive nothing but a path of sounds suspended in giddy heights, linking unfathomable abysses of silence?" (*Disjecta,* 172). That the sounds

would link *silence,* rather than each other, shows the positivity and imbrication of silence in the significatory system, and not its absence from or opposition to it.

3. In English this reads: "the letter g abolished the syllable Ma, and as it were spat on it" (17).

4. See David Watson's analysis of this passage in terms of the *"fort-da* dialectic," which is closer to mine than Hill's is in terms of the treatment of ambivalence and utterance (64–65). Hill's work on translation and the proper name (54–55) shows a fine sensitivity to the cultural and semiotic imbrications of naming, which should preclude the sort of analysis he makes of this passage.

5. This reading is largely indebted to Serge Doubrovsky's *La place de la madeleine: écriture et phantasme chez Proust,* which offers a brilliant and exhaustive psychoanalytical reading of the "madeleine" scene, in all its religious and erotic implications.

6. All further references to the poem will be by line number and will refer to this volume.

7. For an explanation of the allusions and a look at the source passages and historical situations from which Beckett constructed his poem, see the excellent, detailed study of "Whoroscope" in Harvey, pp. 3–66, from which most of the preceding information was taken.

8. "That day we read no further," *Inferno,* canto 5, line 138.

9. This seems to be the logic behind Belacqua's desire for a cicisbeo and is also resonant with *Ulysses,* in which Bloom fantasizes of matching up Stephen Dedalus and Molly, and in the "Nighttown" chapter has rather gratifying visions of Blazes and Molly having sex.

10. It should be noted that Belacqua's euphemism for what he seeks in the forest in "Walking Out," when he searches for the secluded lovers, is "sursum corda"—the raising of the heart. His lover, Lucy, wryly responds, "Corda is good" (*More Pricks,* 107).

Chapter 2

1. Cousineau, *"Watt:* Language as Interdiction and Consolation," in Gontarski, 64.

2. See Ross Posnock for a cogent account of *Watt* as "Beckett's critique of the traditional novel" (51). Steven Connor, in his fine chapter on the book, acknowledges that "Reading *Watt* is, of course, a slow and painful process" (31); and in a recent article, Martin Kevorkian begins by stressing that the text "seems to prohibit certain kinds of reading" (427) altogether. Meanwhile, the famous passage on the unnamable "pot," among others, opens the way for Wittgensteinian reflec-

tions on an essential alienness or unnaturalness of language with regard to what it designates. On a biographical level, it is often recalled that Beckett started writing in French after finishing *Watt,* perhaps in response to the seeming exhaustion of English in this work. See Astro, p. 49, for one example. Stressing Beckett's "sceptical" outlook, Michael E. Mooney asserts that "Watt's sojourn in Knott's house teaches him the futility of attempting to impose meaning on events or to concern himself 'with what things were in reality' (*Watt,* 227)" (see Butler and Davis, 163). Leslie Hill posits Mr Knott as "a figure of paternal indifference, engulfment and indeterminacy, apathy and invisibility" (27), and claims that Watt's relationship to his largely extratextual, presumed biological father "turns on a failure of incorporation" (27). For Hill, the novel's central concern is "the possibility of a form of language in which the spectre of the father can be incorporated" (28). Gottfried Büttner writes of "Watt's path into nothingness or rather Mr Knott's house and garden," which he later asserts quite simply "are to be found in another realm of existence" (Butler and Davis, 172–73). The fullest examination of the issue of Beckett's residence in a new tongue is Ann Beer's "*Watt,* Knott and Beckett's Bilingualism," which repeatedly views the novel as a tentative plunge into the foreign: "Written in English, the novel seems exiled from any familiar realm of English literature and language; but it is also foreign to the French linguistic home which Beckett was to make his from 1945" (37). Another characteristic statement is the following: "In *Watt* Beckett begins to examine and externalize a language which is gradually shifting from its status as a mother-tongue, habitual and instinctive, to that of a language whose relative and arbitrary nature is clear" (37). Beer also mentions, critically, the argument of Patrick Casement, who attempts to forge a link between the "mother tongue" and Beckett's biological mother (43) in explaining Beckett's seeming attack on English and move into French. In this argument, linguistic appurtenance and monolinguism are inscribed into an overriding discourse of the natural and the native generally, in which the "naturalness" of the native tongue and culture will be likened to a supposed natural bond between mother and child. A whole series of oppositions ensues: native language/foreign language, maternal love/paternal law, womb/world, immediate perception/hermeneutic mediation. Beckett's works generally, and certainly *Watt* among them, call all of these oppositions into question.

3. It has not been determined whether this piece was actually broadcast or not. See Gontarski's note in *Complete Short Prose,* 285–86.

4. On June 6, 1944. That it was, in fact, the allies who destroyed the town in their bombardment of German positions in conjunction with D day is the sort of irony to which Beckett's work is consistently sensitive.

5. The following chapters on the trilogy and the *Texts for Nothing* will develop this idea in much greater detail.

6. James Knowlson's recent biography confirms the extent of Beckett's knowledge of psychoanalytic theory, already easily inferred from his writings. According

to Knowlson, Beckett took lengthy and detailed notes on most of the leading figures and theories of his day, including the specialist on group psychology McDougall, whom I shall refer to later in this chapter (see Knowlson, 172–78).

7. For an examination of the question of mirroring generally in *Watt,* see Ramsey, "*Watt* and the Significance of the Mirror Image." Ramsey discusses Watt's inversions on pp. 31–34.

8. An exception would be Arsene's "imprevisible," which is not strictly speaking an English word. However, as "visible" is, and "pre" and "im" are acceptable English prefixes, Arsene's mistake is due only to chance; his inference is based on many valid examples of the transposition of French to English—for example, "visible" and "invisible"—and follows the general rules of French to English transposition.

9. Of course, the "real" narrator is Sam, but as Sam claims to be for the most part simply forwarding Watt's story, the latter's reliability remains a narratological issue.

10. Obviously, the root of "gallicism" is in fact the Gauls, not the "Galls." But given that all the English words derived from this root drop the *u,* I think the reference is still operative. Michael Beausang links the name to Franz Joseph Gall, an early student of aphasia. See Rabaté, *Beckett avant Beckett,* (153–72). More recently, Richard Begam evokes the possibility that "Beckett, the Gaelic writer writing in Gaul, is tuning his piano, keeping his hand in, and wondering all the time whether it is worth it" (91).

11. I do not believe such a break could be read as either doctrinal or definitive, but rather strategic. However much *Watt* distances itself from a certain kind of Joycean wit that dominates *Murphy* and *More Pricks than Kicks,* stylistically and structurally it remains clearly indebted to the "Ithaca" chapter in *Ulysses,* to give just one example. As Peter Nicholls has recently shown, the term "modernism" itself should probably not be taken in the singular. But I would argue that *Watt* does represent a shift of interest to a different tangent of modernism, and a different kind of interest in France and the French—further investigations of Beckett's work of this period thus necessitate a close look at his relationship to the work of Gertrude Stein.

12. Ironically, this itself would inevitably inscribe a filial debt to Joyce, master of this strategy.

13. See the section "The Taboo upon Rulers" in Freud, *Totem and Taboo.*

14. The above translation comes from Strachey's standard edition, which would not have been available at the time of the novel's composition. A. A. Brill's translation, dating from 1918, rather than quote Frazer with elision, renders the passage this way: "He was not allowed to ride, to see a horse or an armed man, to wear a ring that was not broken, to have a knot in his garments, to touch wheat flour or leaven, or even to mention by name a goat, a dog, raw meat, beans and ivy" (62).

15. Thus, I would agree with Leslie Hill's emphasis on the novel as an attempt

to construct a relationship with the father rather than an attempt to defy the paternal law, though I would differ with his account of the mechanics of incorporation, or his identification of Knott with the "father." See the interesting chapter, "The Loss of Species," especially pp. 23–30.

16. Beckett's 1938 article "Les Deux Besoins" (first published in *Disjecta* in 1984) raises similar questions but in quite dissimilar terms, as it stresses precisely that the artist needs to need, rather than not need, and goes on to chart the relationship between the need to need and the particular need that at any given time is needed. Thus, in "Les Deux Besoins," the sort of ataraxy which Knott is under the injunction to search out is precisely the temptation which must be resisted in order to live "la seule vie possible." A much longer study would be necessary to explore the relation between these two texts, but already it could be suggested that Knott's heroism lies in his (doomed) attempt to reject that which life ordinarily commands as its condition: that you need. A first sketch in this direction is probably provided by William Burroughs in *Junky*, where the attraction of heroin is that it supplants and supersedes all other needs while being itself in constant short supply: "Junk takes everything and gives nothing but insurance against junk sickness" (125); "Junk is a biological necessity when you have a habit, an invisible mouth" (124), but also, "The kick of junk *is* that you have to have it. . . . You cannot escape from junk sickness any more than you can escape from junk kick after a shot" (97).

17. Though Beckett never loses interest in ridiculing the assumptions and conventions of bourgeois society. We need only think of Moran.

18. For a notable exception, see Richard Begam's recent reading of the passage, which also views it as an interrogation of "Cartesian dualism" (72).

19. See chapter 4 in this book for a discussion of anachrony in Beckett and Derrida.

Chapter 3

1. For a sophisticated recent example, see Trezise, 39–42. Although Trezise is careful to construct his interpretation around an allegorical conception of subjectivity as exemplified by the Moran/Molloy pairing, the thrust of his argument is unmistakably that Moran represents an earlier version of some sort of Molloy-effect, in the process of metamorphosis. Trezise asserts that Moran is "inexorably impelled toward the Molloy he himself has yet to become" (54), argues that "it is indeed as though Moran were a younger Molloy, and Molloy's story a later and, as it were, yet more impoverished version of Moran's" (40), and concludes that *Molloy* reverses in the telling the chronology of the stories told (41). Meanwhile,

Richard Begam has also recently evoked the hazards in attempting to designate one member of the pair as the "originary" term (110).

2. For a variation on this, see Angela Moorjani's argument that Moran's tale is the subject's "conscious discourse" while Molloy's is the "unconscious subtext" (in Smith, 58). In addition to the untenable reduction of the conscious/unconscious distinction here to a stable duality, rather than a differential, meaning-producing economy, this schema also reduces the repetitive irony and self-differentiation of Beckett's text. Once more, a stable referent is introduced—in this case, not Moran's "history" but Molloy's "subtext," which Moran's "conscious discourse" of repressions would be "representing." It is clear, however, that Moran has an "unconscious subtext" of his own—his story is laden with symptomatic actions and expressions that belie an economy of desire quite different from Molloy's. There are other recent examples. As sophisticated a reader as Trezise, as already pointed out, feels comfortable asserting the temporal priority of Moran's tale, which he qualifies as the "beginning" of the novel (41), and this after intelligently querying the status of *Molloy* as the "origin" of the trilogy (39). Charlotte Renner, for her part, shows exemplary subtlety in studying the complexities of the relationship between Moran and Molloy, carefully following the textual clues planted by Beckett. I have already mentioned how the figure of Moran itself serves to parody all acts of clue deciphering, however, and Renner's acceptance of Moran's transformation into Molloy seems to deny the undecidability of this relationship. Everything in Beckett would lead one to believe that the reader should confront the puzzle's insolubility rather than try to (dis)solve it. If the *failed attempt* to solve it is a necessary moment in this confrontation, one can do no better than Renner (in Bloom, 95–114). Finally, for an intelligent discussion of the critical investments in these interpretations, see Cousineau, "*Molloy* and the Paternal Metaphor." Particularly apt is his point that these interpretations tend to privilege the figure of Molloy as "more profound" or more "'real'" than Moran, when on the contrary both seem to be rather distant from any sort of full consciousness of desire or subjectivity (82).

3. In his "Presocratic Scepticism," Michael E. Mooney argues that the crucial Descartes for Beckett is the Descartes of skepticism, not of certainty. One can only agree, adding that Beckett's interest in the cogito is to pry it open to the skepticism Descartes so peerlessly manipulates.

4. This was noted recently by Trezise, p. 102.

5. Stephen Connor makes a similar argument, discussing how the "I" of *The Unnamable* is often given a centrality or authenticity denied its "surrogates" or the characters found in the other novels. As Connor remarks, "Such a conception proves difficult to maintain in any absolute sense" (79).

6. In his fascinating article, "All Here is Sin: The Obligation in *The Unnamable*," Dennis A. Foster makes a similar point: "For all the critical protestations

that the narrator is unnamable, by calling him Unnamable they link the pronouns in a consecutive association, binding them to a unified individual who by the end of his one hundred and twenty pages . . . has acquired considerable weight and authority" (82–83). Stephen Barker also insists that "what the voice is *not* is substantial character," and that no "sense of conventional identity resides in such a voice" (in Butler and Davis, 198).

7. Stephen Barker has also noted the pertinence of this passage for thinking through Beckett's writing practice. See his interesting article, "Conspicuous Absence: *Tracé* and Power in Beckett's Drama" (in Butler and Davis, 181–205).

8. Richard Begam has also noted the similarities between Derrida's "unnamable" and Beckett's, and focusing on a somewhat different set of questions from my own sets out to show how Beckett "takes up the philosophical problems and procedures associated with *différance* and then reconfigures them in ways that are essentially narrative—how he, in effect, narrates *différance*" (154).

9. For example, "The unnamable is attempting to denounce the identity designated by *je* from a place where *he really is, a place outside language*" (Watson, 44, my emphasis), although Watson quickly follows with the assertion that "it is only within language that a subjectivity can exist" (44).

10. Watson similarly argues, "The unnamable's 'unnamability' is a reaction to the alienating demands to identify with the 'empty' signifier, the father's *nom* which corresponds to his *non*" (43). Once again, one might ask, empty as opposed to what? How can a signifier be full?

11. This opposition seems problematic in any case. To oppose a "maternal body" to a "paternal name" is to overlook the metaphorical, substitutive value of these figures—they are not master signifiers, nor is the "body" of the "mother" a transcendental signified. The "mother's body" is itself a "name."

12. I have diverged here from the Grove Press text (*Three Novels*), which states: "I understood it, I understood it, all wrong perhaps." Given the context and the French text, "Je l'ai compris, je le comprends, de travers peut-être" (*Molloy*, 292), the Grove Press text appears to be inaccurate, and I have adopted the Picador text for this sentence.

13. This problem continues to be central in Beckett right through the final texts. See chapter 6 for a consideration of the "Who asks? Who asks Who asks?" motif in *Company* and *Worstward Ho*.

14. The humor of this passage comes from Beckett's designation of a figural metaphor as "appropriate" or proper (Trezise also comments on this, p. 76). But the oxymoronic notions of "proper figures," along with "figural propers" are an essential part of the textual strategy of the trilogy.

15. Shira Wolosky has done a fine job of pointing out the implicit Platonism of Descartes's thought with its valorization of inwardness and the eternal at the expense of the senses, the body, and the temporal. Wolosky is correct in highlighting, in relation to Beckett's reading of Descartes, the ambivalent position of

language, at once temporal and external, yet also the seat and index of inwardness itself (216).

16. See chapter 5 of this study for a discussion of this.

17. See Carey and Jewinski, eds., 31–42. In addition, in a recent discussion of the passage where Molloy, taking off from Geulinx, describes himself as "free, on the black boat of Ulysses, to crawl towards the East, along the deck . . . a sadly rejoicing slave, I follow with my eyes the proud and futile wake" (*Three Novels*, 51), Mary Lydon asks, "Who can fail to hear the echoes, in this passage, of Joyce's name, not to speak of the names of his two great works: *Ulysses* and the *Wake?*" (9). In discussing the differences this introduces between the French and English texts, Lydon offer speculations similar to my own concerning this issue.

18. For an interesting discussion of these issues, along with the especially problematic place of the proper name in terms of translation, see Hill, 40–58. Hill rightly points out that Beckett's changes in the English text of the trilogy cannot be considered revisions as Beckett often fails to reincorporate them into the French text (Hill, 49).

19. Hill makes a similar point concerning the relationship between the French and English texts, though he reaches a slightly different conclusion: "the trilogy exists and survives as the sum of its own differences and variants" (42). I would argue that the variations rather render the trilogy noncommensurable and preclude a "summing up" of its differences.

Chapter 4

1. See Connor, 70.

2. An example can be found in Martin Esslin's recent claim that Beckett's work is "strictly an exploration of his own experience, of his own 'being in the world,'" or similarly that it represents a "direct distillation of a living experience" (in Smith, 205–7). See Trezise for an excellent discussion of the limits of the phenomenologist and existentialist approaches to Beckett (3–33).

3. I use "performative" here to designate an utterance which, rather than simply describe a referent, is itself, as act, the referent it simultaneously designates. See the introduction for a fuller discussion.

4. See Benveniste, *Problèmes* II, 79–88.

5. "Dispossession," a term to which critics of Beckett make frequent recourse, is also the title of Thomas Trezise's fascinating chapter on *Molloy* in *Into the Breach*. It is to Trezise that my occasional use of the term owes its greatest debt, and his relation of "dispossession" to an "originary absence of origin" (59) is certainly in line with my conception of the stakes raised through consideration of the term. Following Trezise, I would argue that "dispossession" is not an event be-

cause it has always already happened, is prior to the capacity to construct events as such, and is not a state as it precludes the stability and continuity of a "being" and temporality which would allow such a predication.

6. The implications of my argument should necessitate a rethinking of statements like this one by Wolfgang Iser: "The unnamable frequently points out that he has invented the other characters—from Murphy to Watt, and from Molloy to Malone—so that through these ramifications of his ego he can objectify and so render explicable certain conditions of himself" (in Bloom, 77–78). Obviously, I think Iser's schema of the prior, interior, "ego" and its externalized, expressive "representations" is inapplicable here, even if the ego is itself meant to benefit from these objectifications, because the characters' "communications" form part of what would need to be objectified. Iser does note that the delegates also talk to the "voice," but goes on to argue that the delegates' stories are only "fictions" which the "unnamable" reproduces as quotations, "so that he can accentuate the gap between what his characters want to make of him and what he really is" (78). This conservative reading discounts a possibility ceaselessly repeated by the text—that existence cannot be conceived outside these voices, and that there "really is" nothing that can be spoken of as separated and distinguishable from "their" stories. To carry this further, if the objectifications can become a subsequent threat to identity, rather than its representation, does this not indicate that self-representation itself is a form of nonself-identity rather than mimetic doubling? Stephen Connor's poststructuralist reading follows the same presuppositions as Iser's around this issue. Connor claims that the narrator recognizes the "fictional surrogates" as "false repetitions," from which he tries to separate himself (73). Connor goes on to categorize the surrogates as "inauthentic" (73). Similarly to Watson, he argues that language is the site of "artificial stories" as one can never speak "with one's own voice" (74). Certainly, *The Unnamable* characterizes the surrogates as inauthentic and their stories as artificial, but always in the purpose of troubling the categories of authenticity and truth to which they might be opposed. Beckett does not present a double bind in which speech inevitably alienates the subject from its real authenticity; rather he questions the concepts of authenticity and propriety by denying them to the figures that should be allowed to guarantee them, for example, the voice, "silence," and the predicative system. The "mannikins" are not the authentic voice, but they are not a bit more inauthentic than the "voice" is either—there is no authenticity of voice in this text. If the "voice" maintains its separation from the mannikins, it is not because they are false figures, but because they are names, and the text is concerned with what can happen in the absence of names, along with how names are able to make themselves present.

7. See Trezise, *Into the Breach*, 3–27.

8. As David Watson has shown, there is a similar dynamic at work in *How It Is*. Writing about the "figure of citation" in *Comment c'est*, Watson notes, "Although

the narrator addresses the voice in an imperative discursive mode, a *je-tu* structure of locution ('raconte-moi encore finis de me raconter'), he is himself always already positioned as the addressee; the *je* is always already a *tu* ('je le dis comme je l'entends')" (88).

9. Published in English as "Ulysses Gramophone: Hear Say Yes in Joyce," in Derrida, *Acts of Literature*.

10. See Benveniste, *Problèmes II*, 79–88.

11. David Watson's discussion of the "oral fart" in *How It Is* touches on similar problems (92).

12. The "or" as lever of aporia will be looked at in detail with regard to *Company* and *Worstward Ho* in chapter 6.

13. Edouard Morot-Sir comes close to my position here, when he outlines the move from proper names to the pronominal system in terms of the problem of reference in *The Unnamable*. I quite agree with Morot-Sir that "doubt about the pronominal" infects "the last hope for an assured reference—*my* reference to *myself*" (in Bloom, 139). However, Morot-Sir tends to interpret this crisis of self-knowledge and self-reference as an intersubjective issue, as the impossibility of an idealist I to be independent of the "they" or "Collective consciousness" from which individual consciousness arises. In contrast to this, I have been arguing that in Beckett, the "they" is recognized as prior to the construction of a subjectivity, as a supplement to it, and not as an external impediment which would befall a nascent "I." The I is not so much disturbed as never allowed a separate articulation. See "Grammatical Insincerity in *The Unnamable*," in Bloom, 131–44, for the entirety of Morot-Sir's argument. David Watson also comments on the failure of deictic signification, giving a Lacanian reading, which, in its mechanics, is actually quite close to Morot-Sir: "The shifter foregrounds the status of the signifier as never being 'proper' to any given subject, but merely appropriated from the *langue* in the instance of a particular utterance. The 'I' which one imagines to signify oneself is the signifier with which everyone 'signifies' himself or herself. . . . The unnamable decides to abolish the first-person pronoun from his discourse" (43). Watson will go on to characterize this "gesture" as "futile" because, "the *je* always remains, albeit at an implicit level" (44). Perhaps, but it is no longer something one can call a "je"—as I have argued, the problem is not one of adequation, that is, of finding the correct name or pronoun for this implicit "I" or subject, but rather to rethink it in terms of the unnamability which *precludes* the nominational and pronominal systems from the outset. I am closer to Dennis Foster's position, when he asserts that "the 'I' of *The Unnamable* refers to no unified subject, to no single, creating mind that can shape the words into a whole" (81). I would like to extend the ramifications of Foster's interesting speculations on the way *The Unnamable* seems to deny consistent reference or subjective continuity while, as Foster notes, tantalizingly scattering "the pages with 'I's without an explicit indication that the narrator has changed" (82). There is no *explicit*

indication, and the implicit is inevitably aporetic, especially in Beckett. Still, in what follows I shall attempt to push forward all the implicit indicators that the narrator is not constant whose stirrings Foster has quite finely recognized.

14. This sentence is exemplary of the casually aporetic technique of *The Unnamable*. Has Mahood's voice, in fact, mingled "always" or only "often"? We are not told, yet the difference between these two possibilities is much more than one of degree. Likewise, what is the difference between a "mingled" voice and one which is "drowned completely"? Once a voice admits of any degree of this sort of mingling, it can no longer be considered a "voice" in the metaphysical sense.

15. In an interesting postcolonialist reading of "First Love," David Lloyd also relates certain instances of Beckettian scatology to Bloom's sound track for Emmet's epitaph. Lloyd points out that Emmet's "epitaph" is in fact not one at all, being an injunction against the writing of his epitaph until Ireland be free (77). Joyce's parody of this sort of nationalist pathos is obvious, but Emmet's gesture — that of composing an epitaph whose burden is to discount its identity as epitaph, by insisting on an indefinite *future* which would allow it to assume its promised form — bears obvious affinities to Beckett's preoccupations.

16. The French does not extend the punning network as far: for "cogitate" we have "réfléchissais" (*L'Innomable*, 90) and for "ego" the standard "moi" (98). However, "Je résume (96), colliding the thetic "am" with repetition, is promising.

17. See *Beckett Writing Beckett*, 13, 32. Augustine's speculations come in the midst of his discussion of memory in book 10 of the *Confessions*, and the time has clearly arrived for a full-length study of memory in Beckett. A starting point for such an enterprise would certainly be to trace the question from Augustine through Descartes to Proust, all of whom contribute crucially to Beckett's elaboration of the issue.

18. See chapter 1 of this study.

19. The version of the Passion Beckett gives us, with all its tormented interpretive ruminations, evokes Freud's description of the "Wolf Man's" ambivalent investments in the story of the Passion, particularly those regarding the difficulties of Freud's patient in coming to terms with the physical aspects and excretory functions inseparable from the concept of Christ as man. The analysis of Madeleine's ministrations echoes Freud's analysis of the "Wolf Man's" religious fervor in childhood: "A violent defensive struggle against these compromise-formations then inevitably led to an obsessive exaggeration of all the activities which are prescribed for giving expression to piety and a pure love of God" (*Three Case Histories*, 311).

20. For incisive comments on the long tradition of dualist Cartesian readings of Beckett, see Thomas Cousineau, "Descartes, Lacan, and *Murphy*." Cousineau shares my sense that Beckett ironizes this dualism more than he subscribes to it.

Chapter 5

1. These citations are from the famously problematic Shenker interview of 1956, quoted and interestingly discussed by John Harrington, in Carey and Jewinski, 32–33.

2. See Abbott, *Beckett Writing Beckett*, 20.

3. See Rabaté, *Joyce Upon the Void*, xi–xii.

4. Michael Valdez Moses has made a similar point, arguing that although *The Unnamable* may seem "unique," it has, "in fact one prototype for its treatment of novelistic conventions: *Finnegans Wake*. It is from Joyce's last work that Beckett learned how the most fundamental narrative conventions—plot, character, description, narrative voice—could be subverted" (662). I would wholly endorse Valdez's claim, though I differ with his assertion that "What distinguishes Joyce from Beckett . . . is his desire not simply to negate the principal conventions of the novel but to transcend them" (662). I would maintain that Joyce's continued emphasis on parody and pastiche and Beckett's focus on a paradoxical conception of failure render an opposition of transcendence and negation too facile to account for both authors' ambivalent and ambiguous writing effects.

5. I think here of Whitman, Williams, and the later Pound, for example.

6. See Pound, 403–9.

7. See Amossy and Rosen, 77–82.

8. Hugh Kenner makes a somewhat similar point in *The Stoic Comedians*, although his argument is primarily couched in terms of a realist problematic of adequation (15–28). I am considerably indebted to Kenner's genial sketch of the Flaubert-Joyce-Beckett lineage, although I find rather different links between them.

9. This passage is also referred to in Amossy and Rosen, 78.

10. See Rabaté, *Joyce Upon the Void,* 130.

11. Cited in Knowlson, 258.

12. These ideas are explained and expanded in Rabaté, *Joyce Upon the Void,* 112–38.

13. Translated as "Two words for Joyce" in Attridge and Ferrer, eds.

14. As the French text, published after the English version, seems to incorporate some revisions, I have modified the translation accordingly.

15. H. Porter Abbott, also struck by the "comparative neglect" (88) of these works, comes to a similar conclusion, speaking lucidly of the "absolute frustration of structural 'onwardness' which accounts for the neglect into which this beautiful work has fallen" (*Beckett Writing Beckett*, 89).

16. The critical neglect of the *Texts for Nothing* should not be over stated: there *is* a long tradition of commentary, much of it attempting to take the *Texts* on their own terms. If virtually all the criticism seems inevitably drawn to attaching the

Texts to *The Unnamable*—and mine will be no exception—it is precisely because the *Texts* don't have their "own terms." As I have indicated, it is just this lack of individuality or aesthetic self-definition and integrity within Beckett's canon which interests me. Still, the (inevitable) marginalization of the *Texts* can be seen in much older books—like John Fletcher's *The Novels of Samuel Beckett*, published in 1964, which states that after *The Unnamable*, Beckett "will no longer modify it [his work] in essentials," and that the latest fiction "adds little or nothing that is new to his vision" (196)—as well as in much more recent books. For example, Stephen Connor's 1988 *Samuel Beckett: Repetition, Theory and Text* fails to mention the *Texts* after page 1; Alan Astro declines to dedicate a section of his excellent introduction to Beckett to the *Texts,* and Thomas Trezise, Leslie Hill, and David Watson, in books specifically addressed to the fiction, make only very few, very brief, passing references to the *Texts* and always in the context of other arguments concerning other works. Astro's irreproachable definition of the *Texts* as "a series of prose pieces where we find, in abbreviated form, many of the same concerns voiced in *The Unnamable*" (93) sums up the phenomenon which interests me here. However, for an interesting recent look at the *Texts for Nothing* in relation to Kantian and Platonic philosophy, see Alain Badiou's article, "L'écriture du générique: Samuel Beckett," in his book, *Conditions*. Within recent Beckett criticism, there is Susan Brienza's chapter on the *Texts* in her *Samuel Beckett's New Worlds*.

17. Thomas Trezise writes eloquently of the "obligation to move and the inability to do so" so often found in Beckett's texts, describing it as "Reminiscent of an ambivalence commonly experienced in dreams" and asserting that it "may be predicated as well of the compulsion and the inability to rest" (140). Trezise's emphasis on ambivalence seems well placed here, and in the following chapter, I will attempt to show how this ambivalence extends to the point where its two component agents—movement and repose—can no longer be entirely differentiated from each other.

18. Roch C. Smith has also noted the parallelism of these forms of going on, writing of the "replacement" of Molloy's wanderings in the trilogy with "narrative wandering" in *The Unnamable,* where "to 'go on' is to write, to produce more words" (in Bloom, 117; see also 115–22,).

19. For example, see Watson, p. 46.

20. See Dina Alkassim's master's thesis, "Devising You," for a brilliant investigation of the second person in relation to *Company.*

21. In this respect, Beckett can be compared to Lacan, who also tries to address and expand the place of the second person in psychoanalytic theory, through concepts like the Other, and his extensive focus on transference.

22. Beckett's "whose" escapes the need to refer to the other in terms of number or person, however the "his" which qualifies "babble" gives pause. Is this attribution of not only number and person but also *gender* retroactively invalidated by the following sentence? The grammar of the French text differs significantly, but

the problem is the same as Beckett has his numberless, personless other conjugate a verb in the third-person singular ("divague," *Nouvelles and Textes pour rien*, 199).

23. "To Kant's famous, 'What can I know? What must I do? What can I hope for?' the *Texts for Nothing* answer with the triplet: 'Where would I go, if I could go? What would I be, if I could be? What would I say, if I had a voice?' " (my translation). Badiou goes on to argue that after 1960, Beckett's works add a fourth question: "Qui suis-je, si l'autre existe?" [Who am I, if the other exists?].

24. Shira Wolosky has also drawn attention to Beckett's mention of the accusative case in the *Texts* and has drawn conclusions in line with my earlier assertions concerning the impossibility of "being" outside of language in Beckett. Wolosky writes, "To exist here is a grammatical state, 'accusative.' And however much the 'I' twists and turns, insisting that this is only inexistence, it is always and only to this grammatical selfhood, with its pronouns and cases, that the 'I' returns" (226). In my discussion of "accusative existence," I hope to shed some light on how existence in the mode of this particular "grammatical state" might differ from others.

25. Let us remember Lady Pedal from the last pages of *Malone Dies*—the French text gives Mme. *Pédale,* which, as Leslie Hill notes, is also a derogatory term for homosexuals. Hill comments on this constellation of puns and allusions in relation to Molloy's bicycling rather than "Sanies I."

26. For a sophisticated discussion of the impossibility of representing the body in language, see Watson, 104–26. While I appreciate Watson's astute applications of Kristevan analyses to Beckett, the following pages should make clear why I find Watson's framing of the body problem in terms of linguistic adequacy not entirely acceptable.

27. For example, Watson's statement, "The body cannot appear fully in language; it cannot find for itself a name other than a signifier in the symbolic order" (117) or, "The crisis of Beckett's fiction is the crisis of the body unable to name itself within language, but forced, in the attempt to satisfy its drives, into the order of language" (122). In Beckett, the *name* is unable to name itself within language—the opposition Watson implicitly invokes between language and the real, the ideal and the concrete, and finally, the sign and the referent, seems resoundingly deconstructed (in the strict sense of the term) by Beckett's texts.

28. "Un corps . . . c'est de la parole comme telle qu'il surgit," cited by Felman, *Scandale,* p. 129.

29. Leslie Hill makes a similar point, stating "the body cannot claim any existence prior to the motions of language" (119), and "If the body has no inner consistency, or any distinctive attributes, it is because it is subject to a constant process of differentiation and erasure by language" (119). I wholly subscribe to these statements, along with the assertion that in Beckett the body is "a form of writing and a text" (120). However, I would differ from Hill's equation of the textual body with some sort of "non-semantic" movement, "expulsion from sense" (120), and an "exercise in breathing and punctuation" (120) arising from the text's

oral performance. This reappropriation of the textual "body" as *orality* and voice, therefore physical presence, is exactly what Beckett's sense of the body, writing, and text as exteriority renders problematic.

30. "[S]e diffère, cela veut dire sans doute qu'il se tisse des différences et aussi qu'il envoie, qu'il délègue des représentants, des mandataires; mais qu'il n'y a aucune chance pour que le mandant <<existe>>, soit présent, soit <<lui-même>> quelque part" (*Marges*, 21).

31. In his article " 'Shat into Grace,' " William Hutchings argues that *How It Is* represents a passage through the intestines, or as he puts it, a "peristaltic pilgrim's progress" (73). Hutchings compares this to the "peristaltic" aspects of the "Lestry-gonians" chapter of *Ulysses* and draws interesting comparisons between Beckett's use of scatological imagery or allegories, and those found in Joyce and Dante. David Lloyd's "Writing in the Shit" discusses scatology in Beckett in its relationship to the discourse of Irish nationalism.

32. Mary Doll has dedicated a chapter of her *Beckett and Myth: An Archetypal Approach* to the story of Narcissus and Echo, and Judith Roof has offered a suggestive reading of narcissistic concerns in Beckett's drama, using Freudian and Lacanian theory, but without considering Beckett's many allusions to the actual myth; see "A Blink in the Mirror: From Oedipus to Narcissus and Back in the Drama of Samuel Beckett," in Burkman, ed., 151–63. Thomas Hunkeler's recent *Echos de l'Ego dans l'œuvre de Samuel Beckett* is the first full-length study of the myth in Beckett's work.

33. The recently published *Dream of Fair to Middling Women* shows an extensive interest in Narcissus, often contrasted to Apollo in terms of erotic economies. Belacqua's contradictions of character, for example, are exemplified by the conceit that he is both "Phoebus chasing Daphne, Narcissus flying from Echo" (120), and later we are given the contrast: "We give you one term of Apollo: chasing a bitch, the usual bitch. And one term of Narcissus: running away from one" (125).

34. See James Knowlson's biography for details of Beckett's torturous flirtation with his first cousin, who died of tuberculosis.

35. Charles Singleton's prose translation of *Paradiso* reads: "As through smooth and transparent glass, or through clear and tranquil waters, yet not so deep that the bottom be lost, the outlines of our faces return so faint that a pearl on a white brow comes not less boldly to our eyes, so did I behold many a countenance eager to speak; wherefore I fell into the contrary error to that which kindled love between the man and the fountain" (27).

36. See Foster for an excellent consideration of Beckettian "impotence," which he finds usually read so as to make it "the delusional consequence of a desire for potency" (97) through the very act of its critical valorization as an escape from desire. He continues: "The impotence of Beckett's various speakers, far from being their problem, is their deluded triumph, the confirmation of a lost paradise.

Consequently, any reading of *The Unnamable* that approaches the text as . . . an exploration of impotence and silence is already working within the maladies" (98).

37. See "Inhibitions, Symptoms and Anxiety" in Sigmund Freud, *On Psychopathology,* especially pp. 249–73.

Chapter 6

1. Leo Bersani, in his "Beckett and the End of Literature," in Bloom, 61, gives a contrary interpretation. Regarding this passage, he writes of "Beckett's efforts to approach that reality of consciousness about which language lies, to torture words out of their 'limpidity' and significance so that they may let us hear just 'how it was' in the silence." Likewise, Wolfgang Iser cites this passage to oppose "actual reality" to "the convention of narration," concluding that "any narrative representation must inevitably be a lie" (in Bloom, 73). This opposition of reality/representation, truth/narrative seems to be under near-constant attack in Beckett. In any case, it is certainly a reduction of the problem this passage sketches in terms of language, consciousness, and "truth."

2. This is another instance in which Beckett develops and emphasizes a dynamic already inaugurated by Joyce—namely the ambivalent attitude toward mimesis found throughout *Ulysses,* and particularly in terms of the representation of "interior monologue." The mediation of Proust, with his myriad of strategies of problematizing the anteriority of the recounted, might be crucial here.

3. The formulations "saying nothing" and "not having said" cannot be considered as identical to silence, as shall be seen later, in our consideration of Beckett's late emphasis on the "missaid."

4. A similar play on lodgings, entry, transit, home, and the womb can be found in Blaise Cendrars's fascinating meditation on the Paris hotel in which he alleges to have been born, in his poem, "Au coeur du monde."

5. If Milton's *Paradise Lost* casts Lucifer as the usurping oedipal rebel, it is perhaps even more striking in its depiction of Adam's refusal of oedipal debt. "Darkness" also calls up these lines of the first son:

> Did I request thee, Maker, from my clay
> To mould me man? Did I solicit thee
> From darkness to promote me?—

This passage serves as the epigraph for Mary Shelley's *Frankenstein,* a book which Moran's tale seems to echo at points. On Beckett's wealth of allusions to Milton, see Marjorie Perloff, "Une Voix pas la mienne: French/English Beckett and the French/English Reader," in Friedman, Rossman, and Sherzer, eds., 36–48.

6. I use the term "siglum" deliberately—I will discuss the various plays on "on" in my analysis of *Worstward Ho*. For the moment, we should note the ambivalence of "on" in Beckett: on the one hand, it implies continuation, extension, and possibility, but to that very extent, it also implies the impossibility of ever finishing, concluding, or arriving. To go on, then, means to never be able to stop going on, to halt or to rest. In terms of its interminability, going on seems very much like standing still. Even in common usage, "to go on" is always divided between a thrust toward change and movement and another toward continuation and repetition.

7. The resemblances between Beckettian wanderings and those of "Dante-Poet" have not escaped critics. See, for example, Rubin Rabinovitz's "Beckett, Dante, and the Metaphorical Representation of Intangible Reality," in Friedman, Rossman, and Sherzer, (57–64); and Neal Oxenhandler, "Seeing and Believing in Dante and Beckett." See Kevin O'Neill, "A Moment without Bounds," for a consideration of the motif of the voyage in Dante and Beckett.

8. This strategy is clearly in some ways analogous to the rhythms of subsequent affirmations and denials which weave the web of *The Unnamable* and the *Texts for Nothing*. Kateryna Arthur has already demonstrated the ways in which *Company* and the *Texts* can be seen to deal in similar ways with the questions of memory and consciousness. See "Texts for *Company*," in Acheson and Arthur, eds., 136–44.

9. Another way to think this is through reference to the paradoxical status of the signified in classical semiotics—as object of the signifier for the addressee, it is "last" while as "presemiotic" impetus for expression for the sender it is "first." This linear figuring of communication, addressed by Derrida in "Signature, Event, Context," is deconstructed throughout Beckett.

10. Obviously, I exclude the tramps themselves from the "memories." They seem rather to occupy a middle ground between the "memories" and the meta-discursive commentaries, and perhaps should be read as allegories of the passage between them. Their distance from the "memories" is indicated not only by tone and the often surrealistic content (or the fact that one refers not to the hearer but to his father), but also by a use of the present tense which is even more decisive than in the "memories," which usually contain at least a phrase or two to ground them in the preterite. Still, if Beckett does not file the tramps comfortably among the "memories," neither is he the sort of the writer to allow a clear and unambiguous separation from them.

11. "Gist" comes from the Middle French "gesire," "to lie," and let us not forget the hearer's prone position as he listens to this story.

12. Alan Astro makes this point succinctly and intelligently, writing of the "otherness of one's voice and memories" (202). See pp. 198–203 for his development of this problem.

13. L. A. C. Dobrez also notes that although the hearer is posited as "artist,"

with the deviser becoming "his work of art," this conception is eventually also rejected. Dobrez writes of the end of *Company:* "No identity at all remains. Solitude is now total, it is, as it were, the solitude of no one" (75).

14. Hill's terms are reminiscent of Derrida's reading of Hegelian economics in *Writing and Difference,* where Derrida traces Bataille's attempts to think loss, negativity, and meaninglessness in a way that would escape their immediate recuperation into a greater positivity. Throughout the article, Derrida points out that merely by giving "negativity" this meaning we deny its very negativity. Because of this, we can never have, know, or arrive at negativity—our desire to do so makes the goal impossible. At most, we can remain cognizant of our relationship to the meaninglessness and loss which we cannot help but deny.

15. Charles Krance, working from a Heideggerian perspective, has also linked the question of failure as discussed in the "Three Dialogues" to *Worstward Ho.* See Butler and Davis, 129–30.

16. Ruby Cohn has also noted this. See her *Casebook,* 13.

17. This graphic play on "no/on" should give pause to certain privilegings of the admittedly aural components of the late work, like these from Barbara Trieloff: "Thus these literary texts seem Janus-faced, pointing away from their status as written literary artifacts, while indicating their aural/oral dimension" (in Butler and Davis, 89) and "the effects of Beckett's rhetorical devices on the reader . . . eventually prompt the reader to reject the written text and to entertain the text as an aural work" (93). The question of pointing, and thus of positionality, which Trieloff raises, is inevitably a question of the written, that is, the placelessness (always emphasized in Beckett) from which a text points.

18. Meanwhile, see Abbott for a magnificent account of how *Worstward Ho* and Beckett's work generally plays off a certain set of Victorian figures for fortitude and perseverance which he dubs "the trope of onwardness" (*Beckett Writing Beckett,* 32–42).

19. In a similar vein, in *Company* Beckett bids farewell to Dante's Belacqua, "To whom here in any case farewell" (60), who had been a frequent companion ever since *More Pricks than Kicks.*

20. The reference to *Worstward Ho* is obvious. The mention of "Venus" calls up the first sentence of *Ill Seen Ill Said,* "From where she lies she sees Venus rise" (7).

Conclusion

1. Although it could be objected that the filmed version of "Not I" eliminates the position of the "Auditor," the camera's disturbing full-screen focus on "Mouth"'s mouth throughout is hardly neutral as framing. An analysis of the

film would have to discuss how the penetrating eye of the camera replaces the more neutral "Auditor" of the stage, and the effects that this change of emphasis produces.

2. Such hats were favorites of Joyce; meanwhile, the "allée des Cygnes" in the Seine was one of Beckett and Joyce's favorite walking places. See Knowlson, p. 665.

Bibliography

Abbott, H. Porter. *Beckett Writing Beckett: The Author in the Autograph*. Ithaca: Cornell University Press, 1996.

———. *The Fiction of Samuel Beckett: Form and Effect*. Berkeley: University of California Press, 1973.

Acheson, James, and Kateryna Arthur, eds. *Beckett's Later Fiction and Drama: Texts for Company*. New York: St. Martin's Press, 1987.

Alkassim, Dina. "Devising You: Samuel Beckett's *Company* and the Legacy of the Pronoun." Masters thesis, University of California at Berkeley, 1990.

Amossy, Ruth, and Elisheva Rosen. *Les Discours du cliché*. Paris: Editions SEDES, 1982.

Anzieu, Didier. *Beckett et le psychanalyste*. Paris: Editions Mentha, 1992.

Armstrong, Gordon S. *Samuel Beckett, W.B. Yeats and Jack Yeats: Images and Words*. Cranbury, NJ: Bucknell University Press, 1990.

Astro, Alan. *Understanding Samuel Beckett*. Columbia: University of South Carolina Press, 1990.

Attridge, Derek, and Daniel Ferrer, eds. *Post-Structuralist Joyce: Essays from the French*. Cambridge: Cambridge University Press, 1984.

Augustine. *Confessions*. Translated by R.S. Pine-Coffin. London: Penguin Books, 1961.

Badiou, Alain. *Conditions*. Paris: Editions du Seuil, 1992.

———. *Beckett: L'increvable désir*. Paris: Hachette, 1995.

Bair, Deirdre. *Samuel Beckett: A Biography*. New York: Harcourt, Brace, Jovanovich, 1978.

Bataille, Georges. *L'erotisme*. Paris: Les Editions de Minuit, Collection "Arguments," 1957.

Beckett, Samuel. *As the Story Was Told: Uncollected and Late Prose*. New York: Riverrun Press, 1990.

———. *Collected Poems in English and French*. New York: Grove Press, 1977.

———. *Collected Shorter Plays*. New York: Grove Press, 1984.

———. *Company*. New York: Grove Press, 1980.

———. *The Complete Short Prose, 1929–1989*. Edited by S. E. Gontarksi. New York: Grove Press, 1995.

———. *Disjecta: Miscellaneous Writings and a Dramatic Fragment*. Edited by Ruby Cohn. New York: Grove Press, 1984.

———. *Dream of Fair to Middling Women*. London: Calder Publications, 1993.

———. *First Love and Other Shorts*. New York: Grove Press, 1974.

———. *Ill Seen Ill Said*. New York: Grove Press, 1981.

———. *L'innomable*. Paris: Les Editions de minuit, 1953.

———. *Mercier and Camier*. London: Picador-Pan, 1988.

————. *Molloy*. Paris: Editions de minuit, 1951.

————. *More Pricks than Kicks*. New York: Grove Press, 1972.

————. *Murphy*. New York: Grove Press, 1979.

————. *Nouvelles et textes pour rien*. Paris: Editions de minuit, 1958.

————. *Quad et autres pièces pour la télévision, suivi de "L'Epuisé" de Gilles Deleuze*. Paris: Editions de Minuit, 1992.

————. *Stories and Texts for Nothing*. New York: Grove Press, 1967.

————. *Three Novels by Samuel Beckett: Molloy, Malone Dies, The Unnamable*. New York: Grove Press, 1965.

————. *Watt*. New York: Grove Press, 1981.

————. *Worstward Ho*. New York: Grove Press, 1983.

Beer, Ann. "Beckett's 'Autography' and the Company of Languages." *Southern Review* 27 (1991): 771–91.

————. "*Watt*, Knott and Beckett's Bilingualism." *Journal of Beckett Studies* 10 (1985): 37–75.

Begam, Richard. *Samuel Beckett and the End of Modernity*. Stanford: Stanford University Press, 1996.

Benveniste, Emile. *Problèmes de linguistique générale I*. Paris: Editions Gallimard, 1966. Translated by Mary Elizabeth Meek under the title *Problems in General Linguistics* (Coral Gables: University of Miami Press, 1971).

————. *Problèmes de linguistique générale II*. Paris: Editions Gallimard, 1966.

Bernard, Michel. *Samuel Beckett et son sujet: Une apparition évanouissante*. Paris: Editions l'Harmattan, 1996.

Blanchot, Maurice. *L'Entretien infini*. Paris: Editions Gallimard, 1969. Translated by Susan Hanson under the title *The Infinite Conversation* (Minneapolis: University of Minnesota Press, 1993).

————. *L'Espace littéraire*. Paris: Collection Folio: Essais, Editions Gallimard, 1955. Translated by Ann Smock under the title *The Space of Literature* (Lincoln: University of Nebraska Press, 1982).

Bloom, Harold, ed. *Modern Critical Interpretations: Samuel Beckett's Molloy, Malone Dies, The Unnamable*. New York: Chelsea House Publishers, 1988.

Brienza, Susan D. *Samuel Beckett's New Worlds: Style in Metafiction*. Norman: University of Oklahoma Press, 1987.

Burkman, Katherine H., ed. *Myth and Ritual in the Plays of Samuel Beckett*. Rutherford: Fairleigh Dickinson University Press, 1987.

Burroughs, William S. *Junky*. London: Penguin Books, 1977.

Butler, Lance St.John. "Two Darks: A Solution to the Problem of Beckett's Bilingualism." *Samuel Beckett Today/Aujourd'hui* 3 (1994): 115–35.

Butler, Lance St. John, and Robin J. Davis, eds. *Rethinking Beckett: A Collection of Critical Essays*. New York: St. Martin's Press, 1990.

Carey, Phyllis. "Samuel Beckett's *Coup de Grâce*." *Notes on Modern Irish Literature* 1 (1989): 23–26.

Carey, Phyllis, and Ed Jewinski, eds. *Re: Joyce'n Beckett*. New York: Fordham University Press, 1992.

Chabert, Pierre, ed. *Revue d'Esthétique: Samuel Beckett*. Paris: Editions Jean-Michel Place, 1990.

Clément, Bruno. *L'Œuvre sans qualités: Rhétorique de Samuel Beckett*. Paris: Editions du Seuil, 1994.

Cohn, Ruby. *Back to Beckett*. Princeton, NJ: Princeton University Press, 1973.

———, ed. *A Casebook on "Waiting for Godot."* London: Macmillan, 1987.

Connor, Stephen. *Samuel Beckett: Repetition, Theory and Text*. London: Basil Blackwell, 1988.

Cousineau, Thomas J. "Descartes, Lacan, and *Murphy*." *College Literature* 11 (1984): 223–32.

———. "*Molloy* and the Paternal Metaphor." *Modern Fiction Studies* 29 (1983): 81–91.

———. "*Watt:* Language as Interdiction and Consolation." *The Beckett Studies Reader*. Edited by S. E. Gontarski. Gainesville: University Press of Florida, 1993.

Cronin, Anthony. *Samuel Beckett: The Last Modernist*. New York: HarperCollins, 1997.

Dante Alighieri. *Inferno*. Edited and translated by Charles Singleton. Princeton: Princeton UP, 1980.

———. *Paradiso*. Edited and translated by Charles Singleton. Princeton: Princeton UP, 1980.

Deane, Seamus. "Joyce et Beckett." *Europe* 770–71 (1993): 29–40.

De Man, Paul. *Blindness and Insight: Essays in the Rhetoric of Contemporary Criticism*. Minneapolis: University of Minnesota Press, 1983.

———. *The Resistance to Theory*. Minneapolis: University of Minnesota Press, 1986.

———. *The Rhetoric of Romanticism*. New York: Columbia University Press, 1984.

Derrida, Jacques. *Acts of Literature*. Edited by Derek Attridge. New York: Routledge, 1992.

———. *L'écriture et la différence*. Paris: Editions du Seuil, 1967. Translated by Alan Bass under the title *Writing and Difference* (Chicago: University of Chicago Press, 1978).

———. *Marges: de la philosophie*. Paris: Les Editions de Minuit, 1972. Translated by Alan Bass under the title *Margins of Philosophy* (Chicago: University of Chicago Press, 1982).

———. *La Voix et la phénomène*. Paris: Presses Universitaires de France, 1967. Translated by David B. Allison under the title *Speech and Phenomena* (Evanston: Northwestern University Press, 1973).

———. *Ulysse gramophone*. Paris: Editions Galilée, 1987.

Descartes, René. *Discours de la méthode suivie des Méditations*. Paris: Union Générale des Editions, 1951. Translated by F. E. Sutcliffe under the title *Discourse on Method and The Meditations* (London: Penguin Books, 1968).

Dickinson, Emily. *Selected Letters*. Edited by Thomas H. Johnson. Cambridge: Harvard University Press, 1986.

Dobrez, L. A. C. "Samuel Beckett and the Impossibility of Lit. Crit." *Southern Review* (Adelaide) 16 (1983): 74–85.

Doll, Mary A. *Beckett and Myth: An Archetypal Approach*. Syracause: Syracuse University Press, 1988.

Doubrovsky, Serge. *La Place de la madeleine: écriture et phantasme chez Proust*. Paris: Mercure de France, 1974.

Ducrot, Oswald, and Tzvetan Todorov. *Encyclopedic Dictionary of the Sciences of Language*. Translated by Catherine Porter. Oxford: Blackwell Reference, 1981.

Emerson, Ralph Waldo. *Selected Essays*. Edited by Larzer Ziff. New York: Penguin Books, 1982.

Felman, Shoshana. *La Folie et la chose littéraire*. Paris: Editions du Seuil; 1978.

———. *Le Scandale du corps parlant: Don Juan avec Austin ou la séduction en deux langues*. Paris: Editions du Seuil, 1980. Translated by Catherine Porter under the title *The Literary Speech Act: Don Juan with J. L. Austin or Seduction in Two Languages* (Cornell: Cornell University Press, 1983).

Flaubert, Gustave. *Bouvard et Pécuchet*. Paris: Editions Gallimard, 1979.

Fletcher, John. *The Novels of Samuel Beckett*. London: Chatto & Windus, 1964.

Foster, Dennis A. "All Here is Sin: The Obligation in *The Unnamable*." *Boundary* 12 (1983): 81–100.

Fowlie, Wallace. "Dante and Beckett." *Dante Among the Moderns*. Edited by Stuart Y. McDougal. Chapel Hill: University of North Carolina Press, 1985.

Freccero, John. *Dante: The Poetics of Conversion*. Edited by Rachel Jacoff. Cambridge: Harvard University Press, 1986.

Freud, Sigmund. *Civilization, Society and Religion* (Pelican Freud Library, vol. 12). Edited by Albert Dickson, translated by James Strachey. London: Penguin Books, 1985.

———. *The Ego and the Id*. Translated by James Strachey. New York: W. W. Norton, 1962.

———. *On Metapsychology: The Theory of Psychoanalysis* (Pelican Freud Library, vol. 11). Edited by Angela Richards, translated by James Strachey. London: Penguin Books, 1984.

———. *On Psychopathology* (Pelican Freud Library, vol. 10). Edited by Angela Richards, translated by James Strachey. London: Penguin Books, 1979.

———. *Three Case Histories*. Edited by Philip Rieff. New York: Collier Books, 1976.

———. *Totem and Taboo*. Translated by A. A. Brill. New York: Vintage, 1946.

————. *Totem and Taboo*. Translated by James Strachey. New York: W. W. Norton, 1950.

Friedman, Alan Warren, Charles Rossman, and Dina Sherzer, eds. *Beckett Translating/Translating Beckett*. University Park: Pennsylvania State University Press, 1987.

Gluck, Barbara Reich. *Beckett and Joyce: Friendship and Fiction*. Cranbury: Bucknell University Press, 1979.

Gontarski, S. E., ed. *The Beckett Studies Reader*. Gainesville: University Press of Florida, 1993.

————, ed. *On Beckett: Essays and Criticism*. New York: Grove Press, 1986.

Harrington, John. *The Irish Beckett*. Syracuse: Syracuse University Press, 1991.

Harvey, Lawrence. *Samuel Beckett: Poet and Critic*. Princeton: Princeton University Press, 1970.

Hill, Leslie. *Beckett's Fiction: In Different Words*. Cambridge: Cambridge University Press, 1990.

Hunkeler, Thomas. *Echos de l'ego dans l'œuvre de Samuel Beckett*. Paris: Editions L'Harmattan, 1997.

Hutchings, William. " 'Shat into Grace' Or, A Tale of a Turd: Why it is How it is in Samuel Beckett's *How It Is*." *Papers in Language and Literature* 21 (1985): 64–87.

Jakobson, Roman. *Language in Literature*. Edited by Krystyna Pomorska and Stephen Rudy. Cambridge: Harvard University Press, 1987.

Janvier, Ludovic. *Pour Samuel Beckett*. Paris: Les Editions de Minuit, 1966.

Joyce, James. *Dubliners*. New York: Compass Books, 1963.

————. *Ulysses*. New York: Vintage Books, 1986.

Katz, Daniel. "Mirror-Resembling Screens: Yeats, Beckett, and '. . . But the Clouds. . . .' " In *The Savage Eye/L'Œil fauve: New Essays on Samuel Beckett's Television Plays*. Edited by Catharina Wulf. Atlanta: Editions Rodopi, 1995.

Kenner, Hugh. *A Reader's Guide to Samuel Beckett*. London: Thames and Hudson, 1973.

————. *Samuel Beckett: A Critical Study*. Berkeley: University of California Press, 1973.

————. *The Stoic Comedians: Flaubert, Joyce, and Beckett*. Berkeley: University of California Press, 1962.

Kevorkian, Martin. "Misreading *Watt*: The Scottish Psychoanalysis of Samuel Beckett." *ELH* 61 (1994): 427–43.

Knowlson, James. *Damned to Fame: The Life of Samuel Beckett*. London: Bloomsbury Press, 1996.

Kristeva, Julia, J.-C. Milner, and N. Ruwet, eds. *Langue, discours, société: pour Emile Benveniste*. Paris: Editions du Seuil, 1975.

Lacan, Jacques. *Ecrits I & II*. Paris: Editions Points, 1966. Translated by Alan Sheridan under the title *Ecrits: A Selection* (New York: W. W. Norton, 1977).

———. *Joyce avec Lacan*. Paris: Editions Navarin, 1987.

———. Notes from a seminar given on November 18, 1975.

Lees, Heath. "*Watt:* Music, Toning and Tonality." *Journal of Beckett Studies* 9 (1984): 5–24.

Lewis, Wyndham. *Time and Western Man*. Santa Rosa, Calif.: Black Sparrow Press, 1993.

Lloyd, David. "Writing in the Shit: Beckett, Nationalism, and the Colonial Subject." *Modern Fiction Studies* 35 (1989): 71–86.

Locatelli, Carla. *Unwording the World: Samuel Beckett's Prose Works after the Nobel Prize*. Philadelphia: University of Pennsylvania Press, 1990.

Lydon, Mary. "Stretching the Imagination: Samuel Beckett and the Frontier of Writing." *Journal of the Midwest Modern Language Association* 30, nos. 1–2 (spring 1997): 1–15.

Mallarmé, Stéphane. *Igitur, Divagations, Un coup de dés*. Paris: Editions Gallimard, 1966.

Marinetti, F. T. *Let's Murder the Moonshine: Selected Writings*. Edited by R. W. Flint, translated by R. W. Flint and A. Coppotelli. Los Angeles: Sun & Moon Press, 1991.

McMullan, Anna. "Samuel Beckett as Director: The Art of Mastering Failure." In *The Cambridge Companion to Beckett*, edited by John Pilling. Cambridge: Cambridge University Press, 1994.

Mooney, Michael E. "*Molloy*, part 1: Beckett's 'Discourse on Method.'" *Journal of Beckett Studies* 3 (1988): 40–55.

———. "Presocratic Scepticism: Samuel Beckett's *Murphy* Reconsidered." *English Literary History* 49 (1982): 214–34.

Moses, Michael Valdez. "The Sadly Rejoicing Slave: Beckett, Joyce, and Destructive Parody." *Modern Fiction Studies* 31 (1985): 659–74.

Nicholls, Peter. *Modernisms: A Literary Guide*. London: Macmillan, 1995.

Olney, James. "Memory and the Narrative Imperative: St. Augustine and Samuel Beckett." *New Literary History* 24 (1993): 857–80.

O'Neill, Kevin. "A Moment without Bounds: Voyage in *The Unnamable*." *Constructions* (1985): 57–67.

Oxenhandler, Neal. "Seeing and Believing in Dante and Beckett." In *Writing in a Modern Temper: Essays on French Thought and Literature in Honor of Henri Peyre*, edited by Mary Ann Caws. Saratoga, Calif.: Anma Libri, 1984.

Posnock, Ross. "Beckett, Valéry, and *Watt*." *Journal of Beckett Studies* 6 (1980): 51–62.

Pound, Ezra. *Literary Essays of Ezra Pound*. Edited by T. S. Eliot. New York: New Directions, 1968.

Rabaté, Jean-Michel, ed. *Beckett avant Beckett: Essais sur les premières oeuvres*. Paris: Presses de l'Ecole normale supérieure, 1984.

———. "Berkeley entre Joyce et Beckett." *Etudes Irlandaises* 10 (1986): 57–76.

———. *Joyce Upon the Void: The Genesis of Doubt.* New York: St. Martin's, 1991.

———, ed. *Samuel Beckett: intertexualités et psychanalyse.* Dijon: Interfaces, 1992.

Ramsay, Nicola. "*Watt* and the Significance of the Mirror Image." *Journal of Beckett Studies* 10 (1985): 21–36.

Sartre, Jean-Paul. *L'idiot de la famille: Gustave Flaubet de 1821–1857.* Paris: Editions Gallimard, 1988. Translated by Carol Cosman under the title *The Family Idiot: Gustave Flaubert, 1821–1957,* vol. 1 (Chicago: University of Chicago Press, 1981).

Sherzer, Dina. "Samuel Beckett, Linguist and Poetician: A View from *The Unnamable.*" *SubStance* 56 (1988): 87–98.

Smith, Joseph, ed. *The World of Samuel Beckett.* Baltimore: Johns Hopkins University Press, 1990.

Trezise, Thomas. *Into the Breach: Samuel Beckett and the Ends of Literature.* Princeton: Princeton University Press, 1990.

Watson, David. *Paradox and Desire in Samuel Beckett's Fiction.* London: Macmillan, 1991.

Watts, Eileen H. "Beckett's Unnamables: Schizophrenia, Rationalism, and the Novel." *American Imago* 45 (1988): 85–106.

Wolosky, Shira. "The Negative Way Negated: Samuel Beckett's *Texts for Nothing.*" *New Literary History* 22 (1991): 213–30.

Worth, Katharine. "Yeats and Beckett." *Gaéliana* 6 (1984): 203–13.

Yeats, W. B. *Essays and Introductions.* New York: Collier Books, 1961.

Index